The Uncommon Sense
of the Immortal
Mullah Nasruddin

Stories, jests, and donkey tales
of the beloved Persian folk hero

AN ANNE IZARD STORYTELLERS' CHOICE AWARD WINNER

A STORYTELLING WORLD HONOR BOOK

"These hilarious, and at times, ribald folk tales of the Turkish wise fool take the reader to another time and place, and share the spiritual lessons of Nasruddin."

— From the Preface by ANN SHAPIRO,
Executive Director, Connecticut Storytelling Center

"A fine pick and very highly recommended."

— *Midwest Book Review*

"Identifies the real strength of Nasruddin's stories in context to
world literature and story performance, that is, its power
to build bridges between cultures. The point of these stories is to
speak to the audience in the language and metaphors that are familiar."

— *Storytelling, Self, Society*

"A contemporary reworking of the stories fit for a general audience. . . .
The book has maintained the direct, unadorned style that is a hallmark of folk
tales. . . . A delightful break from the everyday world for an hour or two."

— *Green Man Review*

ALSO AVAILABLE AS AN AUDIBLE.COM AUDIOBOOK
Narrated by Ted Brooks

THE UNCOMMON SENSE
OF THE IMMORTAL
MULLAH NASRUDDIN

*Stories, jests, and donkey tales
of the beloved Persian folk hero*

collected and retold by
RON J. SURESHA

REVISED EDITION

with a preface by
ANN SHAPIRO
Executive Director
Connecticut Storytelling Center

LETHE PRESS
MAPLE SHADE, NJ, USA

The Uncommon Sense of the Immortal Mullah Nasruddin
Stories, jests, and donkey tales of the beloved Persian folk hero
by Ron J. Suresha

Published by Lethe Press, Inc.
118 Heritage Avenue, Maple Shade, NJ 08052-3018 USA
www.lethepressbooks.com • lethepress@aol.com

First printing 2011. Second printing 2013.
ISBN: 1-59021-175-8   ISBN-13: 978-1-59021-175-5
Design: Toby Johnson & Ron Suresha
Cover illustration: Sgott MacKenzie

Library of Congress Cataloging-in-Publication Data

Suresha, Ron Jackson.
    The uncommon sense of the immortal Mullah Nasruddin : stories, jests, and donkey tales of the beloved Persian folk hero / collected and retold by Ron J. Suresha ; with a Preface by Ann Shapiro.
        p.   cm.
    Includes bibliographical references.
    ISBN-13: 978-1-59021-175-5
    ISBN-10: 1-59021-175-8
    1. Nasreddin Hoca (Anecdotes)   2. Nasreddin Hoca (Legendary character) — Humor.   I. Title.
    PN6231.N27S87 2011
    398.2'209561--dc22   2010037750

Contents

The Uncommon Sense of the Immortal Mullah Nasruddin

PREFACE
ANN SHAPIRO, EXECUTIVE DIRECTOR
CONNECTICUT STORYTELLING CENTER

THE UNCOMMON SENSE OF THE IMMORTAL MULLAH NASRUDDIN is a collection of tales of the Persian folk hero, Nasruddin, retold by Ron Suresha.

These hilarious, and at times, ribald folk tales of the Turkish wise fool take the reader to another time and place, and share the spiritual lessons of Nasruddin.

The stories are set up chronologically, starting with his youth, introducing us to his friends, his marriage and his own children, his work, old age, and finally, his death. As Suresha writes, "... by opening the listener's heart with laughter, the tales create a space for wisdom to enter."

Traditionally, the tales are told in groups of seven. Suresha upholds this oral custom by grouping the written short, bare bones, and joke-like stories also in groups of seven. His modern retelling breathes fresh life into the stories while respecting their roots.

One of the joys I experienced reading the book, was discovering variants of stories I already knew from other cultures. Nasruddin stories always provided a twist from the versions I was familiar with, and made me laugh out loud many times.

Suresha's introduction and foreword provide the reader with wonderful background knowledge of Nasruddin, not only as a funny (and he is funny!) character, but also as an important spiritual leader, whose stories offer many ideas to meditate on. The book also includes a helpful glossary and a bibliography that story enthusiasts will enjoy.

The teaching stories included in this volume help to build bridges between cultures by exemplifying Arabic wisdom and universal human humor.

FOREWORD

A s a precocious youngster from an ethnically diverse family with strong oral and literary folklore traditions, I became well acquainted early on with the likes of the famous wise fool Mullah Nasruddin, a character of renowned humor and inscrutable wisdom from halfway around the world in the Near and Middle East.

I listened to my mother, an Israeli American who spoke conversational Arabic, recount a few of the droll follies and foibles of the bald, bewhiskered, bumbling Mullah. Threads of his countless fables, anecdotes, and parables, based in Turkish and Persian folk wisdom, were woven into the first stories and jokes that I learned. "You're acting just like Nasruddin," my mom would exclaim, exasperated by my wholehearted commitment to adolescent contrariness, "always answering a question with a question!" To which an obstinate child must reply in kind something along the lines of: "Really?" or "Is that so?" Even still, such comparisons paled in significance to the times when she would suggest a more direct likeness between the Mullah's little grey donkey and my stubborn, smartass adolescent self.

Quite the prankster myself in high school, on several occasions I skipped class and hitchhiked more than three miles by myself to the local metaphysical bookstore. On one such truant pilgrimage, while browsing the store's single Sufi/Islam shelf, I encountered a delightfully illustrated softcover collection of Nasruddin lore which I might have bought had I not already blown half of my weekly allowance on a small package of sandalwood incense.

After college I was the patient of a gentle, bearded Sufi dentist who made me smile with his thoughtful, sometimes koan-like, Mullah stories, and who invited me to join him one night for a talk at the local Sufi Center.

Soon after that experience, I became involved in a yoga community and lived at several ashrams (residential yoga centers) primarily around the United States, as well as two stays at an Indian ashram, where I learned many more Nasruddin tales. These droll stories were included in daily formal lectures by our teachers to illuminate, often with comedic effect, the uncommon foolishness and occasional common sense of human nature. This exposure to a broad range of Near and Far Eastern religious and spiritual teachings enriched my understanding of the stories as it increased my appreciation for Turkish culture and Sufi philosophy.

When I sought out Nasruddin lore in the ashram library, to my delight I discovered several contemporary printed collections of this folklore, including softcover copies of the illustrated story books I'd seen before in the metaphysical bookshop: three popular collections authored by Sufi writer Idries Shah, issued from British publisher Octagon Press.

Eventually I would discover that the oldest Nasruddin manuscript dates from 1571 CE, and while Nasruddin is known mostly through numerous pithy anecdotes in illustrated books, whole novels and plays have been written about him, and an animated feature film in Turkish was almost made. Until my first trip to Istanbul in 2005, however, my only literary sources in English for Nasruddin folklore were these beloved Shah books. I spent hours copying and memorizing my favorites from these volumes, at times feeling as foolish as the Mullah for studying the hilarious, silly antics of this Sufi folk hero, rather than the many volumes of somber, erudite classics of Hindu scripture, world religion, theology, and philosophy that lined the library shelves.

In 1997, while working as production editor at Shambhala Publications in Boston, I presented a formal proposal for a pocket edition of Nasruddin stories culled from the hundreds of stories in the Shah volumes, but Octagon declined the query. From that initial proposal I developed this project, my own contemporary retelling of the Nasruddin corpus.

Over the past dozen or so years, I have collected and indexed several thousand versions of nearly one thousand stories and parables, anecdotes and aphorisms, and jests and jokes of my longtime teacher and friend, Mullah Nasruddin, in his many incarnations in various cultures around the globe. The present retellings are based on my personal recollection of oral narratives as well as dozens of published sources in English, Spanish, German, French, Turkish, and Hebrew, including tales in English presented online but not in printed form. These primary sources are listed in the Bibliography.

Excluding a few longer narratives that incorporate shorter bits, the stories here are given seven at a sitting as per the oral tradition of Nasruddin's "curse":

Whenever someone makes a joke, fool, at your sole expense,
they'll be compelled to tell, at the least, six more tales thence.

Gathered into seven parts having seven sections, each section containing seven stories (7^3 = 343), the selections comprise the most popular, amusing, meaningful, and compelling ones repeated among my sources. My goals have been to craft fresh, strong, clear presentations of the folklore, to incorporate the best aspects of each known variation, and to adapt the narrative material to contemporary readership. While respecting its traditional cultural roots, the text avoids the more lurid and pejorative sexual, scatological, ethnic, racist, sexist, and violent subjects. Mullah willing, that material will comprise a new collection entitled *Naughty Nasruddin*.

The stories are arranged into a rough biography, starting with Nasruddin's childhood and moving through characteristic life passages: his youth and schooling, his married and family life, travels and travails with his devoted grey donkey, the daily labor of his many vocations, encounters with his village neighbors and teahouse chums, his exploits as a favorite in Sultan Tamerlane's court, his duties and acts as local magistrate and religious teacher, and his old age and death.

To inhabit the town of Akşehir alongside our hero, I named various family members and local characters, rather than use a repetitious, anonymous figure as in: "Once *someone* asked Nasruddin …" In a particularly egregious violation of literary license, I designated a pet name, Karakacan, to Nasruddin's little grey donkey. Turks customarily do not name their pets or animals, but upon my insistence one native Turk suggested this name, and it was endorsed by another. I hope that the kind reader will accept this precious and popularizing treatment, and through this literary device come to know the Mullah and his culture better as he routinely interacts with his family, village, and donkey.

The project was originally much more modest and, to nobody's surprise except perhaps my own, steadily grew well beyond its initial scope, blurring the distinction between erudition and obsession. Gathering these tales has seemed at times like young Nasruddin's futile effort to collect the chickens he released from the basket on his way to market: when the fowls fly away in every direction, it seems perfectly apt to seize the rooster by the neck and threaten to punish him for losing control of his whole flock. So, for any shortcomings of this unruly compilation of his stories, anecdotes, jokes, and donkey tales, please don't blame me — Nasruddin started it all!

INTRODUCTION

W HEN THE WISE OLD FOOL Nasruddin was but a silly young child, he had the
habit of distracting his classmates with antics, jokes, and stories, much to
the dismay of his teacher. Once, when the young Nasruddin was being particularly
troublesome, his irate teacher uttered a curse:

> *Wherever you go or stay,*
> *whatever you do or say,*
> *whether it be night or day —*
> *people will only laugh and laugh at you.*

Now, eight centuries later, people everywhere are still laughing at Nasruddin,
one of the world's most beloved folk characters. Mullah Nasruddin (*mull*-ah nas-
rrh-*deen*, from *nasr-ad-din,* "victory of religion"; often preceded by the honorific
mullah, effendi, or *hoca)* was a teacher, scholar, judge, community leader, courtier,
and jack-of-all-trades. The thousands of tales, anecdotes, and jokes attributed to his
character are told throughout the world in the tradition of wisdom stories, just as
commonly as they are shared with a ribald sense of folk humor. He is a sage fool
who always has some pearl of wisdom to teach everyone — even if the lesson is not
to act like him.

Nasruddin may or may not be an actual historical figure, who was born in
Hortu village in Sivrihisar district of Turkey, in the modern-day town of Eskişehir,
and who lived most of his life in the village of Akşehir, but several sources assert
his birth year as 1208–9 CE. Regardless of the actual place and date of his origin,
Nasruddin is now known in the Middle East, and indeed throughout the world, as
a comic, poignant figure of endless exploits — so much so that UNESCO (the United
Nations Educational, Scientific and Cultural Organization) proclaimed 1996–7
"International Nasruddin Year."

In Europe, Nasruddin can be compared with the German 14th-century prankster Till Eulenspiegel. In some Bulgarian folktales originating from the Ottoman Empire, the same figure appears as antagonist to a local wise man named Hitar Petar ("cunning Peter"). In Sicily, the same stories involve a character named Giufà. In the Ukraine, the figure is called Hershele Ostropoler. Elsewhere in Arabia the famous folk hero is known in variations of these narratives as Djuha, Bahlool, or Abu Nuwas. Cognates of the "wise fool" character have flourished also in Puerto Rico as Juan Bobo ("John Fool") and in Jewish/Yiddish storytelling as Schlemiel ("simpleton") of Chelm.

While many countries and cultures lay claim to Nasruddin, none go so far as the modern city of Akşehir in south-central Turkey, which boasts his gravesite and holds an annual Nasruddin festival in July, where Nasruddin devotees dress in folk costumes and reenact the many exploits of the character. In 2008 the town held a Nasruddin symposium and many other cultural events, and the Turkish postal system issued a set of four commemorative stamps, to mark his 800th birthday.

The themes in Nasruddin anecdotes are woven into the oral tradition and folklore of a number of countries and express the national imaginations of a variety of cultures. While there are dozens of published collections of the countless jokes attributed to him, today most people encounter his tales in the context of their daily lives. In many regions across the Far and Middle East and the Turkish diaspora, the tales of Nasruddin are told and retold endlessly in the teashops and caravanserais, can be heard in every home and on the radio, and are still quoted or alluded to frequently in daily conversation, usually to provide a quick injection of humor and wisdom.

In Khaled Hosseini's bestselling 2003 novel of modern Afghani life, *The Kite Runner*, Nasruddin brings much-needed comic relief to a dire situation. "There wasn't an Afghan in the world who didn't know a few jokes about the bumbling mullah," the main character observes. Although most Nasruddin stories depict a rustic small-village setting, the tales deal with timeless concepts of the human condition. They impart a pithy folk wisdom from a rich storytelling tradition that triumphs over all trials and tribulations.

Superficially, many Nasruddin tales are presented as jests or humorous anecdotes told by one party when another party makes the kind of boneheaded error that Nasruddin parodies. Inherent in many a Nasruddin story, however, is its ability to point out the wrong way in order to know how not to act, the way not to think and behave and treat others. "If the wrong way is not known," asserts the young Nasruddin, "how can the right way be understood?"

Its moral, played out in literary form, thus is portrayed as a man riding his little gray donkey — only facing the animal's rear end, literally ass-backward. One should know better, of course, than to ride backward, or to do the many foolish things that Nasruddin does. In practical, daily affairs as well as in the spiritual life, often we end up riding the wrong way on the donkey anyway — because, we reason to ourselves, this is our compromise with the donkey.

Yet the numerous anecdotes attributed to Nasruddin also reveal a sly, humorous personality with a sharp tongue that spared no one, not even the most tyrannical sultan of his time. The Mullah's interactions with the despot Tamerlane particularly display an intuitive intelligence shrewd enough to outwit anyone. Thus Nasruddin became the symbol of Middle-Eastern satirical comedy and the rebellious feelings of people against the dynasties that once ruled that area of the world.

While it is true that most people tell Nasruddin stories in cafés, bazaars, and around dinner tables for the pleasure of an enjoyable joke or anecdote, many Nasruddin tales are used also as teaching stories in modern Sufi, Hindu, Buddhist, and other Eastern and Western mystic traditions. Often the humor of a Nasruddin tale contains a paradox or an illogical conundrum that occupies the rational mind with its surface meaning while more spiritual concepts — the student's intuitive, gestalt mentality that the mystic is attempting to engage — are awakened in the subconscious. Contemplation of the core enigma of these nonsensical scenarios, like that inspired by the Zen koan, propels the consciousness of the student, and the mystic, a little farther along the long road to spiritual realization.

It is also true that by opening the listener's heart with laughter, the tales create a space for both joy and mystic wisdom to enter. The topper of his teacher's "curse" imposes the condition that at least seven Nasruddin tales must be told aloud at one sitting. This is done to allow the listener enough time to relax and perceive the humor even in the most pressing situation. Thus paradox, unexpectedness, and unconventional wisdom are fully expressed in the irrepressible good humor and inspirational humanity of the immortal Mullah Nasruddin.

In a classic depiction of the Mullah, he rides sitting backward on his little grey donkey, addressing his students as they follow reluctantly. Let us return in our minds to this scenario, centuries ago during Nasruddin's time: contemplate what it was like to be one of those children, walking down a dusty unpaved road behind the Mullah on his beloved donkey. Imagine him facing you, with his white whiskery beard and his prominent turban, riding backward as he teaches you one clever wisdom story of his own devising after another, all the while you are blessed with a view of the donkey's ass. Now, whatever you do, don't laugh at the Mullah.

Mullah Nasruddin
&
his donkey, Karakacan

Original Watercolor by
SGOTT MACKENZIE

THE UNCOMMON SENSE
OF THE IMMORTAL
MULLAH NASRUDDIN

Stories, jests, and donkey tales
of the beloved Persian folk hero

PART ONE

FOOLISH YOUTH

1

Imagine if you can, eight centuries ago, when Mullah Nasruddin was just a child. Like all young Turks his age, Nasruddin attended the grade school for boys, the *madrasa*, in the village of Akşehir.

One morning, young Nasruddin ran stark naked through the town square and into the madrasa. As he raced by, his friend Hussein called out, "Nasruddin, why aren't you dressed properly?"

"I overslept for the big test today," said Nasruddin, trying to cover himself and jog in place to respond, "and so in my crazy rush to make it to school on time, I forgot to put on clothes."

One day, Nasruddin's uncle, Mesut, asked, "Can you point to your nose?"

Nasruddin pointed to the back of his head.

"Wrong, Nasruddin, that's not your nose. Clearly, you don't know your front from your back."

"Not quite true, sir," said Nasruddin. "If the back of something is not known, how can you tell for certain exactly where its front may be? If the wrong is not known, how can you possibly understand what is right?"

Once in the madrasa during class, one student's parent brought the village schoolmaster Halil a pan of *baklava, a* sweet, rich pastry made of filo dough, honey, and nuts. Nasruddin's mouth watered at the thought of eating the baklava, but Halil put the pan away in the drawer of his desk.

Shortly afterward, Halil was called out of the schoolroom on an urgent family matter. Before he left, he gave his students a complicated mathematics assignment to finish within the hour. "And I shall expect you to get everything right," he said, "or there will be trouble." He glared at them. "Big trouble."

"One thing more," Halil said as he made for the door. "I have enemies. Many despicable enemies. I keep being sent poisoned meats and poisoned sweets. Even," he added menacingly, "poisoned baklava. I have to test everything before I eat it. So be warned. If you hope for a long life, don't touch anything that has been sent to me. Especially baklava."

As soon as the teacher was gone, Nasruddin went to the desk and took out the pan of baklava.

"Don't eat that!" Hussein cried out. "They may be poisoned!"

"Don't be ridiculous. Of course they aren't poisoned," Nasruddin grinned, picking up a piece of the delicious sweetmeat. "Halil just wants to keep them for himself." And he started in on the baklava. "They really are quite delicious," he said, grinning widely. He ate another one, and another.

When Nasruddin's buddies saw that he didn't fall to the floor in a writhing heap, they gathered round the desk and gobbled up the baklava. The pan was completely clean in a matter of seconds.

"But what will we tell the teacher when he finds it all gone?" Hussein said, wiping the crumbs from his mouth.

Nasruddin smiled and replied calmly, "I know what to do. Just leave the rest of this matter to me."

A while later, when Halil returned, he went right to his desk and looked in his drawer. He glared at his students.

"Someone," he said, "has been at my desk."

There was a long silence.

"Someone has been in my drawer."

Still more silence.

"And someone has eaten the baklava."

"I ate it," confessed Nasruddin.

"It was *you* who ate it! After what I told you?"

"Yes."

"Perhaps you have some explanation," said Halil, "for disobeying me and risking your life. If so, I would like to hear it before you die."

"Well," said Nasruddin, "the assignment you gave me was far too complicated for me to complete. Every problem I've started, ended up horribly wrong. I knew you would be very angry and tell my parents, and they would be very disappointed and punish me. I felt so ashamed at my ignorance that I decided my only option was — forgive me, teacher, for I know it is a sin — to end my life. So that's why I ate all your poisoned baklava. It was the only way I could think of to save myself from shame. But the weird thing is, nothing's happened yet. I feel perfectly fine. I wonder why that is."

Halil examined the boy's innocent expression. "I suspect it is just a slow-acting poison," he said, "and your imminent death is just delayed — in which case, I ought to take a look at the schoolwork you have done."

HALIL THE SCHOOLTEACHER ASKED, "Nasruddin, how old are you now?"

"Twelve," the boy replied.

"But I remember that last year you told me that you had just turned twelve."

"Listen," retorted Nasruddin. "The truth has not changed. The facts have not changed. Nasruddin has not changed. Once I have uttered the truth, would you then have me go back on my word?"

YOUNG NASRUDDIN HAD THE habit of distracting all his classmates within earshot with incessant, silly banter. He was always telling ribald jokes and acting out whimsical stories, pulling pranks and puerile antics, much to the dismay of the teacher, Halil, who seemed powerless to control the children while under Nasruddin's charismatic sway.

One day in the madrasa, Nasruddin was particularly disruptive, making his classmates giggle so hard that all their little fezzes fell off their heads. As the kids were laughing and yelling, the irate schoolteacher grabbed Nasruddin's ear and pulled him forward to the front of the class. Even still, the children giggled and tittered.

"Did you instigate this mayhem in my classroom?" fumed Halil.

"I just watched and laughed," replied Nasruddin haughtily. "Do you think I started it?"

"You just 'watched and laughed,' you say, but every eye in the room was on you. Of course it's you. Do you deny it?"

"Are you accusing me of starting it?"

Halil recoiled, saying, "In all my days as a teacher, I don't believe I have ever seen a more insolent child than you, Nasruddin. How dare you address me this way! Why must you always answer a question with another question?"

"Do I?" said Nasruddin, with a smile.

Nᴀsʀᴜᴅᴅɪɴ's ᴛᴇᴀᴄʜᴇʀ, Hᴀʟɪʟ, ʀᴇʙᴜᴋᴇᴅ his student, "I ask you again — did you start this pandemonium here in class?"

"No! I told you, all I did was watch and laugh," answered Nasruddin sharply, gesturing with a particular finger. "*You* started it."

The affronted teacher stood back, cracked his knuckles, and pointed at the upstart. Then in a fiery voice, Halil uttered this curse uniquely appropriate to a foolish child telling a laughable lie: "Nasruddin, wherever you go, whatever you say, whomever you encounter; whenever you try to tell a story, or attempt to teach anybody about anything at all; whether your words are fact, fantasy, fiction, or something in between — people will only laugh and laugh at you!"

Nᴀsʀᴜᴅᴅɪɴ, ᴡʜᴏ ᴋɴᴇᴡ ʜᴏᴡ to add insult to injury, and how a curse could be a blessing, winked at the schoolteacher. Halil indignantly added, "Not only that, but whenever someone tells one joke at your expense, they will be compelled to tell *at least seven stories* at a sitting!"

This curse, of course, was greeted with great happiness by Nasruddin's classmates, who let out a cheer for their young friend and champion.

And so, because of Nasruddin's curse and blessing, still eight centuries later, his stories make us laugh as they make us think. Fortunately, when asked why we cannot help but laugh at Nasruddin, or why we must keep telling his stories, we can always point to him and say, "Don't blame me — he started it."

2

Oɴᴄᴇ, ᴀs ᴀ ʏᴏᴜɴɢ child, Nasruddin happened to gaze into a large jar full of water, and saw his reflection. He cried: "Mother! There is a young boy hiding in the water pitcher — he must be a thief!"

His mother, Leyla, looked into it likewise, saw her reflection, and shrieked as she recoiled in horror, "Yes, by God, it is true! And with him is an ugly old woman!"

Nasruddin toppled the water jug onto the floor, where it broke and water gushed forth. His mother, trying to save the jar and the boy at the same time, slipped in the water and fell. She cried out, "*Aiii!* The thief grabbed me!"

And the boy shouted: "Help! Come all you people! We are beset by thieves!"

❧

ONCE WHEN NASRUDDIN WAS too young to attend school, but Leyla, his mother, had to go to the well, she pulled his ear and told him, "Mind you, do not leave the door for even a moment. Keep your eye on it." Then she left, gossiping with her friends Turan and Setare, along the way to the well. Once they got going, they could keep chatting at the well with the other village women for most of a day.

Nasruddin sat in a chair staring intently at the front entrance, for the first hour. He paced around the house keeping an anxious eye on the front door always for the second hour. Finally in the third hour, Nasruddin's uncle, Mesut, came by and told Nasruddin to tell his mother that he and his wife and their new baby were coming that night to join them for dinner.

After Mesut left, Nasruddin found himself in a tricky situation. The boy was restless and thought he should find out what was keeping his mother so long or at least give her the message. However, he remembered she had pulled his ear and admonished him to not leave the door, not even for a moment, and he wasn't about to suffer his mother's wrath for disobedience. Before another minute passed, Nasruddin devised a solution.

Nasruddin's mother was standing at the well, still gossiping with her friends, when one of the women pointed behind her and said, "Leyla — isn't that your boy, coming down the road, there?"

Leyla was beside herself when she saw her son dragging something behind him, which she couldn't make out clearly. "Nasruddin, you simpleton! I told you to attend the door while I was out!"

As Nasruddin trudged forward, they could all see that he had lashed the front door to his back. He called out, "No need to worry, Mother. I brought the door with me, so we can both keep an eye on it!"

❧

NASRUDDIN'S MOTHER, LEYLA, DISCOVERED the boy as he was throwing handfuls of sesame seeds around the yard.

"What in the name of the Prophet are you doing out here," Leyla exclaimed, "wasting my valuable sesame seeds?"

Nasruddin answered, "Sesame is an effective large cat repellant, Mother. Keeps the tigers away."

"But there are no tigers in these parts except in the circus," she objected.

"See what I mean?" replied Nasruddin. "It works!"

❦

ONCE YOUNG NASRUDDIN HAD his little chicks walking around the yard with tiny black cloths tied around their necks. Nasruddin's friend, Hussein, came by and noticed the bird pecking at the dust for grains wearing the black bands and asked, "Nasruddin, what's that about?"

"Shhh, be quiet!" Nasruddin whispered, "Show some respect for the grieving chicks. Last night, their mother went on to the other world — and now they are in mourning."

❦

ONCE YOUNG NASRUDDIN TOOK his father's chickens to market in a large wicker basket. "Don't open the basket until you get there," his father had instructed. Halfway there, Nasruddin grew concerned that the basket was too hot for the fowls, and so he let them out.

Immediately upon being set free, the chickens scattered in every direction but that of the market. Instead of trying to capture the birds, Nasruddin seized the rooster by the neck and admonished him, "You have the good sense to know when to crow at sunrise, but you can't keep your flock together to take a simple family walk to the market! What kind of leader of the roost are you?"

❦

WHEN NASRUDDIN WAS A small boy, his family moved to Akşehir, a town much bigger than the simple rural village of Sivrihişar. The mosque in his hometown was quite small, so when young Nasruddin saw for the first time the Akşehir mosque, which was large with a tall *minaret*, the scale of the edifice amazed him.

Just then the *muezzin* appeared at the top of the minaret to call the believers to prayer. Since the muezzin was singing in Arabic in a loud voice, Nasruddin couldn't understand and so he misinterpreted the cries of the man.

Nasruddin ran up to the side of the minaret and shouted up to the muezzin, "I know you're calling for help, but shouldn't you have thought of that before you went up there and got yourself stuck? If you were caught in a tree, I could have climbed up the branches to save you, but how do you expect me to climb up this smooth tower?"

❦

NASRUDDIN WAS CONTRARY AS a child, and his parents would always have to use reverse psychology on him to get the lad to do anything right. Meaning that, if they told him to go right, he went left. If they wanted him to go forward, they would tell him to turn around and go backward. In this way, his parents managed to get Nasruddin to accomplish his chores without too much fuss.

On his fourteenth birthday, young Nasruddin was accompanying his father as they negotiated a donkey-load of flour back home across the river, when they came to a bridge too small for the donkey to cross.

"By no means lead the ass across the river," instructed Yousef. "I'm going to walk over the footbridge." This was a tried-and-true trick to get the boy wet while staying dry.

Sure enough, as his father hoped, Nasruddin took the donkey across the stream near the bridge. Midway across, Nasruddin's father noticed that the sack of flour was weighted too far on the right of the donkey's back, and would get wet unless rebalanced promptly.

Nasruddin's father called out, "Nasruddin, heave up the load on the left." The boy thought for a moment, then opposite to his usual reaction, he did exactly as he was told, raising the sack on the left, which caused it to slip off the ass and into the rushing water.

"You ridiculous fool, Nasruddin," his father shouted in utter exasperation, "I have never known you to do as you're told. Why suddenly did you comply with my directions, which was clearly the opposite of what I meant?"

Nasruddin replied, "Father, today I turned fourteen and have now in the eyes of society become a rational adult. I just now realized while midstream that I have become a man, and instead of my constant contrariness as an immature child, I decided to obey your specific instructions, in reverse to every contrary way I have done things up to now."

3

ONE DAY, YOUNG NASRUDDIN went into his backyard and started digging a hole. He was getting fairly deep when his friend, Hussein, happened to stop by and ask what he was doing.

"Isn't it obvious?" said Nasruddin as he kept shoveling. "You see that huge pile of rubble left over from the repairs to the roof of my house? Nobody seems to know what to do what all that material, so I am digging a hole where I can bury all of it."

"But Nasruddin," Hussein asked, "where exactly do you plan to put the dirt from this hole?"

"Simple. I'll dig another hole," said Nasruddin, shoveling away, "and put that dirt in there."

"You're going to remove the dirt from one hole and dump it into another hole? And what will you do with the dirt from the second hole?"

"Oh please, give me a break," wheezed Nasruddin. "You can't possibly expect me to have worked out every last little detail, do you?"

❦

ONCE, YOUSEF, NASRUDDIN'S FATHER, made young Nasruddin appear in court to testify on his behalf in a case about disputed possession of some grain. Before he testified, Yousef made it clear that the boy was to perjure himself while on the witness stand — or else suffer dire consequences.

When Nasruddin was called as a witness, the judge asked, "Did you witness the transaction?"

Nasruddin began, "Yes, sir. I clearly saw the sacks of barley change hands—"

"Hold on there, boy," said the judge, "this case is about stolen wheat, not barley."

Nasruddin replied, "Barley, wheat — tell me, your Honor, what do the details matter if I am not supposed to tell the truth in the first place?"

❦

ONE DAY NASRUDDIN WENT to Lake Akşehir with a bowlful of cultured yoghurt and a long spoon. He squatted at the water's edge and began ladling yoghurt into the lake.

His pal Hussein saw him and asked what he was doing. Nasruddin replied, "I'm adding starter to the lake to make it into yoghurt."

Hussein asked, "Are you serious? Do you really believe you can turn the lake into yoghurt?"

"I know I can't. I know it won't," stated Nasruddin. "But just imagine — what if I could, and what if it did?"

❦

ONCE NASRUDDIN'S UNCLE, MESUT, instructed the boy to walk to carry a valuable and fragile ceramic bowl to deliver to market. As he was looking around at all the people and things in the place, he tripped on a jutting rock and the glassware flew out of his hands, crashing to pieces on the street in front of him. Everyone turned to see what happened.

Nasruddin picked himself up and dusted himself off as a small crowd gathered to see the source of the commotion. Nasruddin glared at them and yelled, "What are all of *you* looking at? Haven't you ever seen a fool before?"

IN NASRUDDIN'S DAY, GLAD tidings brought quickly were always rewarded somehow. His friend Hussein, wanting a gift for bringing good news, rushed up to Nasruddin one day and announced, breathless, "I just saw a huge tray of delicious *baklava* being delivered —"

"Okay, but what's it to me?" asked Nasruddin.

"The baklava was being delivered," Hussein gasped, "to your house!"

"I see," said Nasruddin. "That makes a difference. Well then, what's it to *you*?"

ONCE YOUNG NASRUDDIN WAS sitting by the side of the lake when he saw a flock of ducks swimming in the water. He was quite hungry so he thought he'd try to catch one of the birds. As he tiptoed to the edge of the water, though, the ducks honked and flew away.

For a moment Nasruddin stood in frustration, then, thinking quickly, took a loaf of bread out of his pocket, broke it up into small pieces, then dipped the pieces of bread into the lake, and ate them.

Hussein was passing by and noticed Nasruddin squatting and chewing at the water's edge. "Say, Nasruddin," he called out, "what are you doing?"

"What I am doing . . . should be . . . perfectly obvious," Nasruddin replied, between bites. "I am eating . . . duck soup."

ONE DAY, YOUNG NASRUDDIN'S buddies decided they would try to nab his pointy slippers. They waited around a tall cypress tree until Nasruddin walked along, then two of the boys, Hussein and Faruk, started to pretend they were having a loud argument.

"Nobody could climb that tree. It's way too tall. No way!" yelled Hussein.

"Of course somebody could climb it," argued Faruk. "Nasruddin, please tell this dunce that this tree is not too tall for someone to climb."

"I doubt that anyone could climb this tree," said Hussein, "certainly not even Nasruddin."

"Of course he can climb it!" retorted Faruk. "He can do nearly anything! Couldn't you climb it, Nasruddin? I bet if anyone could get up to the top of the tree, it is you."

Nasruddin bowed slightly and replied modestly, "I can climb it, no doubt."

"Let's see you do it, then," said Faruk.

"I'll hold your slippers for you while you go up," said Hussein, perhaps a little too eagerly.

"Well, guys, all right then." Nasruddin stood back and assessed the tree, and the group of boys, and then the tree again. He rolled up his sleeves, removed his slippers and tucked them into his belt, then spit into his palms as he prepared to scale the tree.

"Wait, wait, Nasruddin!" said Faruk. "You won't need your shoes in a tree."

"Yes, leave them here down here with us for safekeeping," chimed in Hussein.

With a gasp and a grunt, Nasruddin heaved himself upward. "You never know — there might be a road at the top of this tree." he called out as he climbed, "Be prepared, I always say."

4

Young Nasruddin decided to learn an instrument, so he called upon a music instructor.

"How much do you charge for private lute lessons?" asked the boy.

"The lute is not an easy instrument to learn," answered the teacher. "I charge three silver coins for the first month, and one silver piece for each month after that."

"Fine," agreed Nasruddin. "I'll start with the second month."

Ever the compulsive rascal, once young Nasruddin climbed his neighbor Hamza's fence and started loading a large sack with everything from the vegetable garden that he could uproot.

Hamza found the boy digging around in his garden with the sack nearly full of melons and pumpkins.

"Nasruddin, what are you doing in my garden?"

"Strange that you should ask," the boy replied. "I was just wondering that myself."

"Well, boy, what is your explanation?"

"As best as I can tell from the available evidence, it would seem that I was blown into your yard by a strong sudden gust."

"And what are my vegetables doing in your sack?" asked Hamza.

"The wind, obviously," answered Nasruddin, "blew your veggies into my bag."

"And why were you carrying the sack full of fruits and vegetables back toward your house?"

"I decided to hold on to them for the extra weight, to keep from being carried away by another unexpected gust of wind."

NASRUDDIN WANTED SOME OF the delicious apricots hanging from the tree in his neighbor Hamza's backyard, so he put his ladder on the adjoining wall, climbed up, pulled the ladder over, and was almost to the ground on the other side when Hamza came right up behind him and said, "Just what exactly do you think you're doing in my garden?"

"I was hoping, my friend and neighbor," Nasruddin said, "to interest you in this fine ladder that I have available to sell."

"You young fool," snarled Hamza. "You mean to say that you were going to sell me a ladder in my own backyard?"

Nasruddin defended himself, saying, "It's my ladder, and I can sell it wherever I choose."

"No, Nasruddin, I'm not buying it," said Hamza.

"You overlook the obvious, *effendi*, which is that I've just demonstrated that the ladder works perfectly. Truth is, one may sell a ladder of this high caliber absolutely anywhere," said Nasruddin, as he stepped back on to the ladder. "However, since I can tell you're not the sort of buyer who is interested in acquiring only the finest model of ladder available, I'll just take my wares elsewhere."

AS A YOUNG BOY, Nasruddin was overly fond of apricots, and so once while traveling by himself back from market, very hungry and tired, he saw a farmer's orchard filled with the most delicious-looking fruits. The boy couldn't control himself, so he ran into the orchard and started stuffing both his mouth and his pockets with apricots.

Shortly Nasruddin heard the farmer and his dog approaching, and climbed up one of the apricot trees. The dog sniffed out the boy and started barking, which made the farmer look up at Nasruddin.

"What're you doing up there in that tree, boy?" he growled, waving a long, heavy stick.

Nasruddin said, "Warbling, actually. I am a nightingale."

The farmer had thought he'd heard it all, but he had to laugh at that one. "Alrighty, little miss nightingale — let's hear you sing."

Nasruddin intoned a string of inharmonious notes that sounded more like an old cat screeching in dire pain. Even the farmer's dog put his paws over his floppy ears. The farmer howled with laughter, slapped his knee, and declared, "Never heard any sort of nightingale song like that before!"

"Well, I may be a bit out of practice," chirped Nasruddin, as he preened on his perch. "Still, it's clearly evident that you haven't traveled far from your farm. That happens to be the rare, exotic song of a Chinese nightingale."

ONCE HUSSEIN ASKED NASRUDDIN, "Do you know how tall minarets are built all the way up at the top of the mosque dome?"

Nasruddin replied, "Very simple. Minarets come from deep wells — turned upside down."

ONCE YOUNG NASRUDDIN HAD a sum of money that he wanted to hide, so he stashed his cash in a covered urn in a corner of the house. He felt secure knowing he'd found a safe place to hide his money, and he smiled at his cleverness as he left for the teahouse.

No sooner had he reached the door that a thought entered his head. He spun around, looked at the urn in the corner where he had hidden his cash, and said: "I'd better move my money from there. Now that I know my secret hiding place, who will stop me from stealing from myself?"

ONCE, WHEN YOUNG NASRUDDIN was a donkey driver — one of the many things Nasruddin did for work as a boy — he undertook to transport nine donkeys for delivery to a local farmer.

The donkey broker at the bazaar had all the animals lined up next to each other as he went through and counted each and every one of them with Nasruddin to ensure they agreed there were nine exactly — no more, no less.

Nasruddin mounted one of the donkeys and shouted, "Ugh-r-r-r!" which is Turkish for "Giddyup!" and they began the journey with Nasruddin riding behind the beasts facing forward, so that he could keep a vigilant eye on his donkeys. Along the way, however, Nasruddin began daydreaming. He thought, "These fine animals will arrive without so much as a scratch or a bruise. No donkeys in all of Turkey have received better treatment than these nine."

At this point they passed through a grove of trees, and Nasruddin decided it would be good time to count the donkeys.

Still sitting atop one of the animals, Nasruddin counted the donkeys, "One, two, three—" and up to eight! One was missing! "What the—? Only eight donkeys?"

Panic-stricken, Nasruddin jumped down to the ground, looked all around, then counted the donkeys again. This time there were exactly nine.

Relieved but confused, Nasruddin mounted his donkey, this time riding in front, facing backward, so that he could keep both eyes on his donkeys, and they continued on their way.

Eventually Nasruddin's thoughts wandered, and he began thinking about the money he would receive when he delivered these donkeys, and imagining how he would spend it, and before long, he realized he had been distracted.

He once again stopped his donkey and tallied the animals, but to his dismay he discovered that one had gone missing again — there were only eight!

Bewildered, Nasruddin dismounted again and carefully counted the donkeys. Amazingly, he found there were nine.

"This always happens when I don't pay attention," Nasruddin admitted to himself. "Fine, then — I'll just have to walk behind the donkeys the rest of the way to keep my eyes on these tricksters." And so that was how he herded the donkeys all the way to the farm.

"Did you have any trouble getting them here?" the farmer asked when Nasruddin arrived, dusty and disheveled from having walked for many miles behind the pack of animals.

"For a while, I must admit, there were some problems. Just up until I discovered the method of donkey-drivers."

"What method is that, Nasruddin?"

"The trick is this: you must always travel behind them, not in front or in the middle, and watch vigilantly, lest you lose track. Before I figured that out, the sneaky creatures were full of pranks. So, *effendi*, count for yourself and tell me: how many donkeys do you see?"

The farmer said, "Apparently, ten — the tenth donkey only has two legs."

5

ONCE NASRUDDIN WAS TAKING a heavy block of salt to market on donkey-back. He drove his little grey burro, Karakacan, through the stream, and naturally the salt was dissolved. He was angry for the loss of the payload of salt, and the donkey was frisky with the relief of having its burden lightened.

The next time the boy brought the donkey to the river, he was returning with a large load of firewood, which he had worked hard to chop down in the forest. As the animal waded through the stream, the timber became soaked and increased the donkey's burden. The little donkey staggered under its freight.

"Ha!" exclaimed Nasruddin, "you thought you'd caught a break the last time you went through the water, didn't you? Surely you didn't expect you'd always get off so easily, my old friend!"

NASRUDDIN REMOVED THE WOOD from the donkey's back and tried to shake as much water from the load as he could, but the timber was already rather waterlogged. He struggled to balance the bundle on his head and to reseat himself.

As he was traveling, balancing the huge pile of wood atop his head, he encountered his old friend, Hussein, who asked him why he was carrying so much lumber that way. Nasruddin replied, "My ass is so old and tired. All her life she has suffered so much on my behalf."

Hussein said, "I can see that you have great compassion for your donkey, but I still don't understand why you carry the wood on your head."

"She has enough of a load always carrying me around everywhere, poor old thing," Nasruddin explained. "So this time, to spare her the extra burden, I decided to bear its weight myself."

AS NASRUDDIN WAS RIDING his donkey home with a load of wood balanced atop his head, his neck began to ache, and so he decided to stop. He dropped the lumber and dismounted the donkey. After he stretched out a bit, and put the bundle of wood back onto the donkey.

Just as he was about to remount and leave, a doubt appeared in his mind: "What if the firewood is too wet to sell?" He only wanted to check to see if the wood was dry enough to be used as firewood, so he took out a match and lit just one of the sticks. That done, Nasruddin opened his water bag and had a refreshing drink of cool water.

When he turned around, to his (and the donkey's) shock, several logs of wood were burning! Nasruddin tried pouring the last of his water onto the flaming load of wood, but the donkey was freaked by the bonfire now blazing on her back and began running in circles around him. Nasruddin took off his turban and tried using it to put out the donkey's flaming burden, but that did nothing but fan the fire, scare the poor donkey even more — and then his turban caught on fire!

Finally Nasruddin got in front of the donkey, waving his hands and pointing, and yelled, "If I were you, I'd go that way — toward the river!" And the donkey charged off, braying frantically, in that direction.

NASRUDDIN FOUND HIS LITTLE grey donkey, Karakacan, soaking in the river, and after loading the remaining charred wood, they rode back home, Nasruddin seated backward, of course.

The donkey was moving at her usual plodding pace and Nasruddin's cajoling and prodding got no results. Eventually the old grey beast slowed, then came to a complete stop on the road. He tried taking the load off the animal, he coaxed it with soft words and a carrot, he tried pulling, he tried pushing. Although he made minimal progress forward, Karakacan was aged and tired and stubborn and needed a long break, if not an early retirement.

After some time his friend Hussein came by and said, "I see, Nasruddin, that your ass is dragging — if not already completely broken down."

"Yes, sadly it's true, Hussein — her get-up-and-go has gotten up and gone. But what can I do?"

Hussein produced a small brown bottle from his bag. "This contains a special ointment that will boost the animal's energy if applied judiciously to its rear end, I assure you." With that, he gave Nasruddin the bottle of plain ammonia and left quickly.

After calling out to thank the retreating Hussein for his trouble, Nasruddin took a rag and dipped it in the fluid, then dabbed it on the donkey's ass.

Karakacan's eyes widened, her ears stood up straight, and her nostrils flared — she brayed and reared and took off faster than Nasruddin had ever seen her run before! She bolted in the direction of the river again, leaving Nasruddin in the lurch. He shouldered the burden of charred firewood and trudged toward the river.

Nasruddin felt so tired, and he dreaded having to walk all the way home with the load on his own back. "This will get me nowhere fast," he groaned, "but at least I don't have to travel facing my ass's rear. Still, my old bones are weary and I need to move faster."

Nasruddin had a revelation. *If it worked so well for that tired old ass,* he reasoned, *just imagine what it'll do for mine.* He got out his rag and bottle, lowered his trousers and delicately dabbed a small amount carefully on his own behind. Soon enough Nasruddin was running just as fast as Karakacan had been, and before long caught up to her at the riverbank, where she was soaking her rump in the water. When he reached the water's edge, he dropped his burden and jumped into the river himself.

Seeing Nasruddin careening down the trail at top speed, yelling at the top of his lungs, fanning his rump, and splashing around in the water, Karakacan seemed to smile.

Nasruddin was walking along a street when he came across a water hydrant with a large wooden stopper sticking out of it. As he was very thirsty, he thought it would be fine to take a drink of water.

He bent over the water pipe, brought his lips to the opening, and uncorked the stopper.

The water gushed out with such force that it knocked him on his backside.

"Oho, so that's why they plugged your rear up tight," Nasruddin scolded the gushing hydrant. "And still, you have not learned the least bit of restraint."

Once young Nasruddin approached Ahmet and some of his friends with his pockets stuffed and said, "Whoever can guess what I have in my pockets, I'll give all the peaches."

"Peaches," the kids chimed out in unison.

"Goodness," said Nasruddin as he handed out the peaches, "how did you guess? It's impossible to hide anything from you guys."

Ismail, one of the kids, said, "Nasruddin, are you any good at guessing games?"

"Sure I am," Nasruddin said. "Try me."

"Sure you are. Now you guess what's in my pocket," said Ismail.

"Oh, give me a hint."

"Okay," said Ismail, "it's smooth and oval, white on the outside and yellow inside, and it tastes good."

"Oooh, that's a tough one," said Nasruddin. "Another hint?"

"It's shaped like an egg."

"Hmm. Let me take a wild guess: is it a piece of cake?"

"No, Nasruddin, that's wrong. Try again."

"Well, let's see. Oh, I know! It's a hollowed-out turnip filled with a carrot!"

6

ONCE YOUNG NASRUDDIN OPENED a booth at the bazaar with a large sign with brightly colored lettering, reading:

ANY 2 QUESTIONS — ONLY 1 GOLD PIECE

Aslan, Nasruddin's well-heeled neighbor, greeted Nasruddin at his new enterprise. "Isn't one gold piece a lot to charge for just two answers?"

"Yes. Now for your second question."

❧

"I MUST ASK YOU THIS, Nasruddin," said Aslan, "I have spent a vast inheritance, and I'm afraid that I will have to become a beggar on the streets. What can I do to save myself from such misery and suffering?"

"Oh, is that all you're concerned about?" Nasruddin replied reassuringly. "Not a problem. Soon you won't have to worry about poorness."

"What are you saying — that I will recover my fortune?" asked the desperate fellow.

"Not exactly," said Nasruddin. "I meant that soon enough you'll get used to being poor."

❧

ONCE WHEN YOUNG NASRUDDIN was a young ferryman — which was another thing he did for work — he had a customer, a famously brilliant pedagogue. The scholar requested to be taken across Akşehir River, which was very wide in those days. As soon as the raft was in the fast-running river, the weather turned bad. The scholar asked Nasruddin if he thought the trip was going to be rough.

"Don't ask me nothing about it," replied Nasruddin, as he tried to steer the raft, which as it turned out was leaking.

"Have you never studied grammar, you dolt?" insulted the pedant.

"No," said Nasruddin.

"In that case, boy, half your entire life has been wasted."

Nasruddin said nothing. Halfway across the river, a fierce storm blew up and the water turned choppy. The tiny raft was taking on water and was sinking quickly. Nasruddin dropped the pole, removed his shoes and tucked them in his belt, and said, "Haven't you never learned how to swim, sir?"

"No, you fool — I cannot swim a stroke — and you should never use a double negative."

"In that case, esteemed sir, *all* your life has been wasted," said Nasruddin as he prepared to dive overboard. "However, in your remaining time, feel free to use as many — or as few — negatives as you wish."

ANOTHER TIME WHEN NASRUDDIN was a ferryman, five blind men came and requested to be taken across the river. They negotiated a price of five silver pieces for all the men and their luggage.

Nasruddin helped the men aboard, then the dinghy left the dock in choppy waters. Nasruddin was such a clumsy oarsman that as he was trying to control the rocking boat, he knocked one of the blind men overboard. One of the other passengers said, "What happened? I thought I heard a splash."

Nasruddin said, "I have exceedingly good news for you. Once we arrive, you will have one silver piece less to pay for your fare."

ONCE, WHEN NASRUDDIN WORKED as a ferryman on the river, he was shuttling a small group of irreligious persons who made fun of Nasruddin as he warned them to repent their sins and prepare their souls for God's judgment, as death could always take anyone unprepared.

Suddenly a thunderstorm broke out and threatened to swamp the raft, and the passengers feared for their lives. Now they came whining to Nasruddin and cried: "Tell us what we can do so that God forgives us and saves us from death!"

Nasruddin advised them gravely: "Beware of carnal desire and sinful actions! Promise God that you will cease to lead such an unholy life, and I am sure that the Lord will spare you in His mercy and lead us to safety. Trust me!

"And by the way — over there, I can see the pier!"

⌒∽

Young Nasruddin went to the market, bought a small bag of dates, and returned home to eat them. His mother noticed that he was pocketing each pit very carefully and asked, "Why are you keeping the stones from the dates?"

Nasruddin said, "You think I am about to throw them into the street? Not I!"

"Why don't you throw away the pits, like everyone else does?" she asked.

"When I bought them," he replied, "I asked the grocer if the price for the dates included the pits, and he said that it was all included. 'The fruits come with the stones,' he told me, 'no extra charge.' So I may keep them to eat later, or throw them away, as I please."

⌒∽

Nasruddin was leading his old grey donkey, Karakacan, down the street just outside the narrow streets of the bazaar, counting his coins, when a con artist saw him coming and called out to him.

"Young sir! Excuse me! Pardon me!" he said as he walked up to Nasruddin. "You seem like a handsome fellow of exceptional insight and most discriminating tastes!"

Nasruddin was charmed. "Why, thank you, *effendi*. How did you know?"

"I saw you approaching and I can tell that you are a bright young man who is sharp enough to recognize that he needs something I have right here."

"Oooh," said the Mullah, intrigued. "what could it be?"

"This magic nosebag," the man said as he produced out of thin air a nosebag. "Magic nosebag, magic nosebag, give me a rabbit." Then he proceeded to pull out of the nosebag a rabbit. He repeated the magnificent magical manifestations with a flourish, producing next a ball, and then a potted plant.

Nasruddin couldn't part with his money fast enough. He took the magic nosebag and peered inside: it looked deep but empty.

"Just one thing," the salesman said, "before I leave you to discover the delights of your magic nosebag. Please — don't annoy it. These things are quite temperamental, as you can well understand, and very shy. Don't confide in too many people about its special nature. All will be well."

Nasruddin thanked him profusely and rode back proudly with the magic nosebag to Akşehir. Instead of proceeding directly to the teahouse as he would do normally, he went straight home. By now he was quite thirsty, so he sat down and placed the bag in the center of the table in front of him. "Magic bag, magic bag," he incanted, "please give me a cup of water."

He put his hand inside the bag but it was empty.

I get it, Nasruddin thought. *It's temperamental, and so it gives out only rabbits, balls, and potted plants.*

"Alrighty then, let's try this: Magic bag, magic bag, give me a rabbit instead."

No rabbit manifested. Nasruddin stared at the nosebag. "I would think it should be of no offense to ask. Please don't get annoyed with me. How am I supposed to understand the mysterious ways of magic nosebags?"

The Mullah thought, *When my donkey is temperamental, I buy it a new nosebag. So maybe the opposite is true.*

So the Mullah rode Karakacan back to town and bought a new donkey for the magic nosebag. As he returned home, Abdul greeted him and asked why he was leading two donkeys.

"An understandable misconception, Abdul *effendi*," said Nasruddin. "What you are seeing here is not two donkeys. This is actually one donkey and her nosebag, and one nosebag with its donkey."

7

NASRUDDIN WAS A LANGUAGE tutor — for that was one of the many things he did for work — so once he had a young student whose parents brought him for private instruction in Kurdish. Though Nasruddin himself knew only a few words of Kurdish, he thought he could fake teaching the language to the child, who likely wouldn't know any better, in any case.

"First, let's start with the word for 'hot soup'," Nasruddin tutored. "In Kurdish, this is *aash*."

"Sir," the student asked, "pray tell, what is the word for 'cold soup'?"

"There is no word for 'cold soup'— you see, the Kurds only eat their soup hot."

ONCE, WHEN NASRUDDIN WAS a smuggler — for that is one of the many things that Nasruddin did for work when he was a young man — carrying eggs across the border was highly illegal. Of course, that made the worth of eggs all the greater, and all the more reason to carry them across the border as contraband.

As he approached the customs post, Nasruddin was carrying two dozen eggs in a covered basket on his head, trying to keep the border guard, Halil, from peering inside the basket. Halil stopped Nasruddin and asked what he was transporting.

"The smallest conceivable chickens," said Nasruddin.

"There is a ban on importing livestock, so we shall have to impound your chickens," said Halil, locking the basket in a cupboard. "Of course, while we are making inquiries, we shall feed them for you."

Nasruddin pedaled fast. "You should understand that these are special chickens."

"Is that so?" said the guard.

"Indeed, this is so," said Nasruddin. "Why, surely you must have heard of animals who are so attached to their master that they grow old before their time, withering and dying young?"

"Yes, of course," replied Halil.

"Well, these special chickens are so young and sensitive, that if they are deprived of their master's company for even a few minutes, they grow *young* before their time."

"Oh, really? How young?"

"So young," said Nasruddin, "they can even revert to being eggs again."

ONCE YOUNG NASRUDDIN'S NEIGHBOR, Faik, came to him and asked if he would keep a large jar for him while he went away on pilgrimage for a month. Of course, he would want to have the jar back again upon he return. Nasruddin agreed, and stored the pot in the kitchen.

Several days passed, and the boy was curious to find out what was in the jar. Finally his curiosity got the best of him and, when he opened it, he was delighted to find it full of honey. *I'll just take one little taste,* Nasruddin thought. *Nobody will ever notice.*

He stuck his finger in, tasted the delicious honey, replaced the lid onto the jar, and went about his normal activities.

But since Nasruddin had no strong willpower, every day the same scenario repeated itself — with the boy thinking, *It's just one finger-full . . . nobody will miss it.* Naturally before long, he had tasted all the honey and the pot was empty.

When Faik returned from pilgrimage, he came to Nasruddin and asked, "Where's my jar of honey?" Nasruddin handed him the empty jar, and Faik cried out: "It feels so light!" He opened the jar and peered inside, then demanded, "Boy, where is my honey?"

Nasruddin replied: "Oh, how I wish you had not asked this question. And even greater than that desire, how I wish I did not have to answer."

ONE DAY, NASRUDDIN RETURNED home from the grain mill where he worked, ready to cook dinner, when he realized that he had no firewood. So with his trusty axe tied securely in his back of his belt, he walked into the woods to chop down a tree.

It was already well past dusk and dark, when Nasruddin found a good tree to chop down. He spat on his hands as if to get ready to grasp something, when realized he had misplaced his axe. He looked quickly all around the ground in the area, but his search was in vain.

Finally in desperation, he cried: "O Lord! If Thou can find my axe, then I promise Thou eight measures of barley!"

As Nasruddin uttered his prayer, and raised his arms in supplication to the Almighty, his tool slipped from his belt and landed with a loud *kelankk!* on the hard ground behind him. He turned around and, overjoyed to have found his axe again, shouted heavenward: "Truly I offer Thou my thanks, my Lord! But since it is so easy for Thou hear my prayers, let me also just ask Thou to find me eight measures of barley, so that I may I rid myself of the obligation toward Thou!"

ONE DAY YOUNG NASRUDDIN sat down for lunch, and at the first taste of his soup, he burned his tongue.

Nasruddin jumped up and cried, "Fire! Put out the fire!" then he ran into the street, dashing about like a madman.

Hussein called out to him, "Where is the fire?"

With tears streaming down his cheeks, Nasruddin pointed to his tongue and cried out, "Out of the way, brothers! The fire is in my mouth!"

ONE EVENING BEFORE BED, Nasruddin prayed for a financial deliverance. "I must have ten gold pieces to pay off all my debts," he whispered in his prayers. "Nine will not do. Eleven, more than I need. Ten, God willing, would be perfect."

Nasruddin fell into the most wonderful dream: he found himself kneeling and holding out his hands before a fabulous angel, who was smiling beatifically. The angel was holding a large pot full of gold, from which she took out one gold coin after another, counting each piece as she placed it in Nasruddin's outstretched fingers, "One ... two ... three ..."

The gold pot was so large and full, and the angel so generous! With each coin that fell into Nasruddin's cupped hands, he felt a thrilling rush of grace course through his body.

"Four ... five ... six ...," continued the honey-voiced divinity as the gold coins landed happily in Nasruddin's palms. With each clink of the metal coins, he experienced a surge of ecstatic energy. It was almost too much! Could he withstand yet even more blessings?

"Seven ... eight ... nine ..." Nasruddin counted with the angel. "Ten! I got all ten! They are mine!" he shouted jubilantly, finding himself wide awake with his arms outstretched, his hands clutched heavenward, but his palms bare.

Finding his fortune vanished, Nasruddin immediately lay down under the covers and pretended to sleep again. He shut his eyes tight and held up his hands, saying, "Okay, divine angel — I'll settle for nine!"

NASRUDDIN'S FATHER WAS THE head of a large *dargah*, the burial shrine of a great being, where many seekers, dervishes, and pilgrims would go to worship. Nasruddin used to listen to the pilgrims' tales of their search for God, and it inspired him to strike out on his own in search of the Truth. His father, Yousef, begged him to stay and help him take care of the temple, but Nasruddin insisted that he had to find his own way to God. Finally Yousef relented, and gave him a little grey donkey to ride as a sort of blessing.

For years Nasruddin wandered from forest to forest, shrine to shrine, and mosque to mosque, until one day at a remote crossroads, his devoted little grey donkey collapsed and died. Nasruddin was inconsolable in the loss of his dear companion. He rolled on the ground, rent his garment, beat his chest, tore out what little hair was left on his balding head, and wailed, "*Vai! Vai!* My faithful friend and constant companion has died and left me forever!"

As Nasruddin lay there weeping in the dirt at the crossroads, some pious people traveling on pilgrimage saw him in his grief. They took pity upon him and placed leaves and branches over the dead little grey donkey. Others covered it with mud. Someone brought a wooden box to protect the mound from the weather.

Nasruddin just sat there, brooding and silent, staring at the box.

Some charitable folks who lived in a small village nearby passed by the site and, thinking that Nasruddin was the bereaved devotee worshipping at the tomb of a great saint, painted the coffin white out of respect for the Master and his disciple.

Soon the burial site became a regular place of prayer for certain religious persons in the region, who often left heartfelt offerings of flowers, fruit, and incense. One local devotee passed his fez around and collected enough to enclose the box in a marble sarcophagus. Then another eager follower of the anonymous great being within the tomb built an altar before the tomb, and others enclosed the tomb and altar inside a temple, and before long many other true believers began to worship at the shrine of the unknown saint. The local priests were attracted to the new memorial, and of course, soon enough the incense vendors, fruit sellers, and florists heard of the place and set up businesses nearby to sell offerings to hundreds of seekers, dervishes, and pilgrims who came to worship.

Nasruddin by now was very busy running the shrine and had forgotten his sorrow. News spread far and wide that if a person prayed devoutly at the site, his or her prayers would be answered. The shrine drew larger and larger crowds of worshipers, who were all to glad to offer contributions, and from these funds a huge mosque was built. Soon the mosque became quite wealthy and famous, and several hundred people lived in the town that sprang up around it.

Eventually the news of the *dargah* reached Nasruddin's village. When his pious father heard of it, he went on pilgrimage to see the great mosque. When Yousef arrived and beheld that it was indeed his own son as the famous mullah of the new holy land, he was overjoyed. He embraced his long-lost child and said, "I'm so pleased at your success, considering the family of failures you're descended from. But tell me, my son, I am most curious to know — who is the great being buried here in this tomb?"

"O my unjustly proud father, what can I tell you?" Nasruddin wept into Yousef's arms. "The truth is: this is the dargah of the little grey donkey you gave me!"

"How peculiar and wonderful," said Yousef, embracing his son, "that is exactly how it happened in my life. My shrine is that of a donkey my father gave to me!"

⚬⚬⚬

PART TWO

MARRIAGE AND FAMILY

1

FATIMA, NASRUDDIN'S FIRST WIFE, was wed to Nasruddin from a nearby village by arrangement at a tender age. As was the custom those days in her tribe, she did not reveal herself to her husband before the wedding.

On their wedding night after the ceremony, Fatima sat before Nasruddin, parted the veil for the first time, and showed him her face. Unfortunately, she was quite a homely girl (although it should be said that she became less ugly as a young woman and that Nasruddin himself was no prize). Nasruddin cringed.

The next day as they were walking, she asked, "To which of your male relatives may I take off my veil and reveal my face, my love?"

"You may show your face to anyone you like," he groaned, "so long as you never show it to me!"

NASRUDDIN FOUND HIMSELF RAVENOUSLY hungry one evening when he sat down for dinner. With both hands he started to fill his mouth with food from all the dishes as soon as his wife Fatima set them down on the table. Of course, proper etiquette in those days was to eat with the first two fingers and the thumb of the right hand only. Astonished at Nasruddin's boorish table manners, she asked, "Why are you eating with two hands?"

Nasruddin replied slowly, between huge chomps of food, "Because I . . . don't have . . . three."

WHEN FATIMA WAS PREGNANT for the first time, she went into labor early in the evening and was attended closely in the bedroom by their neighbor, Setare, the midwife, while Nasruddin nervously waited outside. Many hours passed before anything else happened. Though he tried stay awake, Nasruddin was ready to fall asleep standing up when finally, at dawn, Setare came out and said, "Congratulations, Nasruddin! It's a boy!"

As the midwife returned to Fatima's side, Nasruddin could see the sun rising through the bedroom window. He was beside himself with pride, and he rushed to tell the neighbors.

"Congratulate me! I have just had a child!"

"Marvelous, Nasruddin!" said Hussein. "Is it a boy, or a girl?"

"Yes — how did you know?"

Nasruddin returned to outside the bedroom. After a few minutes, Setare called out to the Mullah again, exclaiming, "Congratulations, Nasruddin! You also have a darling baby girl!"

As the midwife went back into the bedroom, he could see that the sun had peeped over the horizon. He was certainly still proud, but now he started to wonder how would he feed two more mouths on his meager income as an aspiring young mullah.

Nasruddin stepped back to consult Hussein.

"Congratulate me! I have just had another child!"

"Wonderful, Nasruddin! Is it a girl, or a boy?"

"Yes — but how in the world could you have possibly known?"

The response was interrupted by Setare who once again rejoined Nasruddin, calling out to him, "Congratulations, Nasruddin! It's twin girls!"

Nasruddin suddenly rushed into the bedroom, grabbed the quilt and covers off Fatima, and threw the bedding over the window, then blew out the room lamps.

Fatima shrieked, "Nasruddin, what are you doing?"

"What else can I do?" cried Nasruddin, "Whoever sees the light wants to come out!"

Nasruddin was worried how he was going to support all the newcomers.

As he considered his situation, he thought of the Turkish custom, never broken, to reward someone who quickly delivers good news. He went to the town square and shouted, "Everyone, come hark my words! I have exceedingly great good news to share with you all! Please come close to hear the important information I am about to tell you."

In short order, a crowd gathered around the Mullah. His friend Abdul asked, "So! Nasruddin *effendi*, what is the excellent news you have for us?"

Nasruddin beamed proudly and announced, "My good news for all of you is —
I have been blessed with four children! Someone take up a collection!"

The crowd groaned its disappointment as one, and Abdul asked, "Are they boys
or girls, Nasruddin?"

"Indeed, I will declare again, for the very last time — yes, they are! But I beg of
you, please tell me — how could you possibly have known?"

ONCE WHILE NASRUDDIN WAS walking down a dusty road, he found a dead
chicken, which may or may not have already been dead when apparently it had
been run over by a cart. He took the badly mangled roadkill home, plucked it, and
prepared it. When he set the roasted bird on the table, Nasruddin's wife Fatima
could see there was something afoul with the fowl.

"Where did you get the run-over poultry?" she asked.

"This chicken is Providential," Nasruddin retorted, "as it appeared before me
already dead on the road as I was walking."

Fatima protested, "But Nasruddin, the bird is unclean and cannot be eaten,
because it has not lost its life by a man's hand."

"I believe you misunderstand the dietary laws," replied the Mullah. "Is a
perfectly edible roasted chicken considered unclean, because God has killed it,
instead of you?"

ONCE NASRUDDIN WENT TO the village butcher, Akram, to buy three kilos of the
finest cut of meat he could find, instructing the butcher, Akram, to trim it well. He
brought the select piece of mutton home to Fatima for her to prepare kabobs with
rice for them at dinner, then he went out with his donkey to sell pickles in town,
which was one of the things Nasruddin did for work.

Fatima eagerly set about preparing the kabobs, first grinding the meat very
fine, spicing it exactly to Nasruddin's liking, and then roasting it until the scent of
the delicious food filled their humble home and wafted out the open windows, and
the breeze carried the aroma on to the neighborhood.

As she was close to finishing Nasruddin's meal, three of Fatima's dearest friends
— Ina, Turan, and Setare — who from their homes nearby could smell the delicious
roasting meat, just happened to stop by for a visit. *Hoş geldiniz,* she said, welcoming
them inside the house.

As she served the women cups of sweet steaming tea and they all laughed and chatted, Fatima knew it would seem slim hospitality to serve her friends a second cup of tea when the air was filled with the tantalizing scent of the cooked lamb kabobs.

They won't eat much, Fatima thought, as she made up a platter of the kabobs, covered them with perfectly cooked rice, and poured warmed butter over it all. *There will be plenty left for my husband.*

Fatima was right that they wouldn't eat much — rice. Her neighbors helped themselves and unearthed the savory kabobs, all the while chatting about this and that and complimenting Fatima on her excellent cooking. Fatima beamed at their high praise as they ate, encouraging them to enjoy themselves.

Very soon after the last shred of meat was eaten, the women lauded Fatima as a cook and hostess, thanked her with invitations to come visit, and left to tend to their own homes and chores.

There was hardly any time left for Fatima to rearrange the remaining rice on a smaller platter before Nasruddin arrived home. He sat down for dinner and said, "The lamb smells absolutely delicious, my dear. What a wonderful cook you are!"

He stuck his fork into the mound of fragrant rice, but instead of stabbing a spicy kabob, there were only grains. He plundered the pile, but came up with nothing but rice.

Nasruddin was furious and demanded to know where the lamb he had brought went. "The whole house and yard smell of broiled mutton, but you feed me only rice. Woman, what did you do with the meat?"

Fatima had never seen Nasruddin so angry. "The cat ate it," she blurted out, "while I stepped outside — to get cucumbers from the garden — just before you arrived."

Nasruddin looked from Fatima to the scrawny cat stretched out lazily before the fire, and from the sleeping cat to Fatima.

He got out of his saddlebag the scales and weights he used for weighing pickles. On one side of the scales, he placed three kilogram weights. Nasruddin gently picked up the sleeping cat and placed her on the other side of the scales. He picked up the scales, which wavered back and forth slightly but soon stilled to show an even balance between the weights and the cat.

"The meat weighed three kilos," said Nasruddin sternly. "Now the cat weighs three kilos."

"Three kilos," Fatima echoed faintly.

Nasruddin looked back and forth between the equally loaded sides of the balance, then glared at Fatima, finally.

"If I am weighing the cat, then where is the meat?" asked Nasruddin. "And if I am weighing the meat, then where is the cat?"

Fatima could only shrug her shoulders.

NASRUDDIN LOWERED THE SCALE, cat, and weights to the floor, went to where his axe was mounted on the wall, and grabbed the axe, then turned around and faced the cat.

Fatima exclaimed, "Nasruddin — no! Please don't —"

"Relax, my dear. I'm just going to hide my axe," he assured her, and proceeded calmly to the pantry, where he opened the locked cabinet, fit the axe in sidewise, then closed and locked the cabinet.

Fatima asked, "Why are you hiding your axe?"

He cast her a suspicious look at the cat and then said to Fatima, "If the cat can steal three kilos of meat, certainly she can be only be tempted to abscond with an object worth ten times that."

2

ONE NIGHT FATIMA AWOKE from a sound sleep to see the Mullah standing over her. He shook her gently saying, "Wake up! Get up, Fatima, and find my spectacles — I need them right now!"

As she awoke, Fatima mumbled, "Why in the world you need your spectacles in the middle of the night, Nasruddin?"

"Oh Fatima, I was having the most lovely dream. A gorgeous angel came to me and hovered midair before me in the distance. She promised me a fortune in gold pieces, and indicated to me in sign language that she would return in another dream to deliver the gold."

"So why do you need your spectacles now — and why such a hurry?"

"For the life of me, I cannot make out the angel's face in the dream," explained the Mullah, "and I need my spectacles so I can see her face clearly! How else can I recognize her when she returns in the next dream? Quick, now, go get them — before I wake up!"

Fᴀᴛɪᴍᴀ ᴄᴀᴍᴇ ᴀᴄʀᴏss Nᴀsʀᴜᴅᴅɪɴ in the living room scooting around on his hands and knees, with his turbaned head bumping around, searching intently. She asked, "What are you looking for, Nasruddin?"

"I lost my ring in the basement."

"Then why are you looking for it up here?"

"I looked for it down there, but it was so dark there that I couldn't see a thing. Since I knew the light here is better, I came upstairs. I still can't find it, so next I'll go outside, where the light is even better, and maybe I'll find it there."

Oɴᴇ ɴɪɢʜᴛ, Nᴀsʀᴜᴅᴅɪɴ ʀᴇᴛᴜʀɴᴇᴅ home very late without a lamp, and was fumbling noisily with the gate. Fatima awoke and called out, "Who is it?"

Nasruddin said, "It is me."

"Why are you wandering around outside at this time of night? Can you not find your key?"

"I have the key," said Nasruddin, "it's the lock I cannot find."

Oɴᴇ ɪɴᴄʟᴇᴍᴇɴᴛ ᴇᴠᴇɴɪɴɢ, ᴊᴜsᴛ as Nasruddin and Fatima were settling into bed, Fatima suddenly sat bolt upright, clutching the covers, and gasped, "Mullah, I heard something outside! Light the candle on your side of the bed and go investigate."

Nasruddin, who was none too anxious to leave the comfort of his bed to confront whatever or whomever was outside there in the cold darkness, replied, "I can't even find the candle, Fatima. How do you expect me to tell *my* side from *your* side in the dark?"

Nᴀsʀᴜᴅᴅɪɴ ᴡᴏᴋᴇ ᴜᴘ ᴏɴᴇ night, and started to make a lot of clatter in the kitchen, which woke Fatima. She said, "What are you making such a racket for?"

"I have lost something, and I was looking for it," replied Nasruddin, before resuming his search, this time making even more noise as he went though all the cabinets and shelves.

Fatima got out of bed, lit a candle, and went to him. The kitchen and pantry were in complete disarray and she became furious. "What in the world did you lose that you have to make such a mess and wake me up in the middle of the night?"

"I was sleeping peacefully, having the most beautiful dream," replied Nasruddin, "but then I woke up and my dream disappeared. So I got up and started looking around for it where I thought I saw it last."

Nasruddin was with his friends when Hussein mentioned that one of the two twin brothers who had been in their class had died unexpectedly.

When Nasruddin went to the funeral procession, he rushed up to the boy and asked, "My condolences to you. Pardon the intrusion, but please tell me: which one of you was it that passed on?"

Aslan, a wealthy businessman who enjoyed Nasruddin's company, invited him to go bear hunting. Nasruddin was terrified at the prospect, but he couldn't decline the invitation for fear of offending Aslan, so he joined his bear-hunting party.

Upon Nasruddin's return home in the evening, Fatima asked him how the hunt went.

"It was so marvelous — I cannot even begin to tell you," he replied wearily.

"So then tell me," Fatima said. "How many bears did you kill, Nasruddin?"

"None."

"How many did you chase?"

"None."

"How many bears did you see?"

"None."

"You've been gone all day. How could it have gone so marvelously, then?" queried Fatima.

"When you're hunting bears," sighed Nasruddin, "none is more than enough."

3

For a festival day, the Mullah wanted some halvah, a heavenly sweetmeat made of ground sesame seeds and honey and spices and other fine ingredients, all of which Nasruddin went to the great trouble of buying and bringing to Fatima to ask her to make the halvah. She gladly prepared a large tray of it and they sat together that evening talking and eating and laughing. By bedtime, they had devoured most of the delicious halvah and put the rest away for breakfast.

After they retired for the night, not two minutes passed before Nasruddin sat upright, awake. He tapped his wife's shoulder and said, "Fatima, wake up — I have just had a revelation!"

She sleepily replied, "What is it now, Nasruddin?"

"Go bring the rest of the halvah, and I will tell you."

So she got up and brought him the halvah, which he ate. He burped, handed her the platter, wiped his mouth, said, "Thank you, my dear," and settled in comfortably back under the covers.

Fatima stood there silently until her patience wore thin. "Nasruddin, you numskull, now I won't be able to go back to sleep until you tell me — what was your fantastic revelation?"

"My great thought was: *Never go to sleep at night without eating the halvah that has been made during the day, for it is better in the tummy than in the mind.*"

FATIMA WASHED UP, AND when she returned, she found Nasruddin sprawled out on the bed. "Nasruddin, your halvah-filled belly has indeed taken up the whole bed. Please move over so I can have some room to sleep too."

Nasruddin, already half-asleep, grunted and rolled to one side.

Fatima blew out the candle and settled in to bed again, she said, "Now Nasruddin, it is too hot in here. Would you move over so I can be a bit cooler?"

Nasruddin rolled over an inch or so toward his end of the bed. Five minutes later, Fatima whined, "Now Nasruddin, you're still crowding me on the bed. Move over already!"

Once again, Nasruddin shifted farther on the bed until he was very nearly hanging over the edge. This seemed to satisfy Fatima for a few minutes, until he heard her say again, "Nasruddin, now you're breathing too heavily. Would you please move over so I can have some air?"

Nasruddin got out of bed, dressed quickly, and left the bedroom. He walked out the front door and through the gate, then turned right. He trudged down the road for several minutes, when he encountered Luqman, the *bekche* or town watchman, on his nightly rounds.

"Hello, Nasruddin," said Luqman, "where in the world are you walking at this hour of the morning?"

"I have no idea how far I'm supposed to go," replied the weary Nasruddin, "but I would greatly appreciate it if you would stop by my house, and ask my wife if I've moved far enough, or if I need to go farther? Meanwhile, I'll just wait here."

❧

Once, Nasruddin's friend and neighbor, Hussein, came by and asked to borrow a clothesline.

Nasruddin said, "I'm sorry, the clothesline is in use."

Hussein pointed inside the house and said, "But Nasruddin, I can see the clothesline, right there on the floor."

"That's quite astute of you to notice that the rope is just lying there."

"Well — if you aren't using the clothesline right now, I would like to borrow it, please."

"But the clothesline *is* in use just this moment," said Nasruddin.

Hussein's voice rose, "What do you mean, the clothesline is being used? The rope is not stretched out in the air hanging between two poles as a clothesline should be. It is coiled up on the ground, doing absolutely nothing."

"I'm afraid that you misunderstand," replied Nasruddin. "Its actual use is just that: lying there."

❧

Hussein was not easily discouraged from trying to borrow Nasruddin's rope. He asked, "So tell me, how long will your clothesline stay in use like that?"

"Offhand, I don't know," said Nasruddin, "but Fatima might be able to tell us."

"Well, then, why don't you go and ask her, Nasruddin?" persisted Hussein.

"Okay. Stay right there. Let me check," said Nasruddin, and he slipped inside the house. Ten minutes later Hussein knocked on the door. Nasruddin cracked open the door, emerged, and shut the door behind him. He walked slowly up to Hussein, and said quietly, "I'm sorry, but it turns out the clothesline is no longer in use lying on the floor. Fatima has now decided that she needed to use it."

"Oh, what does she suddenly need to use the clothesline for?"

"She said ... she needs the rope ... to dry ... some flour that got wet."

"That's impossible, Nasruddin! How in the world can you lay wet flour on a clothesline to dry it?"

"It's really not all that difficult — especially if you don't want to lend the clothesline."

❧

Nasruddin and Fatima happened to be in the market when they spotted their neighbor Faik, the potter, bargaining loudly with Hamza, the miller. When Faik saw Nasruddin, he called to him, "Nasruddin, you are the local magistrate. Please — you must settle our dispute."

Nasruddin and Fatima tried to duck around the corner, but it was too late to refuse. Faik said, "I will tell you my side first," and so Nasruddin listened to him give his sales spiel about the excellent quality of his wares and why the price was quite reasonable — in fact, he was offering it at a considerable discount.

Nasruddin stroked his white beard thoughtfully, raised his right finger, and replied, "I believe you are right!"

Hamza then countered the vendor's argument, pointing out the many flaws in the merchandise and citing lower prices at another stall elsewhere in the bazaar.

Nasruddin raised his left finger and stated to his neighbor, "I believe you are right!"

Fatima interjected, "Nasruddin, you nincompoop, don't be ridiculous. They can't possibly *both* be right!"

Nasruddin looked at his wife, raised both of his fingers, and said, "I believe *you* are right!"

NASRUDDIN WAS FED UP with Karakacan, his ill-tempered donkey, and decided to sell the beast at the market. So the next Wednesday, he took her to the donkey bazaar. Nasruddin found Musa, the livestock auctioneer, and handed over the donkey, then stood around and looked at some other donkeys. Then he spoke with some of the donkey traders about their animals. When Nasruddin's donkey was led up to the stand, Nasruddin was standing in the back and couldn't see over the heads of the men in front.

The auctioneer shouted grandly, "And here's a magnificent beast of burden! It's a superb, unequalled, fabulous donkey. Who will start the bidding for this fine donkey at five gold pieces?"

Just five, huh, mused Nasruddin, and as the auctioneer sang the praises of the donkey, he was impressed and raised his hand to start the bidding. Immediately a shill of the auctioneer pretending to be a farmer bid eight gold pieces, and as the auctioneer exaggerated at great length the donkey's many fine qualities, a short bidding tussle began, finally going to Nasruddin. Nasruddin's new donkey would cost him twenty gold pieces, far more than the worth of his old one.

So Nasruddin as the buyer paid the auctioneer twenty, and the auctioneer handed over the tether to the donkey, took his one-third commission, counted out thirteen gold pieces back to Nasruddin as the seller, thanked him for his business, praised him as a upright businessman, and left.

Nasruddin beamed with pride as he returned from the bazaar with his new prize, a donkey of the highest quality. He had to keep tugging the donkey, which, as stubborn as ever, resisted being led back. Nasruddin didn't mind at all. He could think only of all the fine words the auctioneer used to describe the animal. All the way home, dragging his donkey behind him, Nasruddin thought, *I never miss a bargain.*

⸎

WHEN NASRUDDIN's WIFE, FATIMA, saw her husband dragging his old donkey back to the stable, she seemed surprisingly cheerful. As it turned out, she had great news of her own. She informed him enthusiastically, "I caught the yogurt-seller as he was passing by, and asked him for two pounds. While he was looking the other way, I slipped my gold bracelet onto the weight-side of the scale, so he didn't realize that he was giving me a lot more yogurt for the money."

Nasruddin embraced Fatima and said, "My dear, keep up the wonderful work. With you working inside and me working on the outside, eventually we're going to make something of this family of ours."

4

ONE WINTER NIGHT, MULLAH Nasruddin and his wife Fatima were sleeping soundly in their own beds, snuggled up under the covers and quilt, when the loud din of quarreling voices outside wakened them. It sounded like two thieves were drunk and arguing about something, but neither Nasruddin nor Fatima could make out quite what was the source of conflict.

After the noisy row had gone on for a while, Fatima urged her husband to get out of bed and investigate the matter. "They could be thieves," she whimpered, pulling the bedsheets up close. "They could be terrorists."

Yawning, Nasruddin agreed to check out the disturbance. He was far too sleepy to bother to dress in his turban and cloak, which would have shown the shouting hooligans that he was a village judge, a man not to be disturbed in the middle of a heavenly dream. Instead, Nasruddin wrapped the quilt that Fatima had painstakingly hand-stitched around his shoulders and trudged outside to investigate the commotion.

As Nasruddin stepped outside into the cool night air to confront the two boisterous men, they stopped their fighting and faced the Mullah. Before Nasruddin could even say, "Stop fighting, will you?" the two men set upon him with fists and shouts. One of the thieves grabbed Fatima's quilt from off the Mullah's back, spun him around, then tore off into the night with the other man, leaving Nasruddin naked and stupefied.

Finding himself shivering, Nasruddin dashed upstairs to the bedroom, where Fatima was awaiting his return. She asked, "Nasruddin, what happened to the two men? What were they arguing about at this time of night? And where did my beautiful handmade quilt go?"

Nasruddin could only sigh and reply, "They must have been fighting about your quilt, because as soon as they took it, they stopped fighting. Still, I'm glad to report, now that the quilt is gone, the fight is done."

AFTER FATIMA'S QUILT WAS stolen, Nasruddin bought a bow, quiver, and some arrows. It made him feel more secure somehow, knowing that he had a weapon to protect his family and home — and his quilt — so he placed it near his bed.

One breezy night a loud flapping and rustling in the backyard wakened Nasruddin.

Seeing his wife Fatima snoring asleep in her bed, he crept to the window, picking up his trusty quiver and bow. There was definitely something moving out back, some sort of shadowy figure with his arms aflutter in the strong wind.

Nasruddin rubbed his eyeballs twice and blinked thrice and shook his head until his neck cracked, but he could only make out the cloak of the man standing at the far end of the backyard near the tree. The moonlight in the wind scattered clouds that obscured most of the faceless apparition, but Nasruddin peered at the dark figure in the corner of the yard as hard as he could, and he thought he recognized — could it be? — that someone was wearing his cloak? The thief must have nabbed it from the branch where Fatima hung it to dry after she'd cleaned it last night, and now was prancing about in glee at having stolen such a lovely warm cloak.

Nasruddin looked over at the snoring Fatima, his beloved first wife of so many years, and whispered, "Don't worry, my dear. I'll protect you — and my cloak!"

He flung the windows open, hoping the sound would scare the thief leaping in and out of the shadows in the backyard, but still the rascally character danced next to his apricot tree, flailing his arms wildly, now seeming to taunt Nasruddin.

He issued a warning: "Enough of your barbaric thievery! Return my fine cloak to me right now, or I'll shoot you right there!" Still the man — perhaps it was a ghoul or a *djinn*! — seemed to sway and wave his arms as the wind blew sharply around him.

"All right, you scoundrel! You asked for it!" Nasruddin was so terrified and angry that the bow shook in his right hand as he placed his arrow shakily on the notch, pulled back the drawstring with his elbow akimbo — and shut his eyes as tightly as he could.

He released the bow and ducked. The arrow hit something — he heard the sound of fabric ripping and a thud. Nasruddin squinted his ears, if such a thing can be done, listening for . . . the intruder . . . or anything.

As the breeze continued rustling the branches it became clear that the arrow had hit its target! Nasruddin peered over the edge of the window but, with the moon still darting in and out of the clouds, he could not see any movement near the apricot tree. He raised his bow triumphantly, silently praising God for protecting Fatima and his children from such an evil spirit, when suddenly he realized in horror — he'd just shot a man!

Nasruddin gasped, dropped the bow, shut and latched the windows, then ran downstairs and locked and barricaded the front door. Then he ran upstairs and seeing Fatima still sound asleep and snoring, he jumped under the quilt and pulled it around him tight, shivering like a little question mark scrawled in his bed until finally he fell asleep.

Fatima's alarming voice woke him the next morning, entirely too early, but not from beside him in bed. She was yelling for him from outside. Nasruddin tumbled wearily out of bed and cautiously unlocked and opened the window. Now he could hear Fatima's familiar screeching and see clearly, as she stood beside the tree, quite what it was that he'd shot the night before.

Fatima was cursing at Nasruddin as she tried to pull the arrow from his cloak to release it from the branch where she had hung it. Nasruddin's arrow had pinned the cloak right between the shoulders to the apricot tree.

Nasruddin waved his hands high above his head, dancing and singing with glee, "Praise God! God be praised!"

After struggling with the cloak, Fatima ended up tearing a rather large hole in it, leaving the arrow embedded in the tree. She stormed back to the house up to the window where Nasruddin was still praising Allah loudly.

Fatima yelled, "Nasruddin, you nitwit. Why do you keep saying 'God be praised'? You ruined your best cloak!"

Nasruddin embraced and kissed his wife, then held her hands as he danced around the room. "But do you not see, my dear? If I had been wearing my most unfortunate cloak, I would have been shot through the heart and killed myself! Praise, praise Allah — by Allah's grace, I am saved!"

⚘

Fatima realized how lucky indeed they were that Nasruddin was saved, and so that afternoon she repaired the hole in the cloak so that Nasruddin could wear it to the café that evening. When the Mullah returned home late that night, Fatima was sound asleep, snuggled under the quilt, when she was awakened by a loud thumping of something falling down the stairs. She heard a low groaning and called out tentatively, "Nasruddin, is that you? What fell?"

After a pause, Nasruddin groaned, "Nothing, Fatima. It was just my cloak."

"How in the world could your cloak have made such a racket?"

"This time, I was in it."

⚘

Times were tough. Unemployment was rampant, and the economy was in the pits. "I cannot find a job," declared the Mullah, "as I am already employed full-time in the service of the All-Highest."

"In that case," instructed his devoted wife, Fatima, "you should ask for your wages, because every employer must pay."

"That makes uncommon sense," said Nasruddin. "Perhaps I have never been paid because I have never bothered to request a fee."

"Then you had better go right now and ask," advised Fatima.

Nasruddin went into the garden and knelt, and cried out in supplication, "O Allah, this is your devoted servant Nasruddin here. Send me exactly one hundred — no fewer or more, please — gold coins, for all my past services are worth at least that much in back pay."

Nasruddin's neighbor, Aslan, a wealthy merchant whose yard adjoined the Nasruddin household, overheard Nasruddin's plaintive demands for back wages owed, and thought he'd teach Nasruddin a lesson.

While Nasruddin continued imploring Allah for his back wages in the exact amount of one hundred gold coins, Aslan went up to his private chambers where he kept his money, counted out exactly 99 gold coins into a bag. Then he quickly crept out to the roof of his house. Just as Nasruddin's head was bent to the ground, Aslan threw the bag from his window into the next yard, knocking the turban right off

Nasruddin's balding head, landing with a pleasant clinking thud onto Nasruddin's prayer rug. Then Aslan quickly crept down to stand at the latticed window in his wife's room, where he could observe Nasruddin's reaction undetected.

Nasruddin gasped in surprise, then looked skyward in curious and hopeful anticipation. Without offering so much as a word of thanks to Allah, Nasruddin emptied the bag onto his prayer rug and counted the coins, then recounted them. He couldn't seem to believe the result he was getting.

After watching the Mullah recount the coins seven times, Aslan had to stifle his laughter at Nasruddin's puzzlement as he crept away from the window, thinking that he'd keep that old fool Nasruddin in the dark for a day or two before he let him in on the joke and reclaim the 99 coins.

Finally Nasruddin announced, "You can owe me the last one." He rolled up his prayer rug, and took his newfound earnings inside.

Nasruddin sat down across from Fatima, then said, "I am one of the saints." He tossed the bag of gold coins on the table saying, "Here are my arrears."

Fatima was indeed quite impressed.

The next day, made suspicious by the succession of deliveries of food, clothing, and furniture to Nasruddin's front gate, Aslan went to claim the gold coins were his.

Nasruddin said, "You heard me calling for it and now you are pretending it is yours. You shall never have it, as payday has been long overdue me."

Aslan said, "Then we must immediately go to court of summary jurisdiction to have the qadi settle this dispute."

"I cannot go like this. I have a rip in my cloak that Fatima has to mend. If you sue me and we appear in court together and you are dressed so much better than me, the magistrate will be prejudiced in your favor."

"All right," Aslan said, "I'll lend you a proper robe you can wear to court."

"Also, my donkey's leg is lame," said Nasruddin, "and so I'll also need to borrow a horse, saddle, and bridle, if you don't mind." Impatiently, Aslan got Nasruddin properly mounted onto one of his own horses and the two men rode to court.

When Aslan brought his suit before Bekri the judge, he stated impatiently, "The 99 gold coins in Nasruddin's possession are mine, your honor. It was a joke that I was playing, you see, on the Mullah, because I heard him pray aloud to Allah that he would only accept 100 gold pieces. That's why I threw him the bag with 99 coins, to play a joke on him."

Nasruddin asked to approach the bench, then pleaded his case in a whisper directly to the judge. "This man is clearly bonkers. For some strange reason, he thinks everything of mine is automatically his."

"That's quite a counterclaim," said the dubious judge. "What evidence of this do you have, Nasruddin?"

"His very own words will betray him!" Nasruddin asserted. "Not only does he claim that my gold is his, he will even say this cloak is his."

"That robe *is* mine!" protested Aslan.

Nasruddin leaned in even closer, saying, "It's really quite pathological. Now, watch this rascal, next he will say that my horse is his, as well."

"Bur your Honor! That is *my* horse!" Aslan whined.

"Pitiful, pained, and petty," Nasruddin continued, "you can see how troubled he is. Listen: he will claim that even my horse's bridle is his."

"B-b-but that bridle *is* mine!" cried Aslan, who broke down into hysterical sobbing.

"Order in the court!" called the judge, banging his gavel. "I rule in favor of Nasruddin. Case dismissed."

WHEN FATIMA FINALLY REPAIRED the rip in the cloak so that Nasruddin could wear it out, she decided to also wash it, as it had gotten dirty, and she got out the big tub and a small bar of scented yellow soap, which back then was very expensive.

But just as she reached for her small, precious marble of soap to wash the cloak, a big black raven, observing her nearby from a willow tree, cawed angrily, flapped its wings, and flew directly toward her. Startled, Fatima put her arms up to protect herself and dropped the soap sliver, and the raven swooped down and plucked it with his sharp beak, then flew back to his willow tree.

Fatima began to wail at the top of her lungs, "My soap! That's my last bit of soap!" — and what a fine voice she had for wailing, too! Her loud, shrill screeches carried all the way across the village, where Nasruddin heard her and, thinking his wife in dire trouble, ran back to the house to rescue her.

Upon arriving at home, he found Fatima in near-hysterics, but at least now could understand the problem.

"My soap! My last bit of soap!" shrieked Fatima. "That wretched raven stole my precious soap in its horrid beak. When shall I ever get another?"

"My dear, do not worry about the soap," said Nasruddin soothingly. "Didn't you notice the color of the bird?"

"Yes, of course," she said, "the awful thieving bird is black."

"Indeed, blacker than even our dirtiest clothes. Do you not see? Clearly the bird needs the soap so much more than we do. Let him keep it."

c✱o

ONE AFTERNOON, THE MULLAH, fiercely brandishing a large metal spoon, chased Fatima out of their house and down the street, screaming at the top of his lungs,

"Don't try to stop me!" he threatened the terrified spouse as he ran after her down the street. "This is the last straw! Just let me get my hands on you! I'll show you what's what —!"

Since nosey neighbors are never far away, everyone was bound to hear the shouts and screams and rushed out to intercept the livid Nasruddin and to stop the familiar fighting. The men took Nasruddin into Hamza's house to talk him down and dispel his anger, and the women took Fatima to her friend Turan's to comfort and protect her.

As it so happened, Hamza was hosting a wedding party for his cousin. Nasruddin was seated at the dining table, where many trays of delicious baklava, a sweet pastry with pistachios and honey, were to be served the wedding guests. Naturally since the Mullah was so distraught, they encouraged him to help himself to the baklava on the tray in front of him.

Nasruddin immediately seized a piece of baklava in each hand and began gobbling one delicious, consoling piece after another, while he continued to kvetch about his wife, mumbling things like, "If I had caught that woman — I would've turned her around — this indeed was the last straw — how she abuses my tolerance!"

He finished one tray and moved on to the next, continuing his rant. "She should be punished like the spoiled brat that she is — I cannot live like this any longer," and so on and on he went, while chewing tasty chunks of baklava.

Hamza said, "Mullah, we've never seen you so upset. What happened?"

"We were discussing something and had different opinions. The disagreement turned into an argument which turned into a row, and we ended up exchanging slaps and punches."

Just then the women brought Fatima and the hosts did everything to calm and reconcile her and Nasruddin. Soon the Mullah and his wife were sitting together, laughing and gorging themselves on the heavenly sweet baklava and enjoying themselves while they joked at the head table of the wedding party.

Nasruddin turned to his devoted wife, "My dearest Fatima, please remind me to lose my temper more often — then life really would be worth living!"

Hamza brought the newlyweds to introduce them to the Nasruddins and said, "This serves as a fine example of how married couples can learn to get along, no matter what. Now tell us, Nasruddin, what were you and Fatima fighting about that made you so angry?"

"We were arguing about —," Nasruddin explained between big bites of baklava, "the reason that we had not been invited — to this wedding!

"She maintained that it was because your servants forgot to write out our names on the invitation list — but I felt quite certain that you were trying to avoid us because of the last nasty fight we had at one of your family weddings.

"Obviously," said the Mullah as he and Fatima began a new tray of baklava, "I was right all along."

Hussein ran into the teahouse in a panic, saying, "Nasruddin, come quick! Your house is on fire!"

Nasruddin seemed unconcerned and continued sipping his tea. "You see, my friend," said the Mullah, "my wife and I have an understanding: I take care of the outside affairs, and she takes care of all the domestic matters. So, would you be so kind as to run and tell her about the problem?"

5

Once Nasruddin was holding forth with the wags at the teahouse. Abdul, the baker, asserted that the numbers of the sexes were equally balanced.

"On the contrary," interjected Nasruddin, "there are actually only about 10 percent men."

"How do you figure that?" said Abdul.

"It is well-established statistical fact that 90 percent of men do exactly what their wives tell them to do."

Abdul said, "Your wife is a terrible gossipmonger. All day long while you are working, she visits our wives with her endless gossip and mindless prattle. She is always out, wandering from house to house."

Nasruddin seemed unconcerned. "If that were true, she surely would have dropped in to our house sometime to gossip with me — and most decidedly, she has never done that."

"Well, you should speak to your wife about staying home more. It isn't proper."

"Alright," said Nasruddin, "I'll be sure to mention it — the very next time I run into her."

Abdul said, "Your wife also wears the most garish make-up."

Nasruddin replied, "Why not? It looks good on her."

ABDUL SAID, "NASRUDDIN, YOUR wife has a terrible temper! Why, just last week your wife acted so angry — screaming, running around, throwing things at you — it seemed she was clear out of her mind."

"Don't be preposterous," replied the Mullah, sipping his tea. "I never knew my wife to have a mind, so how could she be out of it?"

MALI ASKED NASRUDDIN, "WHY is it that you never speak your wife's name?"

"Because I have no idea what it is."

"What? How long have you been married?"

"Twenty years, I believe."

"You're married now for two decades and you don't know your wife's name?"

Nasruddin said, "When we were wed, by our parents' arrangement, I had no intention of making a go at the marriage, so why should I learn her name?"

FAIK ASKED, "NASRUDDIN, KINDLY inform us: does kissing your wife break the fast following a holiday?"

Nasruddin answered, "Kissing one's spouse definitely breaks the fast when they are newlyweds. The second year of the marriage, hard to say. But most certainly, not after the third anniversary."

"NASRUDDIN," ASKED ALI, "IS it possible for a hundred-year-old man to bear a child?"

"Yes, if he has a 20-year-old accomplice."

NASRUDDIN ABRUPTLY STOOD UP and started to leave the teahouse. Hamza asked where he was going.

"I just had a brilliant idea. My wife has just turned 40, and I plan to replace her with two 20-year-olds."

6

ONE WINTER, WHEN NASRUDDIN shared a small house with his brother, he got the notion that he should sell his half of the property, so he called a land appraiser to come over for an appraisal.

"How much is my half of this house worth?"

The real-estate agent replied, "Not so much. This is not such a good season for this market. Why do you want to sell only half of the house, anyway?"

Nasruddin said, "Well, I decided I don't like living with my brother, so I want to sell my half of the house."

"Why don't you just sell it to him, then, and move somewhere else?"

"No, you see, *I* don't want to move. I love living here. I want my brother to move. So in order to make him move out, I have buy him out, but I don't have the cash. So that's why I have to sell my half of the house first."

NASRUDDIN DECIDED TO TAKE a second, younger wife, Kerima. It was clear from the start that she and Fatima were fiercely jealous of each other, and Nasruddin needed to find a way to appease them both.

Separately, to each of his wives, Fatima and Kerima, he gave a blue bead, and said, "This blue bead will ward off the evil eye. Never tell anyone about this precious blue bead or reveal it to anyone, and the blue bead will protect you."

Later Nasruddin and both wives were walking and Kerima tugged on his left sleeve and asked, "Nasruddin, tell me, which of us do you love best?"

The second wife tugged on his right sleeve and repeated, "Yes, Nasruddin, tell us which one, do you love most!"

"The one with the blue bead," he declared, giving each of their hands a little squeeze, "is the one who has my heart."

NASRUDDIN'S TWO WIVES WERE always vying to be his favorite. Once as they were walking by the river, Kerima, the younger, prettier one said, "Nasruddin, which of us do you love best?"

"Perhaps I could answer that question properly," Nasruddin said, "if you put it into practical terms."

"Okay, then — say, if the three of us were in a boat in the river and it capsized, which of us would you rescue?"

Turning to Fatima, a larger, older, but moneyed wench, he said, "You're a bit of a swimmer, aren't you, dear?"

FATIMA FELT HORRIBLY ILL and asked for the doctor, Berrak, so Nasruddin dressed and was about to get him to come attend her. As he was leaving the house, however, she sat up in bed and called out to Nasruddin, "By God's grace, I'm healed! My pain has left me and I no longer need a doctor!"

Nasruddin said, "Yes, dear," but then he ran out of the house and rushed to the doctor's house.

When the Mullah arrived breathlessly, Berrak asked him, "What is the panic? Why have you run here to get me?"

Nasruddin replied, "My wife was in quite a bit of pain but, just as I was leaving the house, her aching suddenly stopped, so I ran here to tell you before you left not to bother coming."

ONE MORNING, THE WISE fool Mullah Nasruddin woke up, yawned, and put on his dressing-gown, as he did every day.

He decided that he would bathe early, and needed water for his bath, so he called for Ahmet, his son. He handed him a large earthen vase and told him to go fill the container at the nearby well.

The boy took the vessel and turned to go, but just then Nasruddin swatted him across the back and yelled, "And don't break it!" which nearly made Ahmet drop the fragile vessel.

Faruk, Nasruddin's nosy neighbor, who watched the whole thing, reproached Nasruddin after his son left. "Nasruddin, why were you so harsh with your child? Why did you punish him before he's broken anything or done something else wrong?"

Nasruddin regarded his neighbor and said, "Don't be foolish. It wouldn't do any good to reprimand him *after* he broke the vase, would it?"

ONCE NASRUDDIN INSTRUCTED HIS son Ahmet to go outside to see if the sun had risen. When the boy returned from outside, he said, "I cannot tell for sure — it is still too dark to tell if it is sunrise yet."

"You young fool," said Nasruddin, "why didn't you take a lamp with you?"

DECIDING FOR ONCE TO fast all 30 days of the month of Ramadan, Nasruddin devised a method to keep track of the days. Every day he put a pebble in a pot, figuring that when the time was up, he'd just count the pebbles.

Unknown to Nasruddin, his little daughter, Hafiza, noticed his daily habit of putting a pebble in the pot. Wanting to be helpful to her father, she went around the garden and collected lots and lots of rocks, and added one or many to the collection whenever she liked.

Two weeks later, the Mullah's friends Sedat and Ismail stopped by and asked him how many days remained in the fasting month. Nasruddin emptied his pot and counted the stones, then hesitantly returned with the information: "It seems that 49 days have passed."

"How can that be? There are only 30 days in a month!" said Sedat.

"I'm not exaggerating in the least," Nasruddin asserted. "In fact, I was being conservative in stating that number. It is actually much later than you think. Truth is, today is the one hundred and forty-ninth day of Ramadan!"

7

NASRUDDIN WAS CHATTING WITH his friends Jafar and Abdul one summer day when his son, Ahmet, came running and told him that his mother-in-law, Hayat, had fallen in the river. Nasruddin sighed and turned to go upriver.

Jafar stopped him, saying, "Nasruddin, if your mother-in-law fell in the water in that direction, shouldn't you head downstream to rescue her?"

Nasruddin replied, "Listen, I know my wife's mother, and Hayat is undoubtedly the most contrary person on the face of this earth. If the usual place to look for most people is downstream, then the best place to look for *her* is upstream."

ONCE NASRUDDIN WAS STTING by the side of the road by himself, eating a large roast chicken, when Musa, the camel-seller's son, came by and saw him eating the tasty bird. The boy rubbed his tummy and said, "Mullah, I'm so hungry. Please give me some of that yummy chicken."

"Indeed . . . willingly, I would gladly . . . share some . . . of this delicious . . . chicken," said Nasruddin as continued to chomp away and gobble the roast fowl, "but for the unfortunate . . . fact that it . . . belongs to my wife."

Musa pouted. "If it is your wife's chicken, then why are you eating it?"

"Well, you see . . . my child, she gave this chicken to me . . . with the implicit understanding . . . that I should eat it all!"

ONE DAY, NASRUDDIN RAN into his friends, Abdul, Süleyman, and Jafar, and got to talking about many things. Not wanting to end the flow of such good conversation, Nasruddin graciously invited the men over for dinner.

However, he invited them to eat with him without first checking with Fatima. When he arrived back home, Fatima cuffed his ear and said, "Nasruddin, you fool! We don't have the least bit of food in the house — we don't even have wood to cook anything!"

Nasruddin recoiled and, thinking quickly, grabbed a ladle and a large bowl, then calmly walked into the dining room where his friend were waiting for dinner.

Nasruddin went around the table, and mimed as if he was actually ladling out hot delicious soup in the bowls of each of his guests. After he pretended to ladle some hot soup into his own bowl, Nasruddin set down the imaginary pot and ladle, and sat down to eat it exuberantly, making much slurping and ahhhing and blowing on the spoon.

The men just stared at him in disbelief at first, then Süleyman finally asked, "Nasruddin, what are you doing? Where is our dinner?"

He set down his spoon and got up from his seat, then picked up the large soup bowl. He said, "With this huge bowl, I had intended to serve you both the most delicious and hearty soup and invite you to eat your fill. However, seeing as that we have no rice, meat, vegetables, or butter, nor even fire to cook it with, I had to serve you all imaginary soup from this large bowl. I trust you will all enjoy yours as much as I enjoyed mine."

NASRUDDIN AND HIS SON, Ahmet, were taking a summer trip with Karakacan, their faithful little grey donkey, the son riding while the Mullah walked alongside. Although the morning sun was quite warm, the three travelers were happily moving along the road at a pleasant enough pace when they encountered some pilgrims. One elderly fellow in the group glared at Ahmet as they passed each other. The man shook his finger and admonished Nasruddin's son, "Look at you, a healthy young man, letting your aging father walk. Why, the old man looks like he's about to have heatstroke. That's today's youth for you — indolent and disrespectful."

After they passed out of sight and earshot of the men, the boy felt very ashamed and got off the donkey. He insisted that his father ride while he walked, and so they went and everything was fine for a while.

Farther along they met a group of women sitting by the road. They clucked their tongues, waggled their heads, and complained loudly, "Look at that — the lazy father rides the donkey and makes the little boy walk, on a hot day like this. How cruel and unfair is that?"

Embarrassed by the women's comments, Nasruddin pulled his boy up to ride on Karakacan with him, and they traveled like that for a while in silent dread of the next encounter.

Before long they approached some villagers, and one piped up, "What a shame! I feel sorry for that abused little donkey — carrying both of those healthy, full-grown men in this blazing heat. Those buffoons are surely going to break its back. The poor beast looks almost ready to collapse."

After this group passed, Nasruddin stopped the donkey, dismounted, and helped Ahmet get off. He grasped both his son's hand and the donkey's rein and declared, exasperated, "Now nobody can complain," and they resumed their journey.

At the next village, they walked by a shop where several men were standing. When the men saw the trio trudging along on eight legs, they laughed and pointed, taunting them, "Look at those goofballs — walking in this heat with a perfectly good donkey they could ride! Don't they have any brains at all?"

Nasruddin turned to Ahmet and said, "This just goes to show you, my boy, about the wicked criticism of people whom you don't know. Everyone has an opinion and is quick to share it with you — but there is no pleasing anyone in this world. Therefore, you may as well just do as you wish."

A GNARLY BAND OF BANDITS came upon an abandoned monastery in the countryside near Akşehir and decided to inhabit the place. Hoping to cash in on the Sufi reputation as respected teachers of immense insight, they put on stolen white tablecloths, intending to pose as dervishes in order to catch, confuse, and rob hapless travelers. The group began to beat a rhythmic dirge that was sure to catch the attention of some hapless sucker.

As it so happened, the Mullah and his son were traveling in the countryside at that time and came across the freshly converted dervish retreat center. Nasruddin told Ahmet, "Look, night will be falling soon, and this appears to be a highly advanced sect. Let us humbly request their hospitality and stay the night." The pseudo-monks in their white outfits welcomed them in and immediately began the evening service, which seemed to entail mostly of jumping and spinning around in a circle while chanting certain words. The fake dervishes encouraged him to participate, so Mullah handed over the rein of his little grey donkey to his son and began to jump and spin about and sing along with their peculiar chant.

The dervish impersonators intoned, "I surrender all attachment to everything!"

The Mullah obediently repeated the words as he gyrated, "I surrender all attachment to everything!"

Next they chanted, "I forsake all desire for physical possession of anything!"

The Mullah repeated as he spun around, "I forsake all desire for physical possession of anything!"

The fake monks sang, "I renounce my addiction to the illusion of ownership!"

Nasruddin breathlessly repeated, "I renounce my addiction to the illusion of ownership!" over and again, louder and louder, as he whirled round and around.

The false dervishes then began chanting faster, "I give away my saddlebag and little grey donkey!"

The Mullah gasped the words, "I give away my saddlebag and little grey donkey!" as he turned in place, faster and faster as the tempo increased, until finally he was spinning and shrieking at such a hysterical frenzy that he fainted and collapsed to the floor.

When Nasruddin finally came to in the morning, his saddlebag and little grey donkey — and the dervishes — were nowhere in sight. The Mullah awoke his son and started to cuff him, saying, "What did you do, you little fool? You were left in charge of the animal!"

"But Father," said Ahmet, "when one of the dervishes came and led away the donkey, I ran to you, and you kept saying, "I give away my donkey and saddlebag," so often and with such fervor and in front of so many witnesses that I understood that you meant to give them away."

ONE EVENING, AFTER CONSIDERABLE deliberation, as they sat down for dinner, Nasruddin told Fatima, "I have decided to become a vegetarian. I will forego fish, fowl, and meat out of respect for all sentient beings."

Fatima said, "That's too bad, because I made a wonderful fish stew for dinner tonight."

"I'll just have some of the broth from the soup, thank you."

"Suit yourself."

As Fatima poured the soup from the pan, she tried to hold back with a spoon the offending but delicious smelling chunks of fish that were falling into his bowl.

Nasruddin held up his hand and said, "Fatima, please — don't stop the fish, of their own informed consent and free will, from swimming into the bowl."

ONE NIGHT AS THEY retired for sleep, Nasruddin stuck his bald head out the window and looked at the stars and sky to assess the weather for the next day.

"Tomorrow," he announced to Fatima, who was getting into bed, "if it is pleasant outside, I shall plow the field."

Fatima glared a warning at him. "You shall plow the field — *God willing!* Do not forget to say *Insh'allah*, my good husband!"

Ignoring his wife's comment and noting some gathering storm clouds, Nasruddin continued, "If it rains tomorrow, I shall chop wood."

"Speak carefully, Nasruddin!" rebuked Fatima. "Never, never, never say what you will do without adding *Insh'allah!* Like this: 'Tomorrow I shall weave, *Insh'allah*.'"

Less concerned than she was about this particular religious custom, Nasruddin replied, "Either it will rain or it will shine, and I have decided what to do in either case! If it rains, I chop! If it shines, I plow!" And with that he pulled the covers over himself and was soon snoring soundly.

Fatima knew better than to argue with the sleepy Mullah, but that night her sleep was disturbed by dream after dream of the bad luck that occurs when a good Muslim forgets to say *Insh'allah*. Nasruddin, however, slept as soundly and loudly as his little grey donkey.

Morning brought a steady chilling rain, but stoically Nasruddin shouldered his axe and headed to the woods. He was hoping that his wife or one of his friends might say a word of discouragement, at which he would gladly have turned around to return home, but alas, Fatima was silent as Nasruddin left, and nobody was out in the awful weather.

By the time Nasruddin trudged along the rutted main road out of the village, he was soaked and cold. Ahead at the crossroads he saw a group of men, one of whom, Nasruddin thought, might be kind enough to dissuade Nasruddin from working in such harsh weather. As he approached them, however, he could see they were soldiers having some sort of argument. He wished he could avoid encountering them, but it was too late — they had noticed Nasruddin approaching.

"Hey, you!" growled the captain of the soldiers at Nasruddin. "Tell us — which is the way to Konya?"

Nasruddin tried his best to act stupid. "Don't ask me! What do I know?" he shrugged, feigning ignorance. "I am just an old oaf heading to the woods nearby to chop wood," he said, trying to casually pass by the group of mean-looking soldiers.

This show did not impress the captain, who grabbed the Mullah by his cloak and said, "Oh no, you rascal, you don't fool us so easily! We will help you remember!"

The soldiers shoved, slapped, and shook the Mullah, until he cried out, "Funny thing! Ha ha! I just remembered the way to Konya now!"

"Then lead us there, smartass," said the captain. "March!"

Drooping his head so dejectedly that his turban seemed to rest on his shoulders, Nasruddin led the group through the rain on the long muddy road to Konya. Presently the mud sucked his shoes off, and then his feet seemed to turn into balls of mud that made it even harder to trudge forward, but any time he slowed, the soldiers brutalized him with boots and fists.

As he plodded on and on, Nasruddin could only think of Fatima, sitting snugly at home, safe and warm, working at her loom ... wise Fatima, who had common sense and knew enough to have said the night before, "Tomorrow I shall weave, *Insh'allah*."

It was nearly dusk when they arrived at Konya, and the soldiers were only too happy to be rid of their guide. Without a word of thanks, they entered an inn and slammed the door shut behind them. Knowing not a soul in the strange town, lacking even two coins to rub together, Nasruddin decided it would be best to use the remaining daylight to try to get home.

Soon enough after Nasruddin began the trek back to Akşehir on this moonless, monsoon-like night, he could see no farther ahead than his outstretched arm. He had to feel his way along the rutted road with his hands to move forward. He was so exhausted that he would have slept in the soft mud, except for his sneezing and coughing impelled him to press on toward home, where Fatima was no doubt warm and dry, having said the proper blessing, *Insh'allah*.

Well after midnight, Nasruddin stumbled back on the cobblestones of Akşehir. He leaned up against the gate at the entrance to his home and jangled the knocker.

Fatima opened the door to a vision of her exhausted, bedraggled husband, so covered with mud from heels to head that she could hardly recognize him. "Is that you, Nasruddin?" she exclaimed in shock.

"Yes, my wise Fatima," Nasruddin whimpered, "it is me — *Insh'allah!*"

—∞∞—

PART THREE

DONKEY TALES

1

ONE DAY, AN UNKIND neighbor, Faruk, asked to borrow Nasruddin's faithful little grey donkey, Karakacan.

The Mullah stroked his long grey beard for a minute. "I'll have to ask her permission first," he finally responded, "what she thinks about the matter."

The neighbor agreed to this foolishness, saying, "Alright then, go and ask her."

Nasruddin returned from the stable with a long face.

"I'm terribly sorry," he told Faruk, but my donkey is psychic, and she told me that the future does not bode well for your relationship with her."

"Really? I can't imagine why she would say that. What exactly does your prescient donkey see in her destiny with me?"

"I asked her that very question. She said, 'Long journeys and short meals, sore bones and scuffed knees.' Not only that, she said that you are likely to slander me and my family in my absence."

Faruk reacted angrily and began reviling Nasruddin and his donkey, when the Mullah held up his hand and halted his tirade. "Clearly now, the donkey was entirely correct in her assessment of you," the Mullah said, "except that you are apparently willing to slander me to my face."

ON ANOTHER OCCASION, FARUK called on his neighbor to try to convince Nasruddin to lend him his little grey donkey.

"Terribly sorry," the Mullah answered, "but I have already lent out the animal to go to the mill."

No sooner had Nasruddin spoken than Karakacan brayed loudly from inside the stable. "But Nasruddin," said Faruk, "I can hear your donkey, inside there! I'm disappointed that you won't let an old friend like me borrow your donkey."

In his most dignified manner, Nasruddin replied, "Any fellow who believes the word of a simple donkey over that of a respectable mullah with a long white beard like me does not deserve to be lent anything." And with that, he stepped back into the house and shut the door in Faruk's face.

NASRUDDIN WANTED TO SELL his firewood door-to-door, but he needed a new donkey to help carry the load around town. After much haggling at the donkey bazaar, he purchased the milkman's former donkey, and the next morning set off on his rounds. He led the young, perky beast of burden away from the market. The donkey, for her part, was a creature of habit and always remembered the daily route through the streets, helping her master sell his milk, through the streets around Akşehir. Unknown to Nasruddin, though, this donkey had developed the habit, as she reached certain spots along the route where the previous master had sold his milk, of braying loudly as a signal to the locals that they should come out and get their milk.

After Nasruddin loaded up, he began leading the donkey the quickest way toward the market, but the animal stubbornly insisted on taking its previous path. Nasruddin threw up his hands and relented. He thought, *This donkey acts like she knows the way better than I do — so maybe she is right!* He slackened the tether, and let the young donkey lead the way until they reached the first point of sale, where the donkey stopped abruptly and would not budge forward even a hair.

Nasruddin thought that the donkey must know that this is a good spot to sell, so he took a deep breath, and got ready to call out for folks to come buy his wood. He was interrupted, however, by a loud, long bray. One of the local women, Setare, who was long accustomed to hearing the familiar call of the milkman's donkey, brought out the milk cans, but when they saw that it was just Nasruddin selling firewood, she reviled him and went back inside.

As the donkey led the way to the next stop on the route, Nasruddin was rapidly becoming less delighted with the animal. Again he drew in his breath, ready to proclaim his firewood to all — and again the donkey opened her lips wide, almost seeming to smile, and brayed loud enough to drown out Nasruddin as he made the call for firewood. Soon enough, another local woman, Turan, came out with a milk jug under each arm, but soon enough she realized Nasruddin's folly, and returned to her home disappointed.

After several episodes of the same unsuccessful sales tactic, Nasruddin had sold not so much as a matchstick of wood. Finally the Mullah could stand it no more. He faced Karakacan, shook his fists, and yelled, "Let's settle this matter once and for all, you miserable, impudent animal: Who is selling here — you or me? You bray to announce the firewood, and they attack me for not bringing the milk."

BECAUSE OF A LONG drought followed by a protracted winter, Nasruddin had to ration the barley he fed his donkey. So he decided to teach the donkey to eat less. He put the donkey on a diet and started feeding it just a little bit less barley every day. At first, the donkey seemed just as content with what it was offered, so Nasruddin continued gradually reducing the number and amount of the donkey's meals. The donkey was quieter than usual and moved slower, but to Nasruddin the animal seemed fairly content.

After several months of this diet, however, one day Nasruddin walked into the stable to find that the donkey died.

Nasruddin, desperately sorry, lamented to Fatima, "Such a pity. All the donkey needed was just a little more time and the poor beast would have gotten used to hunger. Sadly, she didn't live long enough."

ONCE, NASRUDDIN TRAVELED TO Konya to borrow money from Jalal, his friend who lived there. Jalal, who knew that Nasruddin and his money were soon parted, put the cash into a purse for safekeeping and instructed the Mullah to be extra cautious on the trip home.

All the way back, Nasruddin felt fearful and paranoid, constantly looking over his shoulder. Like most folks, Nasruddin worried about money a lot when he had none, and he worried about it even more when he had some. "I must find a safe place to leave this money," he resolved.

But by the time Nasruddin crossed the town square on his way home, he had not come up with a secure place to stash his cash. As he neared the far edge of the square, he noticed a flagpole and thought, "Here's a obviously safe place — nobody would ever think to look up there for my money." So he shimmied up the pole, left the purse dangling from the top, climbed down, and went home to recover from his journey, knowing his loan was secure.

As soon as Nasruddin left the square, however, some street urchins who had been watching the whole scene ran to the pole. One climbed up, replaced the cash with an ox turd, and set the purse back atop the pole precisely as Nasruddin had left it there.

The next day when Nasruddin came with Fatima to get the money, he climbed up, retrieved the purse, and brought it down to the ground. When he opened the purse, the turd fell out.

Nasruddin and Fatima stood there, astounded. Finally Nasruddin exclaimed, "How in the Prophet's name did an ox get way up to the top of that pole?"

ONCE NASRUDDIN WAS TRAVELING with his small grey donkey Karakacan on a hot dusty road when they came upon a stand of shade trees. Nasruddin dismounted and rested for a while. Karakacan was always ready for a break from the blazing heat. Nasruddin folded his cloak and put it into the donkey's saddlebag, then propped himself up against the side of a tree and promptly dozed off.

A superstitious and nearsighted thief, who had been following and thought he saw Nasruddin put something valuable in the donkey's saddlebag, silently approached behind Nasruddin as he snored peacefully.

Just as soon as the thief opened the saddlebag and grabbed the cloak, Nasruddin's vigilant donkey brayed long and loud. Nasruddin awoke and instantly grasped the situation, jumped up and down and shouted exuberantly, "An ass's bray! An ass's bray! Praise Allah! Success is mine! Victory is mine! I am safe! What an auspicious omen! The prophets say that an ass's unexpected braying always foretells great good fortune! What excellent news! How lucky am I!"

The would-be thief thought, *A donkey's bray may be auspicious for him — but probably not for me! I'd best not press my luck!* Leaving the cloak in the saddlebag, he ran as fast as his thieving legs could carry him.

As Nasruddin settled back down in the shade to enjoy his nap just a little longer, he chuckled and thought, "Well, I guess that was one prophecy that worked out to be true."

NASRUDDIN WAS TIRED OF feeding and washing his donkey, so he asked Fatima to do it. She refused, and the argument rose to the level of a dispute in which it was decided that whoever speaks first should feed the donkey. Nasruddin sat stoically in a corner and skulked. Fatima soon became quite bored and wandered off to visit her friend and neighbor Setare.

Shortly the Nasruddins' thief entered the house, at first thinking it so quiet that nobody must be home. When he saw the Mullah, sitting mute and immobile with his arms crossed petulantly, at first the thief was startled. But then he realized the Mullah was no threat, and went about his business. He proceeded to trash the place and put all the family's valuables in a large sack. As he was leaving, the thief snatched the turban from Nasruddin's bald head.

As dinnertime, Fatima was still enjoying herself, chatting with Setare, and she sent her son, Ahmet, with a bowl of soup to bring to Nasruddin.

Ahmet was understandably confused when he got to their house and found the Mullah there alone with the place in shambles. Nasruddin kept pointing to his head to indicate his stolen turban, but the boy misunderstood the strange gestures and poured the soup on Nasruddin's head, then beat a hasty retreat to inform Fatima what happened.

When Fatima got home, she saw the house ransacked, all the drawers and doors open, the valuables gone, Nasruddin sitting in the corner, silent but scowling, covered with soup. "What have you done, you witless lamebrain?" she shrieked. "Where's our furniture? What —?"

"Yesss! You have lost! Now you must feed and wash the donkey!" Nasruddin exclaimed with glee. "And I hope you're happy with what you accomplished through your boneheaded stubbornness!"

2

ONE NIGHT, NASRUDDIN'S DONKEY was stolen. Instead of consoling Nasruddin, the wags in the teahouse the next morning offered words of remonstration.

"As they say, 'Take care of your donkey, it will carry you from Morocco to Mecca.' So Mullah, why didn't you take care to tie up the donkey securely?" asked Ali, the teahouse keeper.

"How could you have slept through the theft of your beloved ass, Nasruddin?" questioned Faik.

"You should have replaced the rotting door on your shed, Nasruddin," commented Hamza.

"I bet you didn't even close the bolt on the shed door," accused Hussein. "That'll teach you."

"You were just asking for someone to break in, the way you neglect to secure your stable," added Nasruddin's uncle, Mesut.

Nasruddin listened to the wags' criticism for a while, and then retorted indignantly, "Enough! Obviously, it's completely unfair to blame me alone, or even primarily, for the theft of my ass."

"Tell us, Nasruddin," said Ali, "who else was responsible?"

"Don't you think the thief was at least a tiny bit guilty in all this," the Mullah replied, "or was he entirely innocent in your view?"

NASRUDDIN FINISHED HIS TEA and went to the police station to report the theft.

"Mullah," said Luqman, the town watchman, "this is a very serious case. We will spare no effort to find Karakacan. After all, you and your donkey are rather famous. Now, start at the beginning and tell me how it happened."

"How can I possibly tell you about it when I was not even there? If I knew how it happened, it wouldn't be stolen, now, would it? Besides, it is not any of my business to know how a thief would steal a donkey."

THE SEARCH FOR NASRUDDIN's little donkey was not going well. The men and boys of the village were looking everywhere, but his beloved donkey was not to be found. Still, Nasruddin seemed to be happy and unworried.

Exasperated, the *bekche* asked Nasruddin, "We have been searching everywhere for your donkey, Mullah, but without results. I notice that you seem unconcerned with the loss of your animal."

Nasruddin pointed to the horizon and replied, "Do you see that mountain over there? Nobody has searched that far. When we reach that point, then — you'll hear me wail and cry for my donkey like it's everyone's business."

WHEN THEY REACHED THE mountain, the search party was forced to admit that Karakacan, the Mullah's little grey donkey, was lost, and Nasruddin's expression changed from carefree and happy to bereaved and inconsolable. He pulled handfuls of hair from his beard, beat his chest, and rent his garment, and the tears would not end. Nasruddin's friends tried to assuage the pain by passing around the fez to help Nasruddin purchase another donkey.

When they presented him with the collection, Ali said, "Nasruddin, please tell us: why do you grieve the passing of your donkey more than you mourned Fatima, your dear, departed wife?"

"If you recall," said Nasruddin, blowing his nose, "when Fatima died, everyone promised right away that they would help find me an even better new wife. Until just now, nobody had offered to replace my donkey."

ONCE, LUQMAN THE BEKCHE, the town constable, realized that his donkey was missing. Immediately Nasruddin organized a search party to help find the lost animal. He began walking up and down the streets of Akşehir, singing in a loud and rather unmelodious voice. Nasruddin's screeching was indeed so awful that the neighbors shut their windows — even dogs lie down and put their paws over their ears.

Mali, who was in Nasruddin's search party, asked him, "Why are you making all that horrid noise, Nasruddin? Do you really expect to find the donkey by singing like that?"

"Of course, one can sing to find a donkey," the Mullah replied, "if it is somebody else's donkey."

NASRUDDIN WAS RETURNING FROM a business trip when he rushed into the teahouse in a panic, yelling, "I have misplaced my saddlebag! You must find it for me at once, or else — I know what I'll do! If I don't find it, by Allah! I'll have to —"

"Don't panic, Mullah, I'll help you find your old saddlebag," his friend Hussein assured him. "Now just sit down and think for a moment: where was your bag the last time you saw it?"

So he helped Nasruddin retrace his steps to the donkey, and sure enough, they found the saddlebag, right where the Mullah had left it.

As they returned to the teahouse, Hussein asked, "What were you saying that you would have done if we hadn't found your saddlebag, Nasruddin?"

"Well, I would have had to cut up an old *kilim* rug in my shed and stitch it together to make a new one."

ANOTHER TIME, WHEN NASRUDDIN lost his little grey donkey, Karakacan, he was complaining to his friends at the teahouse. "That no-good hairy ass of mine has run away for the very last time. I promise you, if I could get my hands on that beast, I would sell that crappy piece of donkey meat to the first buyer for one lousy dinar." Nasruddin thus named a price that would insult even the lamest common donkey.

Abdul the baker grinned.

"That would be a good bargain, wouldn't you say?" exclaimed Mali the carpenter. He had to suppress a laugh at the thought of getting Nasruddin's burro for just a measly dinar.

Just then they could hear the familiar clip-clop of small hooves coming toward them and a few moments later, they saw Shoja, Abdul's young son, smiling and riding Nasruddin's donkey.

When donkey and rider reached Nasruddin, Shoja jumped off and handed the tether to its owner. "Where did you find her?" asked Abdul.

Shoja said, "I knew where I'd go if I were a donkey. I found Karakacan grazing in the tall grasses just outside of town."

Nasruddin was now just as overjoyed as he was discouraged the minute before. He hugged his donkey, he hugged Shoja for finding her, he hugged Abdul and praised him for having such a clever child. He was about to raise a new wave of praise for Shoja, when he felt a poke at his right arm and a tug at his right sleeve. He turned to his right to see Mali holding up a dinar, then he turned to his right to see Abdul wiggling a dinar at him.

"I will buy your donkey for one dinar," said both of Nasruddin's friends.

"Not at all," replied Nasruddin, tightening his grip on the donkey's tether. "My donkey is not for sale!"

"But you said you would sell it for one dinar if you found it," Mali reminded him, and all the men agreed that Nasruddin had indeed vowed to sell his donkey.

Mullah giggled nervously, "I was joking!"

"It didn't sound like a joke when you said it," said Abdul, who would do anything to get a bargain, "you weren't laughing then."

Nasruddin stroked his beard as he did whenever he had some hard and fast thinking to do, then said, "Oh sure — but it's too bad that the donkey bazaar is not held today. We will have to wait until Wednesday. At that time I will sell for a single dinar my donkey to the one of you that I think will make the best master."

So for the next week Abdul and Mali went to great pains to demonstrate to Nasruddin how kind and generous they were to all the town's animals. Abdul made a point of throwing handfuls of feed to birds when he knew Nasruddin was looking, and Mali made a great show of brushing his many fine dogs and parading them about, and both men groomed and festooned and treated their own donkeys like royalty.

Come the day of the donkey bazaar, Mali and Abdul were equally anxious as to whether they each had impressed Nasruddin enough to make him sell his beloved Karakacan at such a bargain. The two men waited outside with everyone who also came to see the outcome.

Soon enough, the faint but familiar clopping of donkey hooves could be heard approaching. After some time, the buyers realized they heard another noise, not so familiar, the sound of a somewhat displeased cat. They waited as the sound grew louder, until around the corner came the Mullah leading Karakacan by a tether, just as he had promised. Nobody expected to see, however, that tied to the tail of the donkey — was Nasruddin's scrawny cat.

Once everyone had gathered around this spectacle, Nasruddin announced, "I indeed am willing to sell my beloved donkey for one dinar. But my donkey and my cat — I mean, the donkey's cat — are such good friends, it would be cruel to separate them. Whoever buys my donkey must also purchase her dearest feline companion."

It only took two seconds for the would-be buyers to say, "How much for the cat?" in unison, reaching into their moneybags to grab another dinar or two.

"Oh, this is a very distinguished cat," Nasruddin replied, gesturing to the distressed feline, which tried batting at the red ribbon tethering it securely to a big knot in the donkey's tail. "Its past is exotic and fascinating. I know for a certain fact that her great-grandfather lived in the King's palace. And that was from just this precious cat's third life — still six more lives left.

"So," Nasruddin continued, "as much as I hate to part with my dear kit— I mean, the donkey's dear feline friend, the price of the cat is quite reasonable, considering her regal pedigree: one thousand dinars."

Mali and Abdul looked at each other, and broke into wide grins, and everyone laughed. They hugged Nasruddin and slapped each other on the back and all were glad, because everyone knows that a man and his hairy ass should never be parted.

3

ONCE NASRUDDIN WENT TO the donkey bazaar and browsed among the donkeys available for purchase.

"Are you, fine sir, in the market for a donkey?" asked Musa, the camel and donkey seller, taking his sleeve and leading the Mullah toward his flock. Nasruddin nodded yes. "How about one or more of these remarkably handsome and rugged beasts?"

"Not so fast," countered Nasruddin, "First, show me the worst donkeys you have so we can get those out of the way."

"Okay," replied Musa, as he motioned to their right, "these are the worst, over here."

"And which are the donkeys of average quality and price?" continued Nasruddin.

Musa pointed and said, "Those are the moderately priced average animals, in the middle there."

"Thank you," said Nasruddin, as he gestured toward several donkeys on the left. "I'll take the rest."

∽

EVERY FRIDAY ON MARKET day, Nasruddin arrived at market with an excellent donkey, which he sold almost immediately, for his prices were far below the usual asking price.

One day Musa approached him, "I cannot for the life of me understand how you do it, Nasruddin. I sell my animals at the lowest possible price. My servants force farmers to give me fodder free. My slaves look after my burros and horses without wages. And yet I cannot match your prices. How do you do it?"

"Simple," replied Nasruddin. "You steal fodder and labor. I merely steal donkeys."

∽

ONCE IN WINTER AFTER a snow, Nasruddin was riding his donkey to Konya, when a pack of feral dogs surrounded him. Nasruddin jumped down from his donkey and tried to grab some rocks and pebbles from the road, but everything was frozen solid.

As the dogs drew nearer, barking and nipping at the donkey, he cried aloud, "Allah save me! What kind of hellish place is this, where they bind the stones yet let the crazy dogs run free?"

∽

ONCE THE MULLAH WAS returning from a very long journey. After walking for miles under the blazing sun, his feet were blistered and his throat was dry. Finally he stopped to rest under the shade of an olive tree and sincerely prayed, "Oh Lord! I am so weary from my pilgrimage. Please God! If it is not asking too much, I wish you would provide your faithful servant Nasruddin a donkey." He closed his eyes and opened his eyes. And closed and opened his eyes again. And blinked yet once more.

In the distance, Nasruddin could see three figures approaching his seat in the shade of the olive tree. He could make them out, coming down the road ... a young man riding a fine horse and leading — could it be? — a young donkey. He shook his head, squinted, and rubbed his eyes. When he looked again, Nasruddin could hardly believe his eyes that his prayer had been answered, and that this decent-looking fellow would surely offer his donkey to a pilgrim to ride.

In almost no time at all, the fellow approached where Nasruddin sat, smiling beatifically as his providential delivery of a donkey signified the answer to his very prayer of just minutes ago! Nasruddin considered standing up to greet the man, but then he thought it would appear better to the other man if he should appear to be too weak to arise.

The man turned out to be a cavalry soldier who rode right up to Nasruddin, looked him right in the eye. Before Nasruddin could say *Salaam Alaikum*, the brutish soldier yelled at him angrily, "You lazy bum! Why do you just sit there like a sloth under that tree?"

Nasruddin tried to explain, but the man brandished a long cudgel, and shouted at him, "My young donkey is exhausted from our long journey in the scorching sun. Get your sorry ass off the ground right this minute and carry this donkey to the next town!"

Nasruddin was shocked at this turn of events and tried to protest, but under threat of a severe thrashing, he had no choice but to comply with the soldier's demand that he carry the young donkey on his back.

After several miles and many exhausting hours of travel, they reached the next village. The soldier left Nasruddin without a word of thanks, and just rode off on his horse with his donkey, whose perky trot certainly seemed refreshed.

Nasruddin sank to his knees, clasped his hands, and prayed, "*Subhan'Allah*, God be praised for answering my prayers. I have learned my lesson. Next time, I'll be much more specific."

BY THE TIME NASRUDDIN returned home, the night had turned bitter cold. When he arrived at his house and found there was nothing in the pantry, he thought, "It would be so nice to taste some hot, spicy soup. If I had good soup, I would be so content."

So the Mullah filled a bowl with water and got a spoon and conjured up the thought of hot, aromatic soup. He pretended he was eating the most wonderful, seasoned vegetable soup, with yoghurt and mint leaves. He even blew on the liquid, imagining it to be too hot at first to bring to his lips, saying, "Oooh! Ahh! Such delicious soup!" and he chowed down, savoring every delectable spoonful of his bowl of imaginary soup.

Nasruddin was carrying on as if it were the most delicious soup, slurping and blowing and oohing and ahhing when his reverie was interrupted by the sound of a knock at the gate.

He found the neighbor boy, Sedat, standing in front of the gate and holding a bowl. "We are hungry," he whined. "Mother sent me to see if you had any soup to spare — hot, tasty soup."

"For goodness sakes, child, no," said Nasruddin, shutting the gate and returning to his own kitchen, where he sat down to resume his meal.

"Allah help me, I only have to think of soup and my neighbors can smell it."

✑

ONCE NASRUDDIN WAS RIDING along the road, facing backward of course, when he noticed some exquisitely scented wildflowers growing by the wayside. He jumped off his donkey, removed his cloak and placed it on the donkey's back to keep it clean, and rushed around pinching the flowers and gathering them into a sweet-smelling posy to tie to his donkey's bridle. While his back was turned, however, a thief and his son came and swiped the cloak right off the donkey's back.

When he returned, the Mullah was shocked to discover his cloak gone. The Mullah grabbed the startled donkey's bridle, stared accusingly right in her eyes, and yelled, "You thieving beast! Return my cloak immediately!" The donkey just blinked at Nasruddin.

"Very well, Karakacan," the Mullah spoke sternly to the donkey, "what's fair is fair. If you've decided to steal my saddlebag, I have no choice but to take your saddle." So he snatched the saddle from his donkey, strapped it atop his own back, and swung up onto the perplexed animal, shouting "Ugh-r-r-r!" which, of course, is Turkish for "Giddyap!"

✑

TO BUY THE MANGER, Nasruddin sold the mule.

4

ONE FINE MORNING, NASRUDDIN was leading his donkey, Karakacan, out from the stable, on his way to teach at the *madrasa*, for that is one of the main things that the Mullah did for work in those days. Seeing Nasruddin appear on the street, some young students approached him to ask whether they might instruct them and hear their lessons. Nasruddin readily agreed, and invited them to accompany him as he rode his donkey to the schoolhouse.

Nasruddin mounted his donkey from the left, put his right foot in the stirrup, and heaved himself up. Naturally this put him facing backward toward the ass's rear. As they set off, Nasruddin commented, "Remember, kids: a donkey of your own is better than a shared thoroughbred mare."

As they walked on, Nuri asked why the Mullah mounted his donkey in this manner.

Nasruddin said, "Because, my child, the donkey is left-handed."

Ismail objected, "But Mullah, donkeys don't have hands."

Nasruddin replied, "Well, left-footed, then," then nudged the beast with a shout — "Ugh-r-r-r," which is Turkish for "Giddyap!" — and a shove.

"In any case," Nasruddin continued speaking to the students, "what usually happens is that I want to go in one direction, and this stubborn beast wants to go in the exact opposite way. So this is our compromise."

As NASRUDDIN RODE HIS little grey donkey, Karakacan, sitting backward as usual facing his students, he was about to make a point when suddenly they startled by a series of loud pops and bangs — one of the boys, Mehmet, had set off firecrackers!

The frightened donkey bolted with Nasruddin clinging to its backside and the kids running behind them, laughing and yelling. As the terrorized donkey galloped into the village, the Mullah held on for dear life. His turban came undone, but he dare not take one hand off to tuck it back in.

By the time the donkey entered the market with Nasruddin bouncing and bumping on its rear end, shouting for it to stop, his turban waving like a long banner from his bald head, and the kids shrieking as they followed, the whole market turned to witness the spectacle and laugh.

Nasruddin's son, Ahmet, saw him riding backward at full donkey speed and called out, "Oh Father, you are going ass-backward!"

Nasruddin called out to Ahmet, between bumps, "It's not me ... that's sitting on ... my donkey backward ... it's the donkey ... that's facing ... the wrong way!"

The donkey kept running in circles, but Nasruddin could not get it to stop. On their next circling around the market square, someone yelled, "Hey Nasruddin, where are you going in such a hurry?"

Nasruddin yelled back, in a shaken, desperate voice, "I don't know! Don't ask me — ask my donkey!"

By the time the donkey seemed to be slowing down, Nasruddin's turban was nearly dragging the ground, and he knew he would lose it if he didn't try to catch it from slipping off his head. So cautiously Nasruddin took one hand off the donkey and, as he was trying to grab the end of his turban, he lost his balance and tumbled off to the left, landing with a resounding crash right into a market stand of walnuts, scattering the nuts for yards around.

Some small boys nearby clustered around the walnut stand, laughing hilariously and pointing at Nasruddin, who appeared dazed, but unhurt.

"What are you laughing at?" Nasruddin snarled. "Before I was on the floor, and once again as you can see I am on the very same floor. In Allah's name, tell me: what's so funny?"

As Nasruddin slowly picked himself off the ground, he almost lost his footing as he stepped on the walnuts scattered everywhere about him, which caused the kids to almost split their sides all over again. They laughed until finally Nasruddin stood up fully, rubbing his rear. "That's quite enough!" roared Nasruddin, silencing the peals of laughter. "Don't get carried away with the idea, now!"

Nasruddin composed himself as he tried to regain his dignity, saying, "Clearly you never considered that I might have had a perfectly good reason to fall." The doubtful kids could hardly contain their sniggering, as Nasruddin dusted himself off, straightened his coat, and rewrapped his turban. Süleyman, the walnut seller, who had been at the other end of the market and heard the commotion, came into view.

"Besides," Nasruddin said to the kids as he started quickly gathering the walnuts that had scattered everywhere, "I was going to get off anyway, sooner or later."

Süleyman, the walnut seller, was furious at first when he arrived at his vendor stall, but when the kids described Nasruddin's fall, Süleyman laughed along, and everyone helped Nasruddin collect the nuts and put the stand in order. Nasruddin even bought a bag of walnuts to placate Süleyman, for the kids to share.

"Children, I will give you all the walnuts in this bag. But tell me first — how do you want me to divide them: God's way, or mortal's way?"

"God's way," the four boys chimed together as one.

Mullah opened the bag and gave two big handfuls of walnuts to the first boy, one handful to the next boy, just two walnuts to the third boy, and none at all to the last!

All the children were baffled, but the fourth boy pouted and complained, "What sort of distribution is this?"

"This is God's way of distributing gifts among his children. Some will get lots, some will get a fair amount, and nothing at all to others. Now, had you asked me to divide the nuts by the usual mortal's way, I would have handed out an equal amount to everybody."

As the kids were leaving the market, Nasruddin called out after them, "When I was a young man, you should have seen me ride! I was a master donkey jockey, known throughout all of—"

But the boys weren't listening and Süleyman's angry glare cut him short. Nasruddin offered a quick, quiet salaam to Süleyman. Still sore and limping slightly from his fall, Nasruddin beat a hasty retreat.

"Utter nonsense, Nasruddin," he muttered to himself as he hobbled away, "You're not kidding anybody. I know how you were in your youth, and you were just the same."

Nasruddin began searching for his little donkey, which had trotted off without him, oblivious to being riderless. He set off from the market in the direction the animal went, asking everyone he encountered if they had seen his donkey. Nasruddin was always losing track of Karakacan, so it was not particularly unusual to see him wandering the village, calling out for his little donkey, and sometimes braying the way he thought the donkey did.

After more than an hour of this, thirsty and tired, Nasruddin walked into the teahouse and sat down with a huge grin on his face.

"Nasruddin!" the teahouse regulars greeted him. Ali, the tea wallah, brought him a steaming cup of tea.

"Tell us, Nasruddin," said Ali, "why are you smiling ear to ear, as if you have found gold?"

"Allah be praised, I fell off my donkey and she ran away from the market. I have searched for an hour and still cannot find her."

"Why do you say, 'Allah be praised,' when you have lost your dear donkey?" asked Hamza.

"Allah be praised, because if I had been on my donkey when it disappeared, then I would probably still be lost, too!"

⳾

Then Nasruddin announced: "Whoever shall find my donkey shall get that wretched animal, including its saddle!"

Everyone was astounded. "If you are going to just give away the donkey when you find it, why do you bother looking for it in the first place?"

"But ahhh! You have no idea how utterly wonderful it feels to find something you've lost."

5

Karakacan, Nasruddin's little grey donkey, was old and stubborn and needed to go into retirement, so the Mullah went to market and found one that seemed young and mild-mannered, with sturdy legs and good teeth, and bought him. Nasruddin tied up the new donkey to the saddlebag of his old donkey, and away they went.

Unknown to Nasruddin, a thief and his son were following him, planning to steal the young donkey. They kept themselves hidden behind and, before long, as they hoped, Nasruddin nodded off and began snoring as the donkeys traveled down the road.

Quickly the boy removed the new donkey's halter and tied it around himself without disturbing Nasruddin's siesta, as his father led the donkey back to market, where it would surely gather an excellent price.

When the three arrived back at the stable, Nasruddin awoke, rubbed his eyes, and realized that something was amiss. Seeing the boy tethered to his donkey, Nasruddin demanded to know where his other donkey was. The boy pleaded for mercy on his soul, exclaiming, "*I* used to be your donkey, Mullah. You see, I was a stubborn and impudent little boy who constantly disobeyed his mother, and one day, my mother became so disgusted with my misbehavior that she asked Allah to punish me by turning me into the donkey that I must surely be. Suddenly I had four legs and long ears, and a donkey I'd have stayed forever until you, a honest and kind man, bought me and the curse was lifted, Allah be praised. Now that my punishment is over and I'm a human again, please allow me to return to my mother."

The Mullah scratched his long white beard doubtfully, but he removed the boy's halter, cautioning him, "Allah be praised that you have been transformed back to a boy. You must promise me to behave yourself this time and to obey your mother's wishes." The boy thanked Nasruddin profusely and praised him as a great man of virtue, and off he ran to go home. Realizing that he still needed a new donkey, Nasruddin headed back to marketplace. There, much to his surprise, he discovered the mild-mannered donkey waiting to be brought up again to the auction block.

Nasruddin confronted the little donkey, grabbed its tether, and scolded it in a severe tone, "You little fool! I told you never to disobey your mother again!"

ONCE NASRUDDIN TOOK HIS donkey to the market and put it up on the auction block. When someone touched the tail, inspecting it, the donkey jerked away. When someone else put both hands on the animal's rump, the donkey kicked him with both its hind legs. And when one of the men tried to look at its teeth, it bit him. The auctioneer handed the reins back to the Mullah and said, "You just cannot sell this nasty, intemperate creature. No one will buy it. You'd best take it away."

Nasruddin gathered the donkey's rein in both hands, gave it a violent tug, and replied, "I didn't really expect to sell the donkey, anyway. I just wanted to show you and everyone how ill-mannered this beast is and how I've suffered because of its bad behavior."

ONCE NASRUDDIN RODE HIS ass backward through some rain showers to the donkey seller. He intended to sell the beast for a profit, but at the last minute he noticed that the donkey's long tail hair was muddy, so he cut all the hair off its tail with his knife and stashed the mess in his saddlebag.

The first buyer who came around to look at Nasruddin's donkey noticed its shortened tail right away and asked about it.

"Not to worry — the tail is at hand, my dear sir!" Nasruddin asserted, patting the saddlebag confidently. "And it is included — no extra charge!"

ONE TIME NASRUDDIN WAS leading his ass across a precipitously steep ravine when the donkey lost her footing and tumbled down the side of the mountain.

Nasruddin recounted the untimely and gruesome loss of his beloved donkey to the wags at the teahouse, remarking with damp eyes, "She took off decently, and true she didn't fly all that well, but it wasn't a bad effort. It was clearly her landing that needed the most improvement."

NASRUDDIN'S DONKEY DIED, AND the entire town was sad. Everyone respected and loved the little grey animal that had carried their Mullah for so many years.

It is true that a donkey's life is not as long as that as a human. If the donkey had been human, Nasruddin's neighbors would have moaned and groaned just as if a close relative had passed. Instead, they came quietly with small gifts of sweetmeats and whispered, "We are so very sorry for your loss." As night fell and the Nasruddins were getting ready for bed, they felt comforted to know they had such good friends.

Some of Nasruddin's students, however, were always looking to make grief for the Mullah, even in his hour of muted sorrow. "Mullah always treated his donkey as if he was one of the family," said Mehmet, the gang leader.

"Let's play a trick on the Mullah by pretending we are mourners at the wake for the donkey." The boys quickly agreed.

They proceeded through the dark village streets toward the Mullah's house, moaning and sighing and beating their breasts as though they were professional mourners who had been paid many dinars to grieve the death of a great man.

As they marched, sounding woeful and inconsolable, they made a dirge of the donkey's name, howling it in time to their marching.

From the shadows of doorways along the street, other men and boys emerged following the noise to find out what it was all about.

The hooligans' howls reached a crescendo when they knocked at the Mullah's street gate, then they softened their wails to low moans as they expected the response.

"Open the gate, please," they heard the Mullah call to one of his friends. The boys moaned louder as the door creaked open.

"Bring a light, Fatima," they heard the Mullah call to his wife.

"Who in the world can it be?" they heard Fatima ask her husband.

They groaned and wailed the name of the dead donkey.

Then the loud voice of the Mullah carried easily across the walls to the boys in the street and to the men who were watching them. "It must be . . . our dead donkey's family, who have come to mourn in sorrow."

The boys tittered and giggled. The men coughed.

"Yes, it must be the brothers of the donkey!" Nasruddin continued. "Who else but an ass's brother would come at this late hour to mourn her?"

As the boys sneaked off into the darkness, they heard laughing voices repeating, "The brothers of the donkey! The brothers of the donkey!"

***

As Nasruddin entered the teahouse, Ali said, "Here is Nasruddin. Let us see him address a difficult philosophical question."

"But Nasruddin knows only about donkeys!" retorted Musa the camel seller.

"There is indeed philosophy in donkeys, my friends," Nasruddin said as Ali brought him a steaming cup of sweet tea. "Go ahead, try me."

"Okay then," said Abdul the baker, "answer us this one: Which came first, nosebags or donkeys?"

"Simple. Nosebags, of course."

"Nosebags, Nasruddin? Don't be ridiculous!" said Abdul. "It's plainly obvious that donkeys came first."

"Well, then, prove it," said Nasruddin. "What is your proof that donkeys preëxisted nosebags?"

"Well, for one, the donkey can recognize a nosebag, but a nosebag cannot recognize a donkey."

"I take it, then," said Nasruddin sipping his tea, "that you have it on the assurance of a good many nosebags that they have never seen a donkey?"

***

THREE RENOWNED RELIGIOUS SCHOLARS — a priest, a pundit, and a philosopher — banded together and were traveling the world in search of wise men to engage in learned disputation. When they came to Akşehir, they sent ahead a letter asking the mayor to appoint the town's smartest wit to debate them. Naturally, the mayor called for Nasruddin to debate the pundits, promising a feast in honor of the visiting guests.

When the Mullah arrived at the debate, the mayor introduced him to the three philosophers, who looked very scholarly indeed. The first debater, the priest, was the youngest, perhaps in his thirties, with a distinguished black beard a few inches long. The second debater, the pundit, was in his fifties, with an even longer, graying beard that went down to his second coat button. And the third sage, the philosopher, appeared to be in his seventies with the longest, most distinguished, and wisest beard of all.

Each scholar seemed more formidable than the last, but Nasruddin displayed not the least sense of anxiety as he scratched his own scruffy, scraggly, salt-and-pepper beard, which he now wished he'd taken the time to wash and comb before coming to the event.

To Nasruddin's disappointment, he discovered that the display of wisdom was to precede the feast. *Just as well,* he thought, *as a big meal would probably make me a bit sleepy anyway.*

As the first debater to challenge the Mullah, the priest paced the floor, then dramatically swirled around and pointed at Nasruddin, questioning: "Sir! Tell us, please: where is the exact center of the universe?"

The crowd gasped at such a difficult question, and everyone turned to Nasruddin to see his response.

Nasruddin looked calm and collected. "It's apparent, my dear sir. At this very moment, the center of the universe is exactly under my donkey's left hind foot."

The scholars conferred briefly, then the first one asked Nasruddin, "How can you prove that?"

Nasruddin held out his palms to the priest as if to express the obvious truth of the matter, saying, "If you disbelieve me, then you must measure the universe and show me wrong."

The priest wilted and retreated. The pundit now advanced to the center of the hall and addressed Nasruddin with a sly "gotcha" expression. "How many stars are there shining at night in the sky?"

"Precisely the same number of stars above in the heavens as there are hairs on my donkey."

"But how can one count all the hairs on one donkey?" the pundit protested.

"As easily as one can count all the stars that shine in the sky."

The second scholar turned on his heel and slipped back into the crowd. The final and oldest philosopher strutted forward with his long beard flayed like a peacock.

"Tell me, sir: exactly how many hairs are there in my beard?"

"There is exactly the same number of hairs in your beard as there are bristles on the tail of my donkey."

The scholar, who bristled at the comparison between his long, well groomed beard with a donkey's untidy tail, sputtered, "How can you prove that, sir?"

"The simplest matter of proof of all three of your questions. We just pluck out all the hairs of your beard one by one and then pluck all the bristles of my donkey's tail, count, and compare."

The third scholar clasped both hands over his cherished beard as if protecting an infant, and withdrew from the center of the hall.

And with that, Nasruddin scratched his own modest beard and wondered aloud, "So will it be much longer before the feast begins?"

6

ONCE NASRUDDIN WAS RETURNING from the vineyard, his little grey donkey laden with two baskets filled with bunches of luscious grapes, which he intended for sale at market. The village kids gathered around him and pestered him mercilessly for some grapes, and after sufficient nagging Nasruddin finally stopped and handed each of the boys a single grape.

Mehmet, the oldest, complained, "Why are you so stingy, Nasruddin? You have so many grapes. Can't we have more than one apiece?"

"Don't be naïve, boy," said Nasruddin as he made a hasty exit. "All grapes taste exactly alike. If you've eaten one grape, you've tasted them all. So it doesn't matter in the least if you get just one or a whole bunch."

ONCE A YOUNG FARMER came to Nasruddin for some advice about his mother-in-law, as marriage counseling was another thing Nasruddin did for work. "She moved in with us, and is constantly griping and criticizing me and getting in the way," the man complained, "there's hardly any privacy or quiet at all."

Nasruddin scratched his long white beard as he considered the matter, then said, "Your problem, while not easily solved, can be remedied. Do you have any chickens?"

The farmer said, "Yes, we have five."

Nasruddin said, "Move them into the house with you."

"Why in the Prophet's name would I do that? Surely you can't be serious."

"I am. Do as I say, and come back to see me next week."

So the farmer went back and moved his chickens into the house. The next week he came back to see Nasruddin, who asked casually, "So, how goes it?"

"It's worse," the farmer groaned, "now there's chicken poop everywhere, and my mother-in-law squawks every time she steps in it."

Nasruddin said, "Excellent. Do you have a goat?"

The farmer replied hesitantly, "Um, yes, we have two goats."

Nasruddin instructed, "Two goats is even better. Move them both into the house too."

"You've got to be kidding me."

"If you think I'm joking," replied Nasruddin, "just wait until you see my bill. In any case, consider my advice carefully, do what you can, and come back to see me in a week."

With a long sigh of resignation, the farmer returned to his farm and brought the goats in the house. The next week the farmer returned and Nasruddin asked, "So, how's it going?"

"What did you think was going to happen when I moved the goats in?" the weary farmer growled. "Of course, the mess is even worse. The goats are chewing everything in the house they can get their bearded mouths on. And my mother-in-law whines about it all, constantly."

Nasruddin smiled and said, "Ah, to you this may seem like being stuck in an unsolvable problem, but to me it looks like progress. Tell me, do you have a pig on your farm?"

The farmer gave a pained expression as he replied, "No."

Nasruddin arched an eyebrow. "Is that so? A farm with no pig?"

"No. Yes. No. All right, yes, we have one."

Nasruddin said, "Thought so. Move your pig into the house with you."

"Are you out of your mind? Why in the world should I do that? And how did you know?" the exasperated farmer gasped.

"Trust me," Nasruddin advised reassuringly, "and come back to see me in another week. All will be well."

So the desperate farmer went back home and let his pig into the house. The following week, he returned and Nasruddin asked nonchalantly, "So, how are things with you?"

"What kind of cockamamie advice have you been giving me, Nasruddin?" exploded the patient. "I cannot live like this yet another day, with all the animals and birds! The stench is unbearable. It's impossible to move anywhere inside or to do anything without stepping into a fresh pile of crap. It's so filthy and smelly that even my horrible mother-in-law couldn't stand it any longer and left." And the poor farmer broke down and wept like a baby in front of Nasruddin.

"Perfect! Excellent! Well done!" said Nasruddin, clapping his hands. "Now, just move the animals outside again, clean the house, and you will find that your original problem is completely solved."

ↄᢧᢓ

ONCE THE MULLAH LOST a costly silk sky-blue turban with a valuable jewel pinned to it, but he appeared unperturbed by the loss.

Selim, Nasruddin's brother, remarked, "You seem to have complete faith that your beautiful turban will be recovered."

Nasruddin replied, "Yes, I'm quite confident, considering that I placed a reward for its return: half a silver coin."

"But the finder will never part with the turban and the jewel for a measly half silver!" said Selim. "The jewel pin alone is worth four hundred times that."

"I already thought of that," said Nasruddin. "For the reward announcement, I described an old, dirty, torn turban, quite unlike the original I lost, and I omitted any mention of the jewel altogether."

ↄᢧᢓ

NASRUDDIN WAS FED UP with his turban, which didn't fit right. No matter how many times he tried, he just couldn't link the tip to the back of the turban. He was so irritated that he brought it to the bazaar to sell at auction.

Musa, the auctioneer, started the bidding low, and Jafar, standing at the back right next to Nasruddin raised his hand to bid. Then Nasruddin's wealthy neighbor, Aslan, also raised his hand to bid on the turban. Jafar was determined to get the turban, and he and Aslan kept upping the price until it far exceeded its possible worth.

Nasruddin leaned over to Jafar and whispered, "Pssst, my friend — let me tell you something about this turban. I have it on extremely good authority that it has a serious defect."

ↄᢧᢓ

NASRUDDIN'S WEALTHY NEIGHBOR, ASLAN, who for months had owed the Mullah three silver pieces, came into the teahouse. When Nasruddin reminded him of the debt, Aslan ostentatiously handed him a large gold piece. "I only owe you a few silvers, but I'm afraid I have nothing else. Can you change it for me?"

Nasruddin, who was ashamed to be so poor, but not wanting to lose face, took the gold coin in his hand and held it pensively. "This coin is very worn. I cannot change it for you at face value. Try someone else."

Nasruddin tried to hand the coin back, but Aslan put it back in Nasruddin's palm, saying, "I trust you to discount it fairly."

"The coin is underweight, I can tell," said Nasruddin.

"Then just give me the change for whatever you think it's worth," said Aslan, pressing the coin into Nasruddin's palm so hard it hurt.

"But it's really, very, very much underweight," said Nasruddin, trying to ease Aslan's grip on his fingers.

"So then perhaps it's just best that you return the coin to me," said Aslan, as he reversed his grip and started to grasp the coin out of Nasruddin's clenched fist. "You don't mind if I'll have to owe you for just a little while longer, until I can get the right change, do you?"

"I can't really say how light or heavy it is, but it must be close to the value of the debt," said Nasruddin, trying to keep Aslan from prying the coin out of his hand.

"That's a shame!" Aslan huffed, as the two began to wrestle for the gold piece. "If you cannot give me any change back from my large gold piece, doubtless I should pay you later, then."

"I have decided!" Nasruddin declared, and pulled the coin free from Aslan's grasp. Nasruddin hid the coin in both hands locked behind his back, a bit breathless. "With the additional wear and tear, the coin is now so worn and underweight that if I change it for you, you will owe me money. So really it's best if I just take it off your hands completely and let's call it even."

Once there was a serious water shortage in Akşehir, and the town council called on Nasruddin to help, because water divining was one of the things Nasruddin did for work. Instead of procuring a divining-rod, however, the first thing he did was to go home and wash his shirt. Someone asked him what he was doing. Nasruddin wrung out his shirt, carried it outside and hung it in the backyard on the clothesline.

"It is not the washing of laundry that causes rain," Nasruddin said. "Every fool knows that it always rains only when one is hanging laundry outside to dry."

The rain was pelting down when Nasruddin, standing dry and protected under an awning, saw his neighbor Aslan running stooped with his hands above him in a futile attempt to avoid the sluicing water. He called out, "Why do you hide from God's blessings, Aslan? Rain is a sacred miracle for all creation from none other than God. Do not be afraid of the rain, my friend!"

Aslan, normally a very sanctimonious fellow, righted himself and walked proudly and defiantly, saying, "I hadn't thought of it as such." He slackened his pace the rest of the way home and arrived soaked through and miserable. Of course he came down with a horrible cold.

The next week, after Aslan recovered, he went out to the teahouse for the first time in a week to see his friends. As it so happened, just as the man sat down, the heavens opened up with thunder and a soaking rain beat against the front door.

Five minutes later, Nasruddin burst through the door, breathing hard, utterly drenched and dripping.

"*Salaam,* Nasruddin," Ali and everyone said.

Aslan stood up and confronted Nasruddin. "Mullah, last week you told me that rain is a holy blessing and that one should not try to avoid it. I took your sage advice and caught a nasty cold. So why were you just now running to get out of the rain yourself, Nasruddin? How dare you spurn God's sacred blessings?"

"Please don't misunderstand my motives, *effendi,*" said Nasruddin, trying to catch his breath. "It may have appeared to you from my entrance that I was avoiding the magnificent miracle of rain. In actuality, I was running in a sincere and dedicated effort to avoid defiling God's blessing with my feet."

7

A WISE BUT HAUGHTY PUNDIT, who had arranged to debate Nasruddin, arrived at the Mullah's home while everyone was out. He knocked and knocked at Nasruddin's gate but nobody answered the door. Infuriated, he picked up a piece of chalk and scrawled FOOL on the gate.

As soon as the Mullah returned home and saw the graffito, he rushed to the philosopher's house.

"I forgot our appointment," explained Nasruddin, "and I apologize for not being home when you called. Naturally, I recalled our meeting just as soon as I saw that you had signed your name on my gate."

DURING THE PHILOSOPHERS' DEBATE, seven savants and Nasruddin were on the dais to discuss the meaning of meaning. Nasruddin was allowed to speak first.

"Meaning is irrelevant as far as concerns these so-called wise men, who are in actuality ignorant, irresolute, and confused," declared Nasruddin, drawing a murmur from the audience and the ire of the other debaters.

"Explain yourself, Nasruddin," said the moderator.

"Have paper and pens brought, and hand one to each of the so-called wise men," instructed Nasruddin. This was done, and he continued, "Now, have each of the seven men separately write on their paper the meaning of the word *bread*."

The papers were collected and read aloud.

"Bread is sustaining food," was the first response.

"It is flour, water, and salt," read the second.

"Bread is a loaf of leavened and baked dough," was the third answer.

"Bread is a nutritional substance," went the fourth.

The fifth read: "A gift of God."

The sixth answer: "Depends upon the context of the use of the word."

"Nobody really knows what bread is," was the seventh response.

After the responses were read aloud, Nasruddin declared, "If seven savants can't agree as to the definition of a simple loaf of bread, how are we to judge the extent of their wisdom?"

"And just how do you define bread, Mullah?" asked the moderator.

"I do not invoke mere facts of book learning," said Nasruddin. "I advocate experience."

From his satchel Nasruddin produced a loaf of bread, from which he broke off and handed each of the seven wise men, and the moderator, a piece. "The only way to know what bread is, is to eat it."

✎

A SCHOLAR VISITING AKŞEHIR WAS holding forth at the teahouse, spouting fatuous intellectual nonsense nonstop, posing rhetorical questions and then answering them bombastically, and interrupting Nasruddin and everyone else whenever anyone tried to get a word in edgewise. This verbal assault went on for an hour.

"My astounding powers of recollection are so astute," declared the scholar pompously, "that I can recite every word of an hour-long lecture given twenty years ago by one of my most esteemed teachers, which began, 'Dear students, I have come to speak—'."

"I'm sure," Nasruddin finally interrupted the scholar, "that's not what your teacher said."

The scholar was flabbergasted. "How in the world would you know? I was there at the lecture, Mullah, not you!"

"Undoubtedly," quipped Nasruddin, "if you had been there, the teacher couldn't possibly have said more than five words in a row."

❧

ONCE A PRIEST, A yogi, and Nasruddin were talking about their devotion and offerings to God. The priest declared, "Once a month, I draw a circle one meter wide in the sand and stand in the center. All the alms I have collected that month I throw high into the air. Whatever lands outside the circle, I give to God, and the rest I keep for myself."

The yogi stated, "My offering method is more selfless. Every month, I draw a circle a half-meter in diameter in the sand. Then I stand in the center, and all the alms I have gathered that month I toss up into the air. Whatever lands inside the circle goes to God, and the rest I keep for my few needs."

"Nothing personal, my friends," Nasruddin said at last, "but it would seem that I am surrendered to accept whatever the Lord offers me to a far greater extent than either of you."

The yogi and priest both protested Nasruddin's assertion. "Prove yourself!" the priest demanded.

"Clearly, my offering technique is far superior in its altruism," replied Nasruddin. "I don't even need to use a circle in the sand. Every month, all the alms I have collected I throw into the air up to God and cry out, 'Oh God, accept whatever You want!' Whatever God does not need, He returns back to the ground for me."

❧

NASRUDDIN WAS TRAVELING AND very hungry when he happened upon a yogi living in a small but pleasant hut near a hermitage, and they sat together for sangha.

"I have dedicated my life," said the yogi, "to the upliftment and preservation of all small creatures, especially birds and fish."

"I couldn't agree more with the principles you embrace, my friend." Nasruddin nodded enthusiastically. "A fish saved my life once."

"Remarkable," said the yogi, "not even for all my years as the more tireless advocate of animal rights have I had the privilege of experiencing such intimate communion with such creatures as you have! Saved your life! This substantiates our theory of interspecies compassion!"

"Well, I suppose—" Nasruddin began to explain.

"Please, O Master, it would be my honor for you to join me for a humble but tasty vegetarian dinner of bulgur and vegetables."

"Thank you, *effendi*," replied Nasruddin, "I was quite hoping you would ask."

So Nasruddin was the yogi's guest that night, and for two weeks the yogi hosted Nasruddin, serving him personally, and sharing his wonderful vegetarian food. Nasruddin spent an agreeable time being cared for, contemplating his navel, and learning various gymnastic exercises.

"Now that we are better acquainted, Master," the yogi said one evening, as they sat together after another excellent supper, "I do request you to elaborate on your redemptive encounters with compassionate animals and, in particular, the story of the fish that saved your life."

"I am not entirely certain that you want to hear that particular story," hedged Nasruddin, "since I have heard your ideas."

"Surely you cannot misunderstand my motives in wanting to hear of your extraordinary experience," pleaded the yogi. "Please rest assured that I will not judge you for any lack of storytelling ability, but I beg of you to share your vegetarian experience with this poor soul." And the yogi wept tears of kindness and pressed Nasruddin's feet, imploring him for details of the redeeming fish.

At length, Nasruddin relented. "How the fish saved my life is, upon reflection, a very simple tale. I was starving, and I ate it."

NASRUDDIN WAS WALKING ALONG the road when he saw something glittering in the gutter. He picked up a dusty, broken-framed mirror, and immediately upon cleaning off the glass and glancing at the image, he dropped it like a burning ember.

"Ugh! What a horrible portrait," Nasruddin reflected. "No wonder it was thrown away — something so ugly couldn't hold anybody's appeal. I should have realized beforehand that something abandoned that way would not possibly be worth keeping."

NASRUDDIN WAS KNOWN FAR and wide as a sly, witty fellow with a wry sense of humor. Early one morning a traveling pundit arrived at the little town of Akşehir. The stranger saw a man leaning against a wall and asked him haughtily, "Is this the town of the famous Mullah Nasruddin? I have heard that he is not only wise but clever, and I have come to challenge this Nasruddin to a battle of intelligence, which he will surely lose in a matter of seconds."

The man nodded slowly and replied, "I know this Nasruddin fellow, and he is smart enough, but you're right, he is certainly no match for a genius like you."

The pundit smacked his forehead, thinking that of everyone in this town he chose to speak to this bumpkin, and snarled, "Don't be insolent, you idiot. I am undoubtedly much smarter than this Nasruddin. He may be able to fool others but he can't trick me!"

The man said, "Well, I'm just holding up the wall here. What does a simple idiot like myself know about crafty tricks?"

"Apparently not so much, but stop your pointless banter — waste not another second of my precious time! Where can I locate the great trickster, Nasruddin? I demand to see him immediately! Take me to him."

"Kind sir, let me go find him and bring him back so you can challenge him properly."

The pundit nodded dismissively. The man didn't move. "Well, you nimrod, what are you waiting for? Go get him!"

"The problem, as I was trying to tell you," the fellow explained, "is that I am responsible in our community for ensuring that this wall doesn't collapse, and in order to fetch that rascal Nasruddin, someone must stand here and lean against the wall in my place to support it. If you would oblige me the service, I will get Nasruddin for you post-haste."

The pundit crossed his arms impatiently and stood with his back pressed against the wall while the man scurried away to get Nasruddin. The pundit continued leaning against the wall, in the heat of the day, for ten minutes . . . an hour . . . several hours passed, and still no Nasruddin. Certainly the simpleton must have described to Nasruddin the pundit's vast intelligence and no doubt Nasruddin was too intimidated to meet a great pundit like himself for a duel of wits.

The shadows had grown long by the time some townsfolk came by and asked what the pundit was doing. When he explained what had happened, they all laughed uproariously. Hussein, one of the locals, said, "Only one man in town could have fooled you like this. The fellow you spoke to, whose presumed wall you are holding up, could be none other than — Mullah Nasruddin."

PART FOUR

DAILY VOCATIONS

1

ONE SNOWY, COLD NIGHT during a particularly harsh winter, the Mullah sat very comfortably in the cozy teahouse with his friends, stretching his feet in a seat right next to the little fire, enjoying a delicious hot cup of tea. "Oh, this is not such bad weather at all. It is tolerable, in any case."

"Don't be ridiculous, Nasruddin," said Ali, the teahouse owner, looking out the small front window at the snow falling onto the town square. "The weather is awful. It hasn't snowed like this in years. It's terrible outside — obviously, that's why we are *inside*."

"The weather, whether inside or outside, is just the same to me," said Nasruddin, as he took another sip of the delicious hot tea. "Snow and cold really are nothing to a man whose mind is trained to detach from the physical body."

Ali had an idea how to trick the Mullah, and he winked, unseen by Nasruddin, at the men. "Perhaps, Nasruddin, you are feeling a little too smug in your comfortable chair, snuggled all nice and cozy right there in front of the blazing fire."

"True, I am comfortable now, but I have endured far worse than this storm," replied Nasruddin.

Hamza, a teahouse wag, chimed in. "Then you wouldn't mind staying outside on a night just like tonight, for quite a while — overnight, even?"

"Indeed, it would be no challenge to a man of my fortitude," said Nasruddin confidently.

"Don't be ridiculous, Nasruddin," Ali said, "nobody could stand outside in the middle of the town square until dawn on a night like tonight without a fire anywhere nearby."

"Oh, I could most certainly do that," bragged the Mullah. "My view of this corporeal body is completely detached. In fact, I am so objective that I see myself as if I were somebody else entirely."

"Is that so? Such boasting!" said Ali. "If you're so enlightened and free from bodily sensations, Nasruddin, why don't *you* stand outside in the square in the snow all night without a fire?"

"It's not boasting, b-b-but —," stuttered Nasruddin.

"It's nothing *but* a boast!" said Ali.

"You should bet with your body what your mouth brags," piped in Faik, another wag. The men rallied their support of Ali's challenge.

"If you win, we will make you a nice dinner," said Ali. "If we win, you will make dinner for us. That's not such a high wager, is it, now?"

"After all, Nasruddin," added Faik, "one quarter of the night has already passed. It shouldn't be difficult for a man of your stamina to spend the remainder of a pleasant night outside watching the snowflakes, shouldn't it?"

"It's on," said Nasruddin.

Once Nasruddin was stationed outside in the town square with the snow blowing thickly around him, he found it harder to detach himself objectively from the corporeal body than he had ever imagined.

No night has ever had so many hours, he thought as he stood outside alone in the square, shivering and hopping from foot to foot, trying to stay awake and warm himself. Nasruddin dare not lay or sit down in the cold, for certainly the snow would cover him and he would perish by dawn.

From Nasruddin's lonely spot in the dark town square, he noticed a light in the front window of the teahouse, now closed and its occupants long gone home to their warm beds. Ali must have left the candle out for him as a comforting reminder of its warmth. Indeed, as Nasruddin focused on the dim flickering of the distant candle, he found that he could stay awake.

No dawn has ever taken as long to arrive, the Mullah thought.

Finally at sunrise, when Ali and the men came out in the square, Nasruddin was covered in snow up to his knees, and icicles hung from his grey beard. The men carried the exhausted, shivering Nasruddin into the teahouse and sat him in front of the blazing fire with many blankets. After many cups of steaming hot tea, the Mullah revived.

"So Nasruddin," said Ali, "you seem to have proved yourself. None of us can believe that you could ever survive!"

"Yes, by God's great mercy, I am still alive," sighed the Mullah.

"Tell us what happened, Nasruddin," sail Hamza.

"I stood all night in the village square. I nearly froze to death, but I made it!"

"You certainly made it through a rough night, praise God," said Ali, "but how did you manage?"

"That was the hardest part of it," said Nasruddin. "I fixed my eyes on the flame of a candle that you so thoughtfully left in the café window."

"Did you say a candle?" said Ali.

"You used a lit candle?" said Faik.

"A burning candle?" asked Hamza.

"Yes, but—," started Nasruddin.

"Then you have lost the bet!" they all cried, and they cheered and raised their hands in unanimous triumph. "You warmed yourself by that candle! Now you must make us dinner!"

Nasruddin was too fatigued to argue right then, but as he trudged back home he was thinking hard about the meal he had to prepare for his friends.

The next evening, laughing and joking, Ali and the other men gathered at Nasruddin's house for the meal. Nasruddin met them in a jovial and relaxed mood and led them into the living room.

"Well, I hope you are not yet too hungry. Dinner is not quite ready," Nasruddin told the guests.

"Can we help you at all to prepare things?" asked Ali.

"No, thanks, everything's all prepared. It just needs to cook a while longer."

The men sat around and chatted amiably for at least an hour. Ali said, "Well, Nasruddin, it's time for you to fulfill the bet you lost. We are ready for dinner anytime you are."

"Well, I started it yesterday, so it really ought to be almost done now. Please, relax and enjoy yourselves, while I check on dinner," Nasruddin said, as he went into the kitchen. "It's still cooking," he reported when he returned to the group.

Another hour passed pleasantly enough, and Nasruddin seemed completely unconcerned with the meal as he sat and philosophized and argued and discussed matters of great and little importance.

Ali said, "We are quite hungry now, Nasruddin. Shouldn't you check on the dinner?"

"Of course, I'm sure it's done by now. I'll be right back."

When Nasruddin returned he said, "It's taking a bit more time than I thought, but it shouldn't be too much longer. Please be patient."

Another hour went by in Nasruddin's living room as they talked of this, that, and the other. Finally Ali stood up and declared, "Nasruddin, we're famished. I can't smell any food cooking at all. Why in God's name is dinner taking so long?"

Nasruddin shrugged his shoulders and replied, "I have no idea what's taking it so long, but it's not done yet."

"Well, let us come with you to see what you have prepared for our dinner."

"Suit yourself," said Nasruddin, and Ali followed him into the kitchen along with the rest of the men.

As each person filed into the kitchen, a look of surprise and then a sheepish grin passed over his face.

Nasruddin was stirring a big copper pot which he had hung from the ceiling over the oven where no fire was blazing except for, flickering playfully, a single lit candle.

"I'm sure it won't be much longer," smiled the Mullah. "A candle gives off just so much heat, you know."

ONCE NASRUDDIN WAS SITTING and sipping his cup of tea in the neighborhood teahouse where he would pass time leisurely with his friends. As happened often enough, the men started to brag, and Nasruddin claimed that among his numerous professions — for as everyone knows, as a Renaissance man, Nasruddin did many things for work in those days — he had an intimate knowledge of the stars.

"Tell us, then, as an expert astronomer, Nasruddin," piped up Ali, the teahouse owner, "what do they do with the old moons, when there is a new one?"

"They recycle them. The teeth of Time chew each of the old moons and spit them back up into the sky as hundreds of stars," said Nasruddin.

"MULLAH, TELL US, WHICH is more useful, the sun or the moon?" asked Hussein.

"Most certainly the moon. There's already plenty of light out when the sun is showing. And as I said, moons are recyclable."

NASRUDDIN ADDED, "NOT ONLY do I know the stars, I know their portents and signs. I am modest about the unerring accuracy of my astrological forecasts and metaphysical predictions, but please — ask me anything."

Hamza asked, "Mullah, what sign were you born under?"

"I believe that would be: PRIVATE PROPERTY — KEEP OUT!"

"No, Nasruddin — what astrological sign were you born under?"

Nasruddin stroked his beard thoughtfully. "Of course, that would be the sign of the Donkey."

"I've never heard of any such zodiac sign," said Ali.

"Oh well, since they first invented them, I'm sure they have come up with a few more signs."

"I'm telling you, there is no sign of the Donkey."

"That may be or it may not be," replied Nasruddin, after scratching his long white beard. "In which case, I would have to say it would be the sign of the Billy Goat."

"Where do you get this nonsense?" said Hamza. "The Billy Goat is not a zodiac sign either, Mullah."

"*Effendi*, of course I know that. When I was a child, my mother used to tell me that Capricorn was my sign. Surely by now the Capricorn must have grown up to become a Billy Goat."

"I MAY BE COUNTED AMONG the most hospitable of men," bragged Nasruddin to the wags at the teahouse.

"Is that so?" said Abdul. "In that case, invite us all to dinner tonight."

Nasruddin agreed, to everyone's surprise. "Just wait here a few minutes so that I can run ahead and tell Fatima." The group agreed to the request, but as soon as the Mullah left, Abdul said, "I'm certain that Nasruddin is planning to evade our company for dinner. Let's follow him so that he can't squirm out of this one."

Nasruddin arrived breathless at his house and told Fatima, who promptly cuffed his ears for foolishly inviting his friends for dinner when there wasn't so much as a cucumber in the cupboard. Just then they heard the knock at the gate and voices of the men calling for Nasruddin. He hid behind the door and whispered to Fatima to tell the men outside he wasn't home.

"Come on, Nasruddin, we know you're in there!" Abdul called out, when Fatima opened the door. "We saw you come into the house!"

Fatima just shrugged her shoulders and said nothing.

"Nasruddin, you said that you were so hospitable, but why are you hiding from us?" Abdul said.

"We know you're there!" yelled Ali.

Nasruddin stuck his head out the window and yelled, "Hey, you dopes! I could have left by the back door, you know."

"THERE IS NO DIFFERENCE between my youth and old age!" declared Nasruddin at the teahouse one day. "I'm just as strong as I was twenty years ago."

"Is that so?" Hamza replied, always willing to challenge the Mullah on his boasting. "This is a huge rock in the city garden that most men couldn't even budge. If you are indeed as fit as a man of half your age, let's see you pick it up."

Hamza led Nasruddin from the teahouse, with the rest of the men trailing behind, to the boulder. The Mullah glanced at it casually and said, "Oh, is that all? That stone is nothing. I can lift it now just as easily as I could when I was a young man."

Hamza said, "Have at it, Nasruddin. Let's see you move it so much as an inch."

"Fine," said Nasruddin. He spat on his hands and braced himself. Barely able to reach around the stone, he heaved and huffed and hacked, but it showed no signs of locating to a new address. After some minutes of this embarrassed exertion, Nasruddin staggered back, sweating and panting, his face flushed.

"Nasruddin, you said you could have hoisted up the rock with the sheer strength of your youth, which has not diminished with the years," Hamza commented. "Apparently those were empty words!"

"You cannot accuse me of deceptive boasting. Truth is," Nasruddin admitted, "twenty years ago I couldn't have lifted that huge rock, either."

ONE FINE EVENING, NASRUDDIN yawned, set down the book he was reading, and stretched his back. "Time to go to bed," he said to Fatima, "but first, a nice cool drink of water."

He went to the kitchen and took a cup, but the water pitcher had only a few drops in it. He set down the cup and took the pitcher out back to fill it from the water jug, but that was empty too.

Nasruddin snuggled his toes into his pointy slippers and walked to the old town well with the jug. The night air was still and cloudless and the Mullah was glad to be outside on such a beautiful evening, alone with his thoughts.

All along the short walk, he was admiring the full moon shining high in the sky, almost directly above. "Ah, radiant moon," said Nasruddin, "you are as shiny during the night as my bald head during the day."

When Nasruddin arrived at the old well, he removed the lid, attached the rope hook to the handle of the water jug, and gently lowered the jug. He heard the soft clink of the ceramic vessel touching the rocky sides as it made its way down, then a soft splash. He waited several minutes for the jug to tip and fill with the clear, sweet water for which he was so parched, then slowly cranked the rope to raise the filled jug from the well.

Nasruddin was just unhooking the jug when he noticed something glimmering brightly at the bottom of the well. He set the water jug aside and looked more closely down the well.

As the surface of the water stilled, it became clear to the Mullah's eyes that it was the full moon! Somehow his beloved moon must have fallen from the sky and down the well! She seemed to be managing to just stay afloat, but who knows how long the moon could keep from drowning!

Nasruddin yelled down the well, "Hullo, old moon! Don't despair, for help is here! Have faith, I'll save you! I'll throw down the rope and hook, and you grab hold and hold tight. I'll haul you out in no time at all."

Nasruddin let the hook and rope unwind back down the well. This time he could not hear a splash of water, so he kept unwinding it until all but a short amount of rope was left. Slowly he reeled in the rope, turning the crank until he felt it catch something.

Not considering that he might have hooked on to the handle of an old collapsed bucket at the bottom of the well, Nasruddin called down the well, "Get ready, dear moon! When I count to three, jump up and I will pull you out of the well. Okay? One ... two ... *threeeee!*"

Bracing his feet and putting all his strength into his mighty yank, and with all the force of his big belly, Nasruddin jerked the rope. The hook dislodged from the bucket handle and flew up and out of the well and landed with a clatter on the cobblestone courtyard. Nasruddin tumbled backward, his slippers flying overhead, and he landed on his back with a thud not far away.

On his back, Nasruddin looked up and beheld that the moon had indeed returned to her safe and rightful place in the sky.

He, old Mullah Nasruddin, had delivered the moon back where she belonged! Ignoring his backache, he sprang to his feet, found his slippers, and did a little happy hero dance.

Nasruddin admired the moon like it was his loveliest daughter. The moon beamed at the Mullah and he beamed back. "You are so welcome, my dear moon, I'm glad to have been of service." He offered his *salaam* and said, "Just as well I came along, eh?"

The mullah winked at the moon, and it seemed to him as if the moon winked back. He hoisted up the water jug and walked back home to his waiting bed.

2

NASRUDDIN WAS VERY FOND of bragging to the men at the teahouse about his physical prowess. "Once I got a whole Bedouin tribe to run," he declared "How did you manage to do that, Nasruddin?" Hamza asked.

"Not hard at all. I just ran — and they chased after me."

ONE AFTERNOON, NASRUDDIN WAS bragging at the teahouse again — this time about his abilities as a horseman.

"I remember as a young man, there was a wild young stallion that nobody could ride. One by one, all the men and boys in my town tried to mount and ride the crazy horse, but none could hang on more than a few seconds. That horse bucked like a bull!"

Nasruddin made sure he had everyone's rapt attention, then continued, "Well, finally they came to me and asked me to try. At the time I was really quite strong and agile. So I told them to bring it, and I would tame that wild stallion. I grabbed the mane of that horse and jumped on his back and held on—"

Just then, Nasruddin's old friend Hamza, who happened to be with the Mullah when the incident occurred, walked into the teahouse.

"Yes? What happened when you rode it? Go on!" the men pressed Nasruddin to finish his story.

"Um, well — it threw me off. As it turned out, I couldn't ride the crazy horse either."

IN THE TEAHOUSE, THE men were prone to brag quite immodestly. Once, a decorated soldier was back from the wars and the place was agog. "One day, on the Northern Frontiers, I took my double-edged sword and attacked to the left and right of me and cut up the enemy like chaff. Thus when they were all pieced together and counted, they found that I slew no less than six infidels, all with red beards!"

The wags gasped, applauded, and cheered the soldier. Ali saluted him, then turned to the Mullah. "Nasruddin, you can't cap that one!"

After a pause, Nasruddin drew himself up to his full height. "Ahem. I do not boast much, and I am sworn to tell the truth," said Nasruddin. Ali arched his eyebrows.

The Mullah continued, "But I declare that, once, in battle, I severed the leg of a man in one stroke!"

The men grinned, knowing full well that the Mullah was rarely seen in battles in his life.

"Very brave, Nasruddin!" said the soldier, impressed. "But don't you think you would have done better to lop off his head?"

Nasruddin said, "Well, sir, that would have been impossible, you see, for someone had already done that."

THE TEAHOUSE WAGS GRUMBLED their incredulity at the Mullah's boasting, but Nasruddin held up his hand to silence the dissent. "Speaking of disbelief, then," the Mullah announced, "know all of you, that just yesterday, I slaughtered seven unbelievers, with a single stroke."

"Is that so?" cynically remarked a decorated soldier.

"Indeed," replied Nasruddin, casually drinking down the dregs of his tea while standing to leave. "In fact, I need to leave now to attend to their interment."

All the men, having never known Nasruddin as a man of violence, regarded the Mullah with a newfound sense of respect as he strutted out of the teahouse.

Nasruddin then returned home, where, in the drawing room, seven unbelieving beetles lay dead in the shadow of his flyswatter.

ONCE, AT THE TEAHOUSE, Nasruddin was enthusing about the delights of various sorts of halvah when he admitted, "Oddly enough, I have never made halvah myself."

"Really, Nasruddin?" asked Ali. "You're such an aficionado. Why have you never made halvah?"

"It's true," replied Nasruddin. "If we had tahini at home, it always turned out to be that we would be out of flour. Then, if we had flour at home, we never had butter. Or if we happened to have butter at home, we would never have sugar. And if we did somehow manage to gather all the ingredients — tahini, flour, butter, and sugar — all in the house at the very same time, then I was just too busy to make the halvah."

⤳

"Dᴉᴅ ʏᴏᴜ ᴇᴠᴇʀ ɪɴᴠᴇɴᴛ a new dish?" Hamza asked Nasruddin in the teahouse one afternoon.

"Yes, once by necessity," said the Mullah. "I created a new food of bread and snow, but even I disliked it."

⤳

A ᴡᴇᴀʟᴛʜʏ Pᴇʀsɪᴀɴ ᴡᴀs ɪɴ the teahouse and was talking about the tremendous palaces built in his home of Isfahan. He said, "One of the shah's palaces is fifty kilometers square, with at least two hundred rooms."

"Ehh, that's nothing," Nasruddin said, "You should see the palace the sultan has built in Konya, far more magnificent in every way. In fact, one palace covers an area of five hundred kilometers by—" Just right then, a fellow that Nasruddin knew was from Konya walked into the teahouse. Everyone was hanging on Nasruddin's next words.

"—by fifteen meters," Nasruddin finished, mumbling in his beard.

"But Nasruddin, that's impossible," said the first visitor, "how do you fit that width to that length?"

"It would have fit much better if this fellow from Konya who knows the actual dimensions of the sultan's palace there hadn't entered just right now."

3

Aˢ ꜰᴏʟᴋꜱ ᴡᴇʀᴇ ʙʀᴀɢɢɪɴɢ around the teahouse, they spoke about the famous people whom they knew. Nasruddin had just returned from a trip and said, "On my trip to the capital, the King stood right in front of me and spoke five words that I shall never forget."

"My goodness, Nasruddin," remarked Ali, "that must have been something profound that he said to you. What great words of wisdom did the King speak?"

"Get out of my way."

⤳

Tʜᴇ ᴛʏʀᴀɴɴɪᴄᴀʟ sᴜʟᴛᴀɴ Tᴀᴍᴇʀʟᴀɴᴇ, who believed he had suffered greatly at the hands of women, had the unpleasant habit of calling upon learned men and asking them a question, then beheading them if they gave an unfavorable answer. Not knowing anyone else who could stop this horrible spate of killings, leaders from several tribes beseeched Nasruddin to visit the lord to see what he could do.

Tamerlane made Nasruddin sit near him and asked casually, "Are you married?"

Nasruddin laughed and said, "At the ripe time in my life? How could any man remain a bachelor at my age?"

"Oho!" bellowed the sultan, "so you too are one of them! Off with his head!"

As the guards rushed to seize Nasruddin, he held up his hands, saying, "Don't be in such a rush to judgment! You might not have considered everything!"

The lord motioned to let Nasruddin continue.

"Why don't you ask me if I divorced my first wife and then married her again?

"Or if my first wife died and soon I married someone else?

"Or if, in addition to my first wife, I brought home a second wife? Or a third?"

"In summary, this is to say that . . .

"Why don't you ask me why I didn't come to my senses after the first foolish thing I said and then another foolish thing, followed by then yet another one of the same old foolish things once again?

"No, but I really just made this one foolish statement once in all.

"One never knows one's danger until it is too late.

"You know best, your Majesty, but one doesn't cut off the head of a horse when it stumbles just once.

"Remember the proverb, 'A horse that slips will never break its neck'."

Tamerlane was so delighted with Nasruddin's rambling response that he pardoned Nasruddin and rewarded him with a bag of silver.

WHEN TAMERLANE CAME TO visit Akşehir for the first time, Nasruddin was excited at the prospect of having an audience with him. One of the sultan's ministers briefed Nasruddin in advance of the visit. The minister reviewed the standard questions Tamerlane would ask: how old he was, how long he studied to be a mullah, how long his family lived there, how many of his children attended school, and whether he was happy or angry about taxation. Nasruddin prepared and memorized his answers in order.

When the Sultan arrived with his retinue and met Nasruddin, however, Tamerlane switched the order of the questions.

"How many years have you studied, Mullah Nasruddin?"

"Forty, your Majesty."

"Impressive. How long have you lived here?"

"Sixteen years."

"And you are how old now?"

"Twenty years."

"What the—? Are you crazy, or am I?"

"Both, your Majesty."

"Are you calling *me* mad, then, too?"

"We are mad — but not as much as you might think!"

TAMERLANE WAS A STRICT and powerful ruler who terrorized his subjects according to his whim. One day he arrived unexpectedly in Akşehir with a large battalion and occupied the town.

After a week, with no end in sight, Nasruddin was fed up with Tamerlane's imposition, so he stormed into the sultan's tent.

"I must know: are you and your army going to get out of this town, or not?"

Tamerlane was caught off guard by Nasruddin's audacity. "What did you say?"

Nasruddin stood his ground: "I demand to know if you and your army are going to leave."

"Don't be ridiculous!" Tamerlane fumed. "I'm not going to leave, nor are my troops leaving!"

Nasruddin replied calmly, "Well, if you do not leave here immediately, we have a backup plan."

"Just what in the world do you think you can do about it?" Tamerlane yelled.

"Well," replied Nasruddin evenly, "in that case, I'll gather all the townspeople together and . . . "

Tamerlane blew his lid. He screamed at Nasruddin, "And what, exactly?"

"And we'll run out of here as fast as our feet can possibly carry us."

AS THE VICIOUS AND cruel shah Tamerlane and his troops approached the town in which Nasruddin lived, a group of village residents came to Nasruddin's house and awoke him, terrified.

The Mullah sleepily answered the door, and the group implored him to quickly do something to stop Tamerlane from marching through and rampaging through Akşehir.

Immediately Nasruddin took his bed sheet and fashioned a turban upon his nearly bald head as big as a wagon wheel. Then, in his morning robe, he mounted his donkey and rode out to meet Timur.

When Nasruddin approached Tamerlane, the shah exclaimed: "Mullah! What in the world are you wearing for a turban?"

"Please pardon me for wearing it, your Highness," replied the Mullah, "but this is actually just my nightcap. I wanted to be sure to welcome you early, so I have rushed from my bed wearing this instead of my regular turban. Truth be told, the turban that I wear during the day is even bigger than this and requires another cart just to carry it."

Tamerlane was so alarmed by the strange giant clothes of the townspeople that he decided not to pass through this town.

ALTHOUGH HE WAS HELD in esteem as a wise and learned man, Nasruddin was accused of being nearly illiterate. One day Tamerlane decided to test Nasruddin by challenging him to write something for him.

"Gladly, sire, but I have taken an oath never to write even so much as a single letter again," said the Mullah.

"Well, at least write something in the manner in which you used to write, so that I can view what it was like."

"That would be impossible, because every time one writes something the writing changes with practice. If I wrote now, it would show my writing as of now only."

"Then someone, bring me an example of his writing, anyone who has one," ordered the ruler.

Someone brought an illegible scrawl that the Mullah had written to him once.

"Is this a sample of your writing, Nasruddin?" asked Tamerlane.

"Decidedly not, sire," said Nasruddin. "Not only does writing change with time, but you are now examining a piece of writing done by me to demonstrate to someone how *not* to write."

ONE DAY NASRUDDIN ACCOMPANIED Tamerlane as he reviewed the troops.

"Not a bad shot that," Nasruddin remarked at the skillful performance of the royal archers. "But it reminds me of when I used to shoot a bow and arrow."

"Is that so?" Tamerlane arched an eyebrow at the Mullah. "Never knew you were an archer yourself, Nasruddin."

"But of course, sire. I was famous in my youth. People would come from miles around to see me shoot."

"If you're such a great archer," Tamerlane said to Nasruddin as he beckoned a nearby soldier to approach them, "then you'll be happy to give us a demonstration of your fine bowmanship. As you can clearly see, my soldiers could use the instruction."

At Tamerlane's gesture, the archer handed Nasruddin a bow and quiver. The soldiers lined up on either side along the path toward the target.

Nasruddin slung the quiver over his back, walked to the shooting mark, and fit the arrow to the bow. Everyone in the royal entourage and every soldier in the practice field were watching. Nasruddin breathed in deeply as he drew back the arrow and released it. The arrow wobbled forward a few meters and stuck into the earth just short of the closest soldier's foot.

A roar of laughter and derision was launched at Nasruddin, but he held up his hand and shouted, "Silence! I was demonstrating how your soldiers shoot — too eager, but weak and inhibited. That is why he falls far short of his mark and loses fights."

Tamerlane laughed and the soldiers scowled.

Nasruddin took up another arrow from the quiver, fit it to the bow, pulled, and released. This arrow flew halfway to the target, slicing wide to the left. Several troops had to duck to avoid the arrow's path.

"And that, obviously, is how your Captain shoots. Having failed at his first shot, he is too nervous to concentrate, and so he veers far of the mark and loses battles."

Nasruddin took another arrow from the quiver, fit it to the bow, drew back, and released. This arrow wobbled three-quarters down the way and right of the target.

"And that was a demonstration of how your General shoots. Not having gained complete confidence, he overcompensates in his aim and reach and comes closer to the mark but still loses the war."

Nasruddin placed another arrow, drew back the bow, and released the arrow with a resonant twang. The arrow flew straight and very high. It looked as if was going to pass over the target completely, but then a sudden breeze seemed to drop the arrow quickly and it landed in the exact center of the bulls-eye.

Nasruddin turned to Tamerlane and said, "And that, dear sire, is my demonstration of how the famous archer Mullah Nasruddin shoots and wins."

4

NASRUDDIN APPEARED AT TAMERLANE'S court one day wearing a magnificent brocaded silk turban. Knowing the king would admire it, Nasruddin hoped that he could sell it to him.

"Nasruddin, that is a most splendid turban. How much did you pay for it?"

"A thousand gold pieces, your Majesty."

The Caliph, seeing what Nasruddin was up to, whispered to the shah: "Only a fool would buy a turban for that ridiculous amount."

Tamerlane scowled at Nasruddin and said, "Why did you pay so much? I've never heard of such an exorbitant price for a turban."

"True that it the turban is expensive, but I obtained it knowing that in the whole world there is only one king with the good looks and refined style who would buy such an extravagant thing and wear it."

Tamerlane beamed, flattered by the compliment, ordered that Nasruddin be paid two thousand gold pieces, and accepted the turban.

Now it was the Caliph's turn to scowl. After court, Nasruddin approached him privately and said, "My dear Caliph, you may know the value of turbans, but I know the weaknesses of kings."

ONCE WHILE TAMERLANE AND his retinue were on a hunt, he decided to take a break by stopping in the town of Akşehir. The shah came upon the teahouse, where Nasruddin had been left in charge. Tamerlane called for an omelet, and Nasruddin prepared a sumptuous breakfast omelet for the shah and his entourage.

Tamerlane pushed back his plate, dropped his napkin on the table, and exclaimed, "That was delicious, Nasruddin. It is now time to resume the hunt, so tell me what I owe you."

"For you and your five companions, Your Majesty, the omelets will be one hundred gold pieces."

Tamerlane raised his thick royal eyebrows. "The price of eggs must be exceedingly high in this part of the country," the King said.

"Your Majesty, the price of the omelet reflects the economic principle of supply and demand," replied Nasruddin.

"Surely there is no scarcity of eggs in this part of the country?" asked Tamerlane.

"Eggs are plentiful here," said Nasruddin. "The price reflects the scarcity in this area of visiting royalty."

TAMERLANE DECIDED, DURING ONE of his regular purges of moral impurity among the hoi polloi, that all liars would be caught and put to death. In this way, he reasoned, everyone would be forced to practice truthfulness.

Outside the court, he had a gallows built. When Tamerlane opened court, people found that they had to submit themselves to questioning by the soldiers. If they told they truth, they would be admitted. If not, they would be put to death immediately by hanging.

Before long, heads began to appear on spiked poles outside the sultan's palace. All the townspeople were terrified, of course, and pleaded with Nasruddin to solve the dilemma.

Nasruddin approached the palace gate and said to the soldiers, "Will you hang me if I tell a lie?"

"Indeed, we will, foolish man," said the guard.

Nasruddin said, "The truth is something I have never spoken — nor ever shall!"

"That makes no sense at all," said the guard. "Where do you think you're going?"

"I'm on my way . . . to be hanged."

"We do not believe you!" the guard roared at the Mullah.

"Well then, you must punish me for not telling the truth . . . by hanging me."

"But if we hang you for lying, we will have made what you said come true!"

"That's right," said Nasruddin. "Not only that, it will make what you said false, and thus we will have to put you to death."

The soldiers recoiled in fear of their own lives. "The value of truth is determined by its quantity, a simple matter of supply and demand."

Nasruddin continued to stroll confidently into the court, addressing Tamerlane, "This little demonstration shows you what truth is — *your* truth. Truth is like a coin — it has facts on either side, but its value is in the whole of it."

ONE DAY, THE WISE fool Mullah Nasruddin happened to be present in the court of Tamerlane, the sultan, when a drunken soldier was hauled in before the imperial presence. The soldiers who brought the drunkard asked what to do with him.

The sultan, who was occupied with thoughts of his treasury, waved them away and said carelessly, "Oh, whatever. I don't care — just give him three hundred lashes and we'll call it a day."

Nasruddin started laughing uproariously.

The sultan was incensed by Nasruddin's hilarious outbreak, and yelled at him: "What are you laughing at? Are you laughing at me? You should be ashamed! Explain yourself before I order you *five* hundred lashes of your own!"

Nasruddin responded, "I laughed at your punishment for this man because it means one of two things: either you have never felt the sting of a whip yourself, or you just don't know how to count."

ONCE NASRUDDIN WAS WALKING to Konya when he encountered Tamerlane on his way to go hunting. As usual, the sultan was in a foul mood and yelled at his soldiers, "It is the worst luck to see a Mullah when you are about to engage in a chase. Don't let him stare at me — whip him out of the way!"

The guards did just that.

As it turned out, the hunt was entirely successful. After the royal hunting party returned to the palace, Tamerlane sent for Nasruddin.

"I am sorry, Mullah. I thought you were a bad omen. As it so happened, you were not."

"*You* thought *I* was a bad omen?" exclaimed Nasruddin. "You look at me and receive a full game-bag. I look at you and get a whipping. So tell me, who is a bad omen for whom?"

ONCE THE TURKISH RUNNING team went to compete in trials against the Greeks before the Olympics, and the sultan, Tamerlane, assigned Nasruddin to be the team coach, although Nasruddin had never been particularly athletic himself.

Tamerlane warned that if the Turkish team lost, Nasruddin could expect severe punishment upon his return.

At the races, the Greeks beat the Turkish team.

Nasruddin was upbeat, much to the team's surprise. When asked why, Nasruddin said, "I have sent a messenger with news of the results."

"Why are you smiling?" asked one runner. "Don't you face the prospect of horrible torture or death upon return to Turkey?"

"The message I sent ahead to the sultan was this: *Our valiant Turkish runners, according to their best efforts, have come in just second. Our opponents only came in second to last.*"

THE MULLAH'S WISE AND witty comments made him a favorite in the King's court. Once, while Nasruddin was attending a royal dinner, the royal chef prepared the King and his guests a mouth-watering aubergine dish. The King was delighted with the tasty recipe and asked Nasruddin, "Are they not the most delicious, the best vegetable in the world?"

"Indeed, Majesty," said Nasruddin, "they are the very best. Everyone should eat eggplants every day."

"Splendid idea, Nasruddin. So be it." And he ordered the royal chef to make eggplant for every meal.

Five days later, after the tenth eggplant meal in a row, the Shah had tasted more than enough. He threw his fine linen napkin down and roared to the royal chef, "Take these disgusting vegetables away! I cannot stand the very sight of them!"

"Indeed, they are the worst vegetables in the world, your Majesty!" agreed Nasruddin.

"But Mullah, less than a week ago you praised eggplants as the very best vegetables, and recommended to eat them daily!"

"True," said Nasruddin, "but I am the servant of the King, not the vegetable."

5

ONCE, NASRUDDIN WAS INVITED by the *muhtar*, the mayor, of the town to a banquet at which the *emir*, the governor, was expected to attend. All day long the Mullah had toiled tilling his garden, and as the day wore on he anticipated the delicious food and sparkling conversation in store for him that evening. The Mullah's daydream about the feast made him misjudge the time to complete his work that day, and so he had no time to wash and change into something more appropriate. It was either clean up, dress, and arrive quite late; or go as he was and show up, more or less, on time. Turning up very late for a feast at an important social function was not an option, so Nasruddin hastily ditched his tools, dusted off his dirty work clothes, and hurried off to the banquet.

Although he arrived at the banquet hall not too late, he was greeted with disdain, and treated with disrespect from everyone. All the guests had already taken their seats, so he was seated alone in a dark, drafty corner furthest away from the table of honor. Seeing the Mullah enter looking so unclean, the muhtar and his guests were embarrassed.

Instead of being an honored guest, with the Muhtar and Emir paying keen attention to Nasruddin's ready stories and jokes and lavishing him with praise for his sharp wit, as Nasruddin would normally expect to be treated, the scruffy Mullah felt entirely neglected. When Nasruddin complained that nobody had offered him dinner, he was brought a few plain radishes, which only made him thirsty, and when he asked for water, the servants flat-out refused him.

Shortly the bedraggled guest left the great feast, slipped out the door, and hurried home. He scrubbed himself from his bald head to his toes and perfumed himself. Then Nasruddin dressed in new baggy trousers, a clean shirt, pointy slippers, and yellow silk turban, with an ostentatious brocaded coat, and rushed back to the banquet hall.

This time, Nasruddin was ushered in immediately by the bowing servants and given a place of honor at the head table. The Muhtar and the Emir rose to greet him as he was seated. Throughout the dinner they posed one question after another of the Mullah, who answered everyone with great wit and good humor, as one delicious dish after another was brought out for Nasruddin's enjoyment.

When the Mullah was sure that he had everyone attention, he picked up a choice chunk of meat, brought it to his lips — and then he dropped the food into one of the pockets, and said, "Eat, my fine cloak!"

Neither the Muhtar nor any of the guests or servants could guess why Nasruddin was feeding his pockets with fluffy pilaf, a square of cheese, a few dumplings, pickles — it was a very big coat with large pockets. Each time he fed the garment, he said, "Eat, my fine cloak, eat!"

After Nasruddin's coat made its way though about half the courses, the Muhtar could no longer restrain himself and remain quiet. Finally he inquired, "Nasruddin, *effendi* — what are you doing?"

"Ah esteemed sire, I am just feeding the true guest of this banquet — my cloak. When I came here the first time, I was completely ignored; the second time, I was treated as the guest of honor. I did not change: I am still Mullah Nasruddin. Therefore, I surmise that it must be my cloak to which you offer such great attention, affection, and respect. As such, it is certainly entitled to its fair share of the food, wouldn't you agree?"

ONCE TAMERLANE INVITED NASRUDDIN to join him in a polo game, and Nasruddin rode into the royal court on an aged water buffalo. Everyone in the courtyard laughed at Nasruddin, and Tamerlane taunted him, saying, "Any fool knows that you need a swift pony to play this game, so why did you show up on that stumbling ox?"

"Well, your Majesty," replied the Mullah, slightly red in the cheeks, "It's been so many years since I last played polo, and I forgot how the game is played. But even though the rules may have changed, believe me, when it was a youngster, this beast ran even faster than a horse."

✑

FATIMA ROASTED A SUCCULENT goose for Nasruddin to bring to Tamerlane.

Along the way, Nasruddin tripped on a rock and the cooked, wrapped goose flew unexpectedly one last time. When Nasruddin unwrapped it, he found that one of the legs had broken off. There really wasn't anything Nasruddin could do but eat the leg, and consider how he would explain it to the Sultan.

When he arrived to see Tamerlane, he tried rearranging it on the plate with the wrapping propping up one side.

"Your wife certainly roasts a fine bird!" remarked Tamerlane. "Please offer her my compliments on her fine cooking."

"Ah thanks, your Majesty, she and I are both most grateful," said Nasruddin.

"But tell me Nasruddin, why does the goose have only one leg?"

"Because sire, in this particular part of the country all the geese have one leg."

"Oho, no no, Nasruddin! Everywhere ducks and geese have two legs."

There was a large window in the courtyard that overlooked a pond where a small flock of geese were standing, in the water on one foot. "Witness the fowls in your very own yard."

Indeed, Tamerlane was hard-pressed to deny his own eyes. Nasruddin stated, "I count only twelve birds, and twelve legs. How many do you count, sire?"

"Well, in the capital where I grew up, and everywhere else I've traveled, the geese all have two legs," he muttered. "Still, my thanks to your wife for her excellent roast goose."

Tamerlane called the royal chef, whispered something in his ear, and the chef hastily removed the platter with the one-legged goose from the court.

"I want my chef to taste the bird," Tamerlane said with a twinkle in his eye, "so that he can see how a goose ought to be roasted properly. Meanwhile, let us talk of other things."

Suddenly a clattering and banging came from the kitchen, then seemed to proceed out the back door and toward the pond, and shortly the chef came into view, along with four other members of the kitchen staff, making a ruckus with the pans and pot lids. They walked single file like a makeshift marching band toward the goose pond and, in short order, the geese all woke up from their nap, and lowered a second leg, just before they flew away, scattering in the four directions.

Tamerlane turned to face Nasruddin, who was ready with a response: "My liege, if any of us had such a din poured into our ears while we were asleep, we too would have grown another leg in order to fly away as fast as we could!"

ONCE TAMERLANE WAS HOLDING court and became bored, so he issued a challenge. "I will give three thousand gold pieces to anyone in my court who can teach a donkey to read in three years."

Nasruddin stepped forward. "Your Majesty, I can teach a donkey how to read and write."

"You had better be able to do just that, lest I have you beheaded," the king threatened, as he tossed the bag of gold pieces to the Mullah.

"I can do it, but I need ten years to accomplish the task."

"Very well, you may have ten years."

After court, the dignitaries and courtiers crowded round Nasruddin.

"Mullah, can you really teach a donkey how to read and write?" the Caliph asked.

"No," said Nasruddin, "of course not. Don't be foolish."

"Then the next decade will bring only tension and anxiety for you," remarked the Caliph, "for you will surely be put to death. What folly to endure ten years' mental suffering and mortal dread for the sake of gold!"

"I have absolutely nothing to worry about," replied Nasruddin calmly. "You have overlooked one important fact: the king is seventy-five years old, and I am near eighty. Long before the time's up, other elements will surely have entered the situation. Either he will die beforehand, or I will be dead, or most likely, the donkey itself will have expired."

ONCE WHILE CONVERSING WITH Tamerlane, Nasruddin began boasting about his little grey donkey. "Karakacan is such a noble and intelligent animal that, why, I could even teach it to read!"

"Then go ahead and teach your ass to read," Tamerlane commanded. "I give you three months to accomplish your task. If you can get the donkey to read, I will reward you three hundred gold pieces. If you cannot, you will receive three hundred lashes from the whip instead."

Nasruddin went home and immediately started training the donkey. He placed a few grains of bulgur wheat between each page of a big book and, by turning the pages of the book himself, he let the donkey eat the bulgur. The donkey quickly learned how to turn pages by using its tongue to find the grains. Three days before the three months was over, Nasruddin stopped feeding the animal.

When he presented the donkey to Tamerlane for its literacy test, he asked for a big book to be placed in front of the donkey for it to peruse. The hungry animal turned the pages of the book rapidly one by one with its tongue to find its feed, but when it reached the end of the volume without eating a single grain of bulgur it started braying.

Tamerlane, who had watched the demonstration closely, remarked, "This is surely the strangest way of reading I have ever witnessed!"

Nasruddin shrugged and replied, "But sire! This is how a donkey reads!"

NASRUDDIN WAS IN COURT when the new tax collector, Eren, came to present the accounts to the despotic sultan Tamerlane. The tax collector was brought in, with dozens of long strips of parchment, upon which he had calculated all the taxes in impressive columns, fluttering behind him as he approached the throne.

The sultan was in a despicable mood that day, completely unnerving the new tax collector. The terrified Eren halted and stuttered in presenting his tedious report, and his hands shook so hard that he dropped the dozens of accounting rosters.

Tamerlane fumed, "Surely you cannot think I would be so gullible as to accept your word that this accounting is accurate."

Eren broke down and wept before the King, "*Ai vai!* Please your Majesty, I did not mean —"

"Forget it, you scoundrel! You have revealed yourself as a scamp and a cheat. I shall make you eat your words and figures now."

With the palace guard bearing over him, the tax collector had to chew and swallow all the long slips of parchment he had presented, without so much as a sip of water, and then the guard dragged the new tax collector outside, choking and sputtering.

"Who shall be the new tax collector?" As Tamerlane surveyed the courtiers clustered about, each person there gulped and turned to face Nasruddin, except for the Mullah himself, who was trying to figure out upon whom everyone else in the room seemed to be focusing.

Tamerlane declared, "But of course! I appoint you, Mullah Nasruddin, to act as the new tax collector!"

"Who, me? But sire —" Nasruddin tried to object.

"But nothing! Begin at once, my new tax collector!"

Nasruddin was galled and appalled. Although he knew it was a dreadful position, he gravely but graciously congratulated the sultan on his fine judgment placing his royal trust in a simple mullah to prepare the tax receipts. With that, Nasruddin bowed and excused himself to return home. He was certain there was no pleasing the King with the accounting, but then, an idea struck him that being Tamerlane's new tax collector might be manageable after all.

The day before his first report was due to Tamerlane, Nasruddin had Fatima bake dozens of *yufka* flatbreads for him. Very carefully in an immaculate and miniscule handwriting, Nasruddin copied the accounts on the flatbreads and stacked them in piles.

Finally the day of reckoning had arrived. When Nasruddin appeared in court with a large tray piled with neat stacks of flatbread, everyone in court was amused, except for, of course, Tamerlane, who thundered, "What is the meaning of this, Nasruddin? But whatever gave you the foolish notion to print the accounts on *yufka* bread?"

"I witnessed when the last new tax collector presented his written tabulations to you and you made him eat them. Just in case you decided to force me to devour my accounts as well, I have brought the figures here to you written as legibly as possible on pastries which my wife baked, so that both of us might digest the accounting figures more easily."

Tamerlane, who seemed placated so far, motioned for Nasruddin to proceed.

Nasruddin replied calmly, "Your Majesty, here are the correct sums for all tax collections for this month," and he passed to the sultan a flatbread twice as large as the others that contained the monthly summary chart with their daily tallies printed precisely and neatly. Tamerlane remarked, "Nasruddin, I heard that your handwriting was terrible, but this, I can read."

"Your Majesty, a simple matter of abject necessity required that my penmanship improve so dramatically."

"And it smells delicious, too!" grinned the King.

"And these supporting documents," Nasruddin continued, motioning to the stacks of freshly baked and inked smaller flatbreads, "each contain the details for the monthly revenue accounts. I trust you will find the results fresh, accurate, and delectable!"

Tamerlane was indeed impressed, amused, and pleased with the monthly tallies. "Nasruddin, your accounting has my approval. You may offer my compliments to your wife on her fine baking!"

And he gave Nasruddin a small bag of gold coins to share with Fatima, who made many more flatbreads after that for a very long time.

ONCE NASRUDDIN WAS ON his way to the sultan's palace when he ran into his old friend, Süleyman, who greeted him warmly and asked why he was carrying a tray of beets.

Nasruddin answered, "I have grown these good red beets in my garden, and I have brought them as an offering to the sultan Tamerlane."

"Beets for Tamerlane?" Süleyman gulped nervously. "*Effendi*, with all due respect, I beg of you for your own sake that you bring Tamerlane something more refined, such as figs or olives."

Nasruddin thought this to be excellent advice, so on the way to court he exchanged the beets for some fragrant oranges. As it turned out, Tamerlane was in a jovial mood that day, and he accepted Nasruddin's gift with gracious good humor.

The next time Nasruddin went to court, he remembered that Süleyman recommended figs as a good present, so he brought a basket of beets to barter for some other fruit. The Mullah went to a fruit vendor near the palace but the only figs for sale were quite soft and mushy. Nasruddin was unsure, but he was glad to be rid of the beets and took the figs and went inside.

This day, Tamerlane was in a temper, and seeing Nasruddin's offering of overripe figs put him over the top. He yelled, "Nasruddin, you idiot, you think that I should eat these awful figs? I think that *you* should eat them! Soldiers, give Nasruddin a taste of his own fruit!"

Six guards immediately grabbed the basket of figs and pelted Nasruddin with the mushy fruit. Try as he did to duck the assault, their aim was spot on, and not a fruit missed its mark. *Smack! Squish! Splatter! Sploosh!*

As each soft fig exploded upon hitting his body, Nasruddin cried out, "Thank God, thank God!"

Tamerlane roared, "Nasruddin, you moron! Why in God's name are you thanking God each time one of these figs smacks you in the face?"

Nasruddin said, "Thank God that I never brought you the beautiful hard beets from my garden, as I would have been bruised black and blue now, and no doubt injured severely by the time your guards got to the bottom of the barrel!"

Tamerlane smirked, then jerked his head away, "Ah whatever, you dunce. Guards, now throw the rest of the fruit at this fighead. Hard."

When the basket was empty, Nasruddin was plastered with fig-pulp and fig-seeds and fig-juice from the top of his turban to his pointy slippers. The soldiers chased him out of the courtyard, a green-brown, figgy mess.

Nasruddin tramped away from the court in shock and disgrace, trailed by a gathering swarm of many kinds of flies and stinging insects. On the way he saw Süleyman approaching, and he dropped down on his knees and bowed before him, "*Effendi*, I thank you seven times below the ground!"

Süleyman stood back to take in Nasruddin as the Mullah continued, "And I thank you seven times above and beyond heaven! O my guardian angel! My true friend and benefactor! Süleyman *effendi*! You are a prophet and the son of a prophet! Indeed, I owe you my very life!"

"You look disgusting, Nasruddin," said Süleyman, swatting away the insects from his bespattered friend. "Tell me, what happened?"

"I give thanks to God for sending you as His messenger to save me!" exclaimed Nasruddin. "I took your advice to give the sultan figs, and he had his brutish soldiers hurl them at me. Just imagine my fate if I had brought him an overflowing bucket of those large, hard beets — they surely would have killed me!"

6

SULTAN TAMERLANE HAD THE unfortunate tendency that, whenever he had a bad dream at night and got mad with someone, the next day he would ride out and execute that person.

When the Mullah heard of this bad habit, he was afraid and wanted to leave Akşehir, but a friend implored him to stay, "Do not leave us, Mullah! You're the only one who can appease the sultan! If you go, what will happen to us?"

But the Mullah seemed unconcerned as he got on his donkey and rode away. A minute later he turned around and shouted, "Let somebody else take care of him from now on. Although during the day, I can sometimes calm him down, it's not within my powers to influence his nocturnal dreams!"

❧

DURING TAMERLANE'S REIGN, CITIZENS were banned from carrying any sort of weapon or knife.

One day Luqman, the town constable, stopped Nasruddin on the street and searched him because he thought the Mullah was acting "suspiciously." Hidden under his turban was a big curved knife.

Luqman shouted at Nasruddin, "Fool, don't you know that the sultan has forbidden the use of knives?"

"But I use that to scrape off mistakes and make corrections in the books I read," Nasruddin protested. In those days, small penknives were used to correct errors in books.

"Is that so?" said the captain. "Well then, why do you need such a big knife?"

"Because they are very large books and there are lots of huge mistakes. Sometimes the errors are so egregious that even this enormous knife isn't big enough to handle them."

❧

THE BRUTAL SULTAN TAMERLANE, who had slaughtered hundreds of innocents, once remarked to Nasruddin, "Mullah, as I am certain you must know, all the illustrious benevolent leaders of our superior Persian civilization had some sort of honorific attached to their names, such as 'God-Gifted' or 'God-Beloved'."

"Yes, my liege," affirmed Nasruddin.

"Would you suggest that such a distinguished name should also be bestowed upon myself, your imperious Highness?"

"God forbid," replied Nasruddin.

❧

ONCE NASRUDDIN ACCOMPANIED TAMERLANE to the royal bathhouse. As they were sitting in the *hammam*, enjoying the steam, Tamerlane asked, "Tell me, Nasruddin, if you were to buy me as a slave, what would you appraise my net worth right now?"

Nasruddin stroked his white beard and replied, "In all, I would pay no more than two gold pieces."

The sultan protested, "What? You blockhead! But this belt that holds up my bathing trunks is worth that much!"

"Quite what I was thinking when I named your price," said Nasruddin. "Yes, your royal belt is certainly worth two gold pieces. The value of the man inside the bathing trunks that are held up by the belt, however, is priceless. I cannot place a numerical value on your existence. So the maximum I would pay for you in cash is two gold coins."

ONCE TAMERLANE GAVE TO the gentle folk of Akşehir what he thought was a delightful present: a gigantic male elephant. Naturally, the poor townspeople couldn't afford to keep and feed an elephant, but they were too afraid of offending the sultan, who would likely punish them for not accepting his gift.

They tried to accommodate the monster, but when they could not provide it with enough food, it went berserk and rampaged through farms, vineyards, and gardens in search of anything to stuff in its mouth. After a few days of this disaster, half the town lay in shambles.

Somehow they needed to dump the elephant, but knowing Tamerlane's fierce temper, they thought the best strategy would be to ask him to take the huge beast back.

Knowing that the sultan favored Nasruddin, a delegation of the town elders persuaded the Mullah to represent them in their request. Nasruddin agreed on the condition that a dozen townspeople accompany him as he confronted Tamerlane in court.

The determined group left with Nasruddin bravely leading the way to the palace, but along the way, one by one, they dropped away, mumbling some lame excuse or the other:

"I left something cooking on the stove," said Hussein.

"I've got to pass water," said Agha.

"I forgot my cigarettes at home," said Ali.

"My lame foot is hurting and I cannot walk farther," said Halil.

In this manner, one by one, each of the townsfolk ditched the delegation. When Nasruddin arrived at the entrance to the court and turned around, not a single person was there to cover his back. He was furious, but knew how to handle the matter.

"Greetings, your Majesty!" Nasruddin spoke confidently to Tamerlane. "The people of Akşehir have asked me to come here to make a request of you."

"Yes, continue," said the sultan.

"Well, the townsfolk are well pleased with your fine gift. We love the magnificent elephant — but we have a problem."

"Yes, what is it?" said Tamerlane impatiently.

"The problem is," said Nasruddin, "the male elephant has been lonesome and desperate without a female companion and has been very destructive. We are afraid that it is too dangerous to keep a single, lonely elephant all by himself."

Tamerlane replied, "Don't worry about the problem of having a bachelor elephant. I will immediately have a female elephant delivered to the grateful people of your town to keep the lonely fellow company."

Nasruddin thanked Tamerlane profusely for his thoughtful generosity and left the court. When he arrived back in Akşehir, the townspeople clamored around him in the town square to hear how things went.

Nasruddin announced: "Brace yourselves for more good news — the female calamity is coming to town."

ONCE NASRUDDIN WAS WALKING through the bazaar when he saw a pair of spectacular birds for sale for fifty silver pieces. *My bird*, he thought, *which is larger than both of these expensive birds put together, must be worth far more.*

The next day he brought his lovely pet turkey to the market. He extolled the virtues of the turkey to no end, but nobody would pay more than five silver pieces for it, and this put Nasruddin in an uproar. He exclaimed to the brokers and merchants: "O people! This is a real disgrace! Only yesterday you were selling birds just half this size for ten times as much!"

"But Nasruddin," Süleyman the walnut-seller explained, "those birds were parrots — they're worth more because they come in brilliant colors, and because they can talk like a human."

"Surely," said Nasruddin coolly, "you are not considering all the hidden assets of my bird. It may be that your parrot can talk, but my turkey thinks. And not only that, his thoughts are blessedly silent, without all that annoying squawking chatter."

ONCE NASRUDDIN WAS IN the teahouse when the wealthy Aslan was going on at length about his property.

"My real estate holdings are so vast," Aslan claimed, "that it takes me almost a full day to ride on my fastest horse from one corner to the opposite border."

"Is that so?" asked Nasruddin slyly. "How unfortunate."

"Why in the world would you say that such a thing is unfortunate?" said Aslan.

"Well, I used to have a horse that slow," Nasruddin replied, "but I sold it."

7

O NE FINE EVENING, FARUK the busybody came across Nasruddin carrying a lamp while walking down the street. He said, "Mullah, you always boast about your excellent night vision and how you can see in the dark. So why do I find you now, carrying a lamp so visibly?"

"The use of a light may not always be obvious," Nasruddin replied. "This lamp, in fact, is highly effective in preventing others from bumping or colliding into me."

O NE NIGHT, LUQMAN, THE town watchman, found Nasruddin prying open his front window.

"Mullah, what are you doing sneaking into your own house?" asked Luqman. "Are you locked out?"

"Shhhh!" whispered Nasruddin. "They say I sleepwalk, so I'm trying to spy on myself, to find out for myself if they are right."

T HE MULLAH AND FATIMA had a burglar problem for a while. Every time the Nasruddins went out of town, they would return to find that one or another room had been cleaned out.

One night Fatima was awakened by a thud in the next room. She crept over to Nasruddin's bed, put her hand over his mouth, and poked him, whispering, "Shush, Mullah — I think there may be another burglar downstairs."

"What is left here worth stealing for him to find?" grumbled Nasruddin as he turned over and pulled the blanket tighter. "We are so poor now that the thief will have to bring his valuables into the house — and then we can rob him."

O NCE AFTER ANOTHER BURGLARY episode, Nasruddin came home in time to see the thief making off with the last of their possessions in a huge sack, leaving only a single moth-eaten blanket.

Nasruddin immediately grabbed the blanket and followed the robber.

Once the thief arrived back at his place, he unloaded the sack and started examining the goods.

Nasruddin walked right into the fellow's place, lay down on the blanket, and pretended to fall asleep.

"Who are you, and what are you doing in my house?" asked the shocked thief.

"I presume," said Nasruddin, recognizing the furniture, "that we are in the process of moving house? If so, then you neglected to take this blanket." He handed the blanket to the stunned robber.

"No need to leave a job unfinished," remarked Nasruddin.

ONE DAY BY MISTAKE, the Nasruddins' robber returned to their house while the Mullah was home. The thief found him cowering in the closet and asked him, "What are you doing in there? I'm here to rob you, not hurt you."

"*Effendi*, I am not hiding in the closet from fear," Nasruddin said, "I am hiding from shame that I have nothing left of value to steal. The obvious exception being this body I have, which is, take my word for it, of no usefulness at all."

ONCE NASRUDDIN FOUND A diamond ring in market, but according to the law at the time, the finder of an object had to go to the market and shout three times the fact that an object had been found.

At three o'clock the next morning, Nasruddin, true to the letter of the law, stood in the center of the marketplace and yelled thrice, "I have found a valuable gold and bejeweled ring!"

By the third shout, Luqman the *bekche* had come out to see what the commotion was about. "What did you just announce?" they asked him.

"The law clearly dictates a threefold repetition," said Nasruddin, "and for all I know I may be breaking the law if I proclaim it a fourth time. But this much I'll tell you: I'm the owner of a diamond ring, all right!"

ONCE NASRUDDIN WENT TO the *hammam* for his bath at the end of the day in his dirty, dingy work clothes. The attendants scoffed at him and gave him a sliver of soap, a rag for a loincloth, and a grungy old towel. Nasruddin had his bath and as he left, he handed the two men a gold coin each.

The two *hammamjis*, the bath attendants, could not believe their good fortune, after having treated the young Mullah so shabbily without a complaint from him. Surely, they decided, they misjudged his true worth and would give him better treatment next time, and so receive an even more generous tip.

The next time Nasruddin went to the bathhouse, the attendants looked after him with much greater attention and deference, and offered him all the nice amenities. Nasruddin was bathed, massaged, and perfumed like a VIP and, as he exited the *hammam*, he handed each of the attendants the smallest possible copper coin. The head *hammamji* protested, "Sir, I ask you — is it fair to leave such a small tip for all the extra services you received today?"

"The gold coins you received before were for this time," Nasruddin replied, "and these coppers are for the last time. Now we're even."

PART FIVE

VILLAGE LIFE

1

ONCE NASRUDDIN AND HIS son, Ahmet, were walking along a road when they saw Bekri, the local *qadi*, or magistrate, romping around half-naked in his vineyard. The elderly magistrate was singing merrily and carrying a large jug of wine, from which he would take a large gulp every so often, and then begin singing again. Shortly the man dropped to the ground as if struck dead, and when Nasruddin and Ahmet went to check that the man was all right, they found him asleep in a drunk stupor, alongside his costly silk cloak and turban, which were abandoned sometime earlier. Nasruddin and Ahmet took the cloak and turban and went home.

When he awoke the next day, Bekri made his way home in disgrace. He called his servant and told him to be on the lookout for the clothes. Sure enough, soon Nasruddin could be found strutting around in his new finery. The servant collared Nasruddin and brought him to Luqman the *bekche*, who promptly escorted him before the qadi while court in session. Nasruddin immediately stated his case directly to the judge:

"Your Honor, last night I was walking with my son Ahmet past your vineyards when we came across some poor drunken fellow, running around stark naked, chugging wine from a jug and singing bawdy songs, the likes of which I'm sure your Honor has never heard before in his life."

A murmur rose from among the people sitting in the scandalized courtroom.

"You don't say," answered Bekri at last.

"I do say," continued Nasruddin. "The unfortunate sot was so intoxicated that before long he heaved and pitched and collapsed in a disgusting ditch. I could not make out the drunken man's face, as he had fallen flat on it into the mess. Such a shameful man!

"In any matter, seeing that he had discarded his fine cloak and turban by the side of the road, and knowing that many thieves and ruffians inhabit the roads, I thought it best that we take the fine garments to keep them safe and clean."

"Of course, Nasruddin," said the judge. "That was indeed quite thoughtful."

"I believe we must consider the likelihood that this grave sinner who trespassed on your treasured vineyard must have been an infidel reprobate from some other place, because as you know drinking is forbidden to all true believers, and only true believers live in your jurisdiction. Would you agree, your Honor?"

"I cannot disagree with your assessment that the man was not from here, Nasruddin. Considering that you have already worn the clothes, keep them. I wish to hear nothing more of this matter — case dismissed!"

THE NEXT MORNING NASRUDDIN was walking along in his fine new clothes when a man came up from behind and slapped him hard on the back, knocking the breath out of him. When Nasruddin turned around to confront his attacker, the stranger held up his hands and said, "Ooh! Forgive me! I thought you were the thief who stole my brother-in-law's clothes — which look remarkably similar to the fine garments you are wearing, my sir."

Nasruddin replied, "It must be the latest style," and collared the fellow to drag him to court, which was in session again with Bekri the qadi presiding.

Nasruddin could tell immediately that, if not indeed a brother-in-law, the man who slapped him was some sort of friend to Bekri, who listened impassively to Nasruddin's complaint. He urged Nasruddin to accept the man's apology as sufficient, but the Mullah pressed him for fair justice.

"I have decided the matter," said Bekri. "The punishment for a slap is a slap. You may slap the fellow back, and then we may call it quits."

Nasruddin was hardly satisfied with this resolution, and he complained further.

"Fine, then," declared the qadi, barely able to hide his delight at Nasruddin's displeasure. He told the defendant, "Pay the plaintiff one copper coin, and be done with the matter."

"But your Honor," protested the man, "I have not even a copper in my pocket."

"Well, then," said the judge, "go and get the coin for Nasruddin, and return to pay him. Case dismissed!"

The man left and Nasruddin waited while court proceedings continued. Finally, after two hours, Nasruddin asked to approach the bench. When he stood before Bekri, Nasruddin reached over and slapped him sharply on the face.

"Take that, your Honor, from me," Nasruddin said, "and when your brother-in-law returns, either he can pay you the coin, or you can slap his face in turn. *Then,* we can consider the matter well settled."

⟨⟩

NASRUDDIN HAD A RICH friend, Aslan, whom he asked if he could join his party when they went hunting. Aslan reluctantly invited him and, when Nasruddin showed up at the hunt one cloudy morning, the man offered Nasruddin the worst horse in the stable, a steady but very slow pony. The rest of the hunting party galloped off, leaving Nasruddin trotting not much faster than a young donkey, and soon enough the group had left him so far behind that he could no longer hear their laughter on the wind.

Not very much farther along, the clouds grew thick and dark, storm winds kicked up, and the skies burst forth with rain. Nasruddin removed and folded his clothes, and sat down on top of them under the pony. When the storm had passed, Nasruddin got up and dressed, returned the pony to the stable, and enjoyed himself in the dry warm comfort of the hunting lodge.

When the hunting group returned empty-handed that afternoon, they had been wet and cold all day, as they had already gone far away into an area where there was no nearby shelter. Somehow Nasruddin hadn't gotten wet, but nobody could figure out how. Aslan asked, "Nasruddin, how did you manage to escape the rain?"

"It was that fantastic horse you gave me!" Nasruddin replied.

Aslan was intrigued by Nasruddin's cleverness, so he extended an invitation to return for another hunt.

Nasruddin came again for the hunt, as it turned out, on a cloudy day, and this time Aslan put Nasruddin on his finest steed, and himself on the slow pony.

This time Nasruddin took off like a thunderbolt, outpacing the host and his retinue. Again by midday an unexpected storm blew up, and rained. Nasruddin took off his clothes and sat under the steed until the storm passed, then doubled back to the lodge, arriving quite dry and happy.

Aslan and his friends, who were obliged to ride apace with the host, returned much later, drenched and shivering.

"It's all your fault, Nasruddin!" Aslan accused. "You made me ride this terrible horse!"

"I made you do nothing of the sort," replied the Mullah. "Did you not consider that you and your retinue had to contribute some effort to the problem of staying dry?"

⟨⟩

ONCE, NASRUDDIN WAS TRAVELING, subsisting solely on alms offered from good Muslims to their religious leaders, who dedicate their lives to the attainment of knowledge and wisdom. He came into a town and asked at the house of a very rich and learned man for alms, and the master of the house brought him in and gave Nasruddin a thin mattress to sleep on.

In the morning, Nasruddin went to the grand dining room and found the rich man seated at the table, which was laden with delicious food: omelets, yoghurt, fruit, and fresh brown bread with honey.

"Before you may join me for breakfast, I will require you to demonstrate that you are worthy of my largess. Please, Mullah, read me a passage from the Qur'an."

Nasruddin read the section indicated with the correct pronunciation and intonation, but the man was not impressed. He took the Qur'an and read the same section, and he recited it about as well as the Mullah had done it.

Then the man asked Nasruddin to write some verses. The Mullah complied, whereupon his host also wrote down in a neat and clear script the same verses.

Then the man asked Nasruddin, "Now you see that I can read and write, just as well as you. You asked me for alms, but why should I give you something? We are equals, and I do not need you!"

"Well," said the Mullah, "while it may or may not be true that you can read and write, we most certainly are not equal."

"Why not?" retorted the man.

Nasruddin replied: "Only when you have wandered across the country on pilgrimage, and then returned, starved, exhausted, humiliated, and empty-handed — only *then* will you be my equal!"

✷

ONCE WHEN NASRUDDIN WAS *qadi* of Akşehir, Hamza, a neighbor with an adjoining piece of land, appeared in his court. With a great show of humility, Hamza confessed, "Mullah *effendi,* I am deeply aggrieved to inform you that your bull jumped the fence, then gored and killed my cow. Is there any compensation I'm eligible to receive?"

"You certainly cannot sue the bull for blood-money. Nor can you hold the innocent owner of an animal responsible for its bad actions. So it would appear, in my opinion, that there is nothing, I'm afraid, that you can do about the matter."

"Oh, my bad!" exclaimed the crafty villager. "I misspoke. What I meant to say is that my bull gored your cow."

"In that case," Nasruddin said, "Clerk, get down that big black law book from the shelf and let's take a look. It is highly probable that there are precedents or mitigating factors affecting the case that must be considered."

ＯＮＣＥ ＮＡＳＲＵＤＤＩＮ ＷＡＳ Ａ guest at his wealthy neighbor Aslan's house. The Mullah craved cheese, and so he started raving about it as they were being seated for dinner: "Cheese is most certainly a pleasant and healthy food! It helps digestion. It's also very nutritious and can be taken on long trips."

Wanting to play a trick on Nasruddin, the host ordered the servant at once to bring cheese. But secretly he told the servant to return and announce that they had just run out of cheese. The Mullah said, "It's better that way. For cheese stinks, makes you thirsty, and rots your stomach."

Aslan acted surprised and said, "First you praise the cheese as healthful and beneficial, and then you damn the cheese as unpleasant and dangerous. What then, is your real opinion?"

"My opinion depends solely," responded the Mullah, "on whether or not there is cheese."

ＮＡＳＲＵＤＤＩＮ'Ｓ ＮＥＩＧＨＢＯＲ, ＦＡＩＫ, ＷＡＳ hosting his daughter's wedding, so he came by to ask if he could borrow two of Fatima's brand new copper pots to cook two of the dishes for the big feast. The Mullah agreed to lend them to his neighbor.

After the wedding Faik forgot for a while to return the pots, but eventually he brought them back to Nasruddin, somewhat battered and dirty.

Inside the two nested pots, Nasruddin saw a third very small pot. Nasruddin asked, "Where did this tiny pot come from?"

Faik, who felt guilty for continuing to use the pots for so long, made up an excuse, "Your two pots also got married at my daughter's wedding and had a child, and so now that the infant can travel safely, I am returning the offspring that was born while your pots were under my care."

"Is that so?" said Nasruddin as he took back the borrowed cooking pots. "Fair enough."

Some time afterward, Nasruddin visited Faik to borrow his neighbor's old, banged-up, black-charred cauldron, but he never returned it. When, after several months, Faik came by to query Nasruddin about it, he said, "I'm terribly sorry, but as it turns out, your old cauldron has died."

"What in the world are you talking about?" the neighbor shouted. "How can an inanimate metal pot die?"

"Quite simple," replied Nasruddin calmly. "We have already well established the common belief that pots are mortal, is that not correct? So, quite logically, if my two new pots could multiply, then it should certainly come as no surprise that your old cauldron should have kicked the bucket, so to speak."

2

Once Nasruddin's brother Selim asked a favor. "Brother, I hear that you have some very fine forty-year-old vinegar. I need a small quantity to prepare some medicine. Would you kindly give me some?"

"Don't be ridiculous," said the Mullah. "If I gave out some of my precious aged vinegar to anyone who asked, do you think there would be even a single drop left for me?"

Jalal, a poor but industrious friend of Nasruddin from Konya, came to ask to borrow money from Nasruddin, saying he would repay the full amount the next week. Though he doubted he'd see the money returned, Nasruddin lent him the requested amount.

One week later, much to Nasruddin's surprise, Jalal showed up at Nasruddin's door and repaid the debt on time.

A few months later, Jalal returned to ask Nasruddin for a somewhat larger loan.

Nasruddin spat in the dirt and said, "Oh no, you don't, you deceitful scoundrel. You'll get not so much as another copper from me ever again!"

"Say *what*, Nasruddin?" said Jalal. "You know fully well that you can trust me and my credit is good, since I repaid the last loan promptly."

"Feh. You tricked me last time by repaying me on time, you prankster. Do you really think I'll let you make me raise my expectations of you like that again? No way. There's an old saying in Konya — I know it's in Akşehir, probably in Konya — that says, 'Fool me once, shame on you. Fool me twice — you can't get fooled again.' I mean — shame on you for fooling me in the first place!"

One morning, the Mullah's old family friend Jalal arrived to visit the Nasruddins. "You're just in time! I'm just about to go on my rounds to minister to my parishioners, and I'd be delighted for you to accompany me."

"But I cannot possibly go visiting without a decent cloak," Jalal complained.

"No problem, I'll lend you mine." Nasruddin lent Jalal a very fine embroidered coat indeed, and the two set off on rounds.

On the first call, Nasruddin introduced his friend, "This is my good friend Jalal, from Konya. But the fine embroidered coat he is wearing — that is mine!"

On their way to the next house, Jalal scowled at Nasruddin, complaining, "Why did you say such a boneheaded thing? 'The robe is mine,' indeed! Don't do that again, you nincompoop."

When they were comfortably seated at the next place, Nasruddin made the introductions again. "This is my old companion, Jalal, who has come to visit me. But you see the fine embroidered robe he is wearing? That robe is his!"

After they left, Jalal was just as annoyed as before. "You asshole, Nasruddin! Why in the world did you say that? Are you crazy or what?"

"I was just trying to make amends," said Nasruddin. "Now we are evens."

"If you would not mind," Jalal enunciated slowly, "let us not speak one word more about the robe."

At the third and final place of call, Nasruddin said, "May I present Jalal, my old friend. And that fine embroidered robe he is wearing — ah, but we mustn't mention that now, must we?"

Nasruddin was greatly pleased with a lunch of liver that was prepared for him at the house of his friend Hussein — so much so that he requested the recipe from his Hussein's wife, Setare, to bring back home to Fatima in hopes she would prepare the dish.

With the recipe written on a slip of paper, Nasruddin returned home, stopping on his way at the butcher's where he ordered three kilos of fine, fresh liver. Tucking the recipe safely in the pocket of his baggy pants, swinging the parcel of liver wrapped in paper and string, Nasruddin hurried home.

Suddenly, while Nasruddin was occupied with thoughts of another fine dish of delicious liver, a large buzzard swooped down, snatched the parcel in its beak, and flew off with it. Nasruddin ran after the bird for a few steps, then realized the futility of trying to chase it.

Still, Nasruddin was not about to let the buzzard have the last word: "Go ahead and take the liver, then, you birdbrain — but it won't do you any good! I still have the recipe!"

ONCE NASRUDDIN NEEDED A court decree from the judge in Konya. Several times he went to Konya only to have the court officer tell him to come back another time.

Having heard from his friend, Jalal, that the judge was a greedy man, Nasruddin decided to suborn the judge. He carefully poured mud into a pot about three quarters of the way, then filled up the rest with honey, and left it at the judge's door. When the judge came home that day, he looked into the jar and tasted the honey, and it was sweet.

At court the next day, Nasruddin appeared at court and mentioned to the judge that he had left something sweet for him. The judge nodded, and granted Nasruddin his decree.

Every day, the judge ate several big spoonfuls of honey. After a few days, wanting to savor the delicious nectar, he stuck his spoon deep into the jar, and proceeded to ladle in his mouth a heaping spoonful of mud. He was furious.

The next morning, the judge called the town watchman and told him, "Find the rascal Nasruddin and bring him to court. Tell him the certificate he was issued is wrong, and he must return to court to have the matter corrected."

The *bekche* collared the Mullah at the market just before he was about to leave Konya and told him, "An error has crept in during the processing of the decree issued you earlier this week. It must be amended to reflect the mistake."

"With all due respect to his Honor," Nasruddin said, "I would greatly prefer not to change the decision. You may tell him, 'If a mistake has crept into the process, it must be the jar's fault, not mine!'"

And with that, Nasruddin slipped out of the market and headed back home.

ONE DAY, NASRUDDIN WENT hunting and by accident managed to bag a quail. He returned home with it, plucked and washed the bird, then spiced and salted it well and put it in a pot on the stove. Nasruddin turned on the oven and soon the delicious aroma filled his house, and went out the open window into the neighborhood.

Shortly, there was a knock at the door. One of the neighbor boys, Ismail, apparently needed Nasruddin's services as a holy man. "Please, Mullah, come now," implored the boy. "My father is very sick and requests your prayers."

Given the direness of the situation, Nasruddin could only comply with the request. He turned off the stove, put on his cloak, and went with the boy to their house to help his sick father, leaving the quail basting in the stove.

As soon as Nasruddin left, the boy's father, Abdul, slipped into the dining room, replaced the cooked bird with a live fowl in an identical pot, and reset everything as before.

When they got to the boy's house and Nasruddin discovered it empty, he asked where Abdul was. The boy could only shrug, and Nasruddin, sensing a deception at hand, immediately spun on his heels and sped out the front door and back to his house.

When he got back to his kitchen and removed the pot lid, the quail flew up and out through the open window as Nasruddin covered his face and shrieked.

Within moments, Ismail and Abdul rushed into the kitchen, asking what was wrong.

"My quail somehow came back to life and flew the coop," said Nasruddin.

"It's a miracle!" exclaimed the other two, barely able to conceal their sniggering laughter.

Nasruddin sniffed at the air, and he detected the lingering aroma of a cooked bird. A suspicious scowl cast across his face like a shadow. "Wait a minute," he said, "although Allah can restore the dead back to life, there is also the matter of the spices, herbs, salt, pepper, butter, and water that were used. Where do you suppose those ingredients went? The miraculous is all very well and good, but after all, as everyone knows, miracles do have details!"

NASRUDDIN HAD A SWEET-NATURED little lamb that he adored. Its gambols were a constant source of amusement to the Mullah and his family, and for several years he fed and cared for the happy creature with great affection.

The teahouse wags coveted Nasruddin's lamb, and conspired to make him surrender it to their molars. One scheme after another failed, until finally, Ali came up with a clever idea.

Ali approached Nasruddin once while he was tending his lone sheep out in the pasture. "Greetings, Nasruddin."

"*Salaam*, Ali. You have come to admire my fatted lamb," said Nasruddin.

"Indeed, Mullah," said Ali. "Your lamb is so delightful, so charming, so . . . succulent — I mean, so sweet! So . . . it is indeed such a shame, alas . . ."

"What shame?"

"You haven't heard? As has been widely prophesied, the world is coming to an end tomorrow. What a shame that such a gorgeous lamb should be wasted when the last day comes."

"The last day is tomorrow? Allah save us!" cried Nasruddin, "Ali, *effendi*, thank you for letting me know about the end of days as foretold. I would never have known otherwise."

"Nasruddin," said Ali, "considering how well-informed you are, I'm surprised that you weren't aware that the Apocalypse that was predicted, indeed, for tomorrow!"

"No! It's true?"

"Yes, Nasruddin," Ali assured him. "That is why it's too bad that your little sheep should be wasted when you should cook and enjoy it. First thing tomorrow, everyone is planning to bring something to share to the picnic area by the lake. I'm sure your lamb would be ready in time for the final feast if you begin roasting it very soon."

The Mullah was quite shocked at the sudden turn of events but it seemed as if there were no way to save his beloved lamb, and so he resigned himself to the inevitable. With deep sadness, he agreed, "You're right, we may as well eat it."

So early the next morning, Nasruddin slaughtered his beloved lamb and brought it for the picnic feast at the lake, and before long the poor creature was skinned and staked and Nasruddin had the unhappy task of roasting it, turning the cooking meat on a spit over a modest fire.

Meanwhile, the men of the village came to the picnic and enjoyed themselves as they waited for Nasruddin's lamb to roast. Someone suggested, "Let's go for a swim in the lake while the meal is cooking, and we shall return refreshed and have our feast at the expense of Nasruddin's little sheep!"

The fellows tossed off their clothes and ran to the lake, hollering and diving into the cool, pleasant water. They laughed and splashed around while Nasruddin sat dejected, turning the roasting lamb on a spit over and over again on the rotisserie.

After Nasruddin's friends enjoyed their most pleasant interlude cavorting in the lake, they decided they had waited long enough. They were more than ready for their fine meal of roast mutton as they came out of the water, dripping, and naked. They laughed at Nasruddin's foolishness for believing that the end of the world was coming today, but now they would confess and tell Nasruddin about their wicked little trick.

But when they ran up to the spot on the bank where they had discarded their clothes, they could find not a stitch of clothing there.

They ran covering themselves best as they could to the fire pit, where they found Nasruddin happily smiling as he turned the roasting lamb over a blazing fire, in which the men could make out charred and burnt remnants of their clothes, turbans, and shoes.

"Nasruddin, you idiot, you imbecile, what have you done?" Ali and the men yelled.

"Why, my friends, I didn't think you would mind in the least," Nasruddin answered innocently, "if I used your clothes for kindling to heat the fire to cook my beloved lamb. After all, if the end of the world is indeed today, and this is indeed our final feast, what need have any of you for clothing?"

3

ONCE IN THE TEAHOUSE, Ali declared, "There is nothing without an answer!" Nasruddin replied, "True, and yet, once a wise and learned scholar challenged me with an unanswerable question."

"Impossible," said Ali. "Come now, Nasruddin, surely there was some sort of response for the question, some solution for the problem."

"Truth be told, at the time I was unable to answer what he asked me."

"What lofty intellectual question did the scholar ask that rendered you speechless?"

"Very well," relented Nasruddin. "This was the question he asked me: *Why are you sneaking into my house through the back window in the middle of the night?*"

NASRUDDIN DECIDED TO DON the robe of a Sufi dervish and travel on pilgrimage. On the way he encountered a yogi and a priest, and the three holy men decided to travel together. When they came to a village to rest for the evening, Nasruddin begged for alms while the other two secured lodging and bedding. Nasruddin collected some donations with which he could only buy four pieces of baklava.

He brought the food back, and each man had one piece of the delicious dessert.

"I deserve to have the last piece of baklava, for I worked the hardest to bring it to us," said Nasruddin, reaching for it.

"I should eat the last piece," objected the priest, "since I am the only representative of a properly organized hierarchical religious body, and therefore I should have preference."

The yogi argued that since he ate only once every three days, the baklava should go to him, since he needed it the most for sustenance.

Nasruddin suggested that they sleep on it, and the triad agreed that, come the morning sun, whoever related the best dream would receive the baklava.

The three awoke at dawn, performed their ablutions, and sat down together. The yogi was eager to go first: "I dreamed that I was walking along a beautiful path in Mount Kailasa, the abode of Lord Shiva, and I met the goddess of food, Annapurna, and worshipped at her feet."

"Not bad," said the priest, "but my dream was better. In my dream, I saw Mary, mother of Jesus, pulling loaves of bread out of Jesus' robes and feeding hundreds of small children."

They turned to Nasruddin. "I dreamed I was home sleeping, and God entered my own bedroom and kicked me out of bed. Then God shook his fist at me angrily and commanded me, 'Nasruddin — don't be a fool — go eat the rest of the baklava — *now!*' And of course, I had to obey."

A SCHOLAR FROM FAR ASIA happened to visit Akşehir and with signs and gestures managed to convey that he wanted to meet the greatest teacher in the village. Naturally Nasruddin was dispatched to engage the scholar in wordless debate.

The visiting sage took a stick and drew a circle in the sand. Nasruddin took the stick from him and drew a single line across the circle, and then the visitor drew a line perpendicular to the previous one, dividing the circle into quarters. Nasruddin gestured like he was taking three parts and leaving the last quarter to the scholar. In response, the scholar brought the fingers of his right hand together and shook his hand with the palm facing down. Finally, the Mullah did just the opposite, turning his hand palm up and wiggling his fingers.

When the meeting was concluded, the scholar explained: "Nasruddin's disputation and grasp of natural science is most excellent. When I began by asserting that the earth is round, he pointed out that it is split in two by the equator. When I divided the circle into four quadrants, he replied that three-fourths of the earth is water and one-fourth of it is land. When I asked what causes rain, he told me that water from the ocean evaporates, rises to form clouds, then turns into rain."

When asked his version of the debate, Nasruddin replied, "That strange and greedy fellow! He started out nicely enough, suggesting we eat a round pan of baklava. I agreed, saying I would gladly share half with him, but then he asked what I would do if he cut it into four pieces. I replied that I would eat three of the pieces. Then he told me he wanted the baklava with chopped pistachio nuts sprinkled on top. I answered, 'Okay, but in that case you cannot cook it on hot ashes, you must use a flaming fire.' He couldn't come up with a reply to that, so he quit."

ON NASRUDDIN'S SMALL FARM, he had a buffalo with large horns set wide apart that looked like a bow. Nasruddin often looked at the animal and thought aloud, "What if I could sit between the horns of my buffalo? Wouldn't it be magnificent to be mounted on the creature's head, holding on to its horns, as I travel about town? It would be like riding a throne! People would see me on the buffalo and comment how regal I look. I could even replace my old grey donkey Karakacan for some of my longer trips . . ." In this way, over time, Nasruddin developed an elaborate fantasy of riding down the streets of Akşehir seated on the buffalo's horns.

One day, Nasruddin's buffalo happened to lie down on the grass right in front of him, and the Mullah saw that this was a perfect opportunity to fulfill his dream. He turned around, backed up two steps, sat down on the creature's head, and grasped its horns.

"Nobody will ever believe I actually did it," he thought.

Immediately the startled buffalo, insulted but not injured, stood up and tossed Nasruddin high and far into some bushes, which broke his fall. Fatima heard the commotion and ran outside to find the Mullah groaning and rubbing his balding pate. "*Ai*, big head — big headache."

As she helped him out of the shrubbery, she asked, "Nasruddin, are you alright? What happened?"

Nasruddin replied, "This mishap is not as bad as it looks, my dear. Indeed, I have created my own suffering, but at least I have finally attained the object of my long-held desire."

ONE AFTERNOON WHILE THE Nasruddins were out, their neighbor Hamza's ox crashed their common fence, mounted Nasruddin's cow, ate some vegetables and fruit in the garden, and took a huge crap outside the back door of the house. Well sated from its afternoon romp, the animal returned to its stable ready for a nap.

The family arrived home presently. When Nasruddin saw the cow, the pile, and the fence, he was furious. He charged up Hamza's yard to the bullpen and into the stable, where the ox was placidly munching hay. He grabbed a whip and started lashing the bull mercilessly. Hamza, unaware anything untoward had happened with the animals, came out of his house screaming at Nasruddin, "Are you crazy, you idiot? What are you doing?"

"Mind your own business," hissed Nasruddin, pausing between lashes. "This matter is just between the two of us."

"Stop it, you hateful imbecile!" cried Hamza. "That is my beloved prize bull! Why in the Prophet's name are you whipping my ox?"

"Believe me, your ox knows its crimes fully well. I even gave this wicked sinner the option to confess, but the stubborn beast would not."

Nasruddin dropped the whip and turned to leave. "So now *you* try to ask the ox why it's guilty."

LATER THAT YEAR, WHEN Nasruddin's cow dropped its foal, it was no surprise that the male calf turned out to be just as mischievous as its father and as stubborn as its owner.

Nasruddin tried to get the young calf into the pen with its mother, but ended up chasing the frisky youngster around the field, yelling at the top of his lungs for the calf to stop, for half an hour. Finally he gave up and skulked back to the pen, where he proceeded to verbally abuse the cow. Fatima came out and asked, "Nasruddin, why are you cursing the cow?"

"I am scolding the cow for bringing up such a stubborn and willful calf. It's all the mother's fault, for she ought to have raised her child better."

NASRUDDIN'S GOOD FRIEND IN Konya, Jalal, brought a nice plump duck when he came to visit for a few days one winter. Nasruddin gave the fowl to Fatima, who prepared a delectable, hearty soup with plenty of juicy bits of perfectly spiced duck and just the right amount of vegetables, herbs and spices, and pepper and salt.

The Nasruddins and their guest sat down to eat this most delicious duck soup for lunch, and they enjoyed themselves with countless quack-quack jokes and other lighthearted conversation that night. There was plenty of the wonderful soup left over and the next morning Jalal said goodbye to his friends and departed.

An hour or so later, a knock came at the gate, and Nasruddin answered.

A man bowed and said, "I am Adem, the best friend of your dear friend, Jalal, who brought you the duck yesterday. I ran into Ahmad on the road, and he told me about the wonderful duck soup, and said that I absolutely had to come right over and taste some, if you would wouldn't mind."

Nasruddin could not think of turning away this stranger, his best friend's dearest friend, so he seated Adem in the dining room. Then the Mullah added a bowl of water to the remaining soup, stirred it over the fire, and served a bowl of the diluted soup to Adem, who ate it smiling without a word. When the man finished, he stood to leave, praised it as the tastiest duck soup he ever tasted, thanked Nasruddin profusely, and left.

About an hour later, there was another knock at the gate, and Nasruddin went to see whom it was. A man bowed and said, "I am Bilal, the closest friend of Adem, who is the best friend of Jalal, who brought you the duck yesterday. I happened to see Adem this morning, and he told me that I just had to come right over and try some of your fabulous duck soup."

Nasruddin certainly could not refuse, his dearest friend's best friend's closest friend, so he admitted Bilal, stirred another bowl of water into the remaining soup, and served it to him. His guest ate quickly, commented it was good duck soup, heartily thanked Nasruddin, and left.

No more than an hour had passed when Nasruddin heard yet another knock at the gate.

"I am Firat, the oldest friend of Bilal, who is the closest friend of Adem, who is the best friend of Ahmet Ahmet, who brought you the duck yesterday you had for dinner. I just saw Bilal on the road, and he insisted that I just had to come right over and try some of your delectable duck soup."

Nasruddin brought in Firat, added another bowl of water to the remaining broth, and served the broth to him, who gave it faint praise, offered quick thanks to Nasruddin, and split.

An hour, more or less, went by when Nasruddin went out the gate to meet whomever else would be there, and sure enough, a fellow bowed and said, "I am Hekim, the dearest friend of Firat, who is the oldest frien—."

Nasruddin wordlessly grabbed the stranger by the hand, led him inside, seated him at the dining table, and served him the last of the remaining watered-down duck soup.

After the first taste, the stranger looked displeased and complained, "What is this malarky? I was told this was the most delicious duck soup to die for, but it's almost clear and tastes like nothing!"

Nasruddin sighed and said, "Hekim *effendi,* just as you are the friend of the friend of the friend of my friend, who brought me the duck, what is in that bowl is the soup of the soup of the soup of the soup of the duck. So now, if you'll just eat it and leave, the duck will have fulfilled its final destiny."

4

ONE DAY, NASRUDDIN WAS traveling down the road, he saw a fellow and struck up a conversation with a stranger, and they stood in the middle of nowhere, gossiping and chatting, for almost an hour.

Nasruddin then held up his hand to pause and asked the man, "Pardon me, *effendi*, what is your name?"

"It is Firat — but didn't you remember me, from somewhere before you started speaking with me nearly an hour?"

"No, actually, I'm afraid I'd forgotten where I knew you from," said Nasruddin as he scratched his thick white beard, "that is, if I ever knew you before. Pardon me for this case of mistaken identity. You see, as you approached me, I noticed that your beard is long and grey like mine, and your turban and robe are the same colors as mine, so I figured that you were me, or at the very least just like me, and since I was lonely, I stopped to have a friendly chat with myself."

ONE TIME, HUSSEIN ADMIRED Nasruddin's silver pinky ring and said: "Nasruddin *effendi*, please give me your ring to wear, so that every time I see my finger, I shall remember you."

The Mullah replied, "I most certainly will not give you my ring. But be comforted, for you'll still have something to remember me by."

Hussein replied, "Oh, what is that?"

"From now on, Hussein *effendi*, every time you look at your finger, you shall recall what I have *not* given you."

WHEN NASRUDDIN WENT TO the ocean for the first time, he stood on the sandy beach admiring the vastness of the water. Then he gingerly tiptoed into the water and splashed in the shallow waves. After swimming around awhile, he became very thirsty, so he started to sip the seawater. Naturally this made him even thirstier, but after several more gulps, Nasruddin began coughing violently and ran out the water, gasping and spitting. He staggered from the beach until he found a well nearby and managed to get enough fresh water down his throat to quench his thirst.

After he recovered, he asked a woman at the well if he could briefly borrow her bucket, and she nodded assent. Nasruddin filled the bucket and then carefully carried the well water back to the seashore.

When the Mullah reached the water's edge, he poured the water from the pot into the sea.

"Someone had to give that big fancy impostor a taste of what real water is like!" Nasruddin said to the woman as he returned her bucket.

∞

After Nasruddin got home and saw his friends in the teahouse, Ali asked if he liked the ocean setting. The Mullah observed, "Overall, it was quite lovely. Pity, though — they filled up the whole land with water. Just imagine how pretty it must have been before that."

"How could the ocean have been so awful?" Abdul asked.

"Such immense grandeur — all that froth and foam and crashing waves — but such a disappointment!" Nasruddin answered. "To think that something with such great pretensions is not worth drinking."

∞

While Nasruddin was traveling in Konya, he was walking with his old friend Jalal at night and remarked, "The air here is quite the same as it is in my hometown, Akşehir."

"What makes you say so, Mullah?" asked Jalal.

"Because I can see, my friend, there is indeed exactly the same number of stars in the sky here that is there," said Nasruddin. "From this I deduce that the air must be the same."

∞

Nasruddin was walking to the market and came across a basket weaver at his work. He went up to the weaver and said: "You should make that tray larger."

The basket weaver was delighted and asked, "Because you will purchase my lovely handcrafted work?"

"No, I don't want to buy it," replied Nasruddin, "but someone might send me something in it someday, so it should be as large as possible."

∞

A new road to the capital was built called the *Shah-Rah,* or the King's Highway, and Nasruddin decided to check it out.

He walked all day until finally sleep overcame him, and he lay down by the side of the road, feeling safe on the Shah-Rah. In the morning, though, he discovered that his turban had been swiped right off his head! Nasruddin was incensed, but he continued down the highway, hoping to come across the thief of his headwear.

At a crossroads, he met several soldiers on the road, marching another blindfolded soldier. Nasruddin asked where they were going.

"This soldier was supposed to guard the highway, but he fell asleep on duty. By the Shah's orders, we are to take him to be hanged."

"That's enough of this cockamamie *Shah-Rah* for me," said Nasruddin, beating a hasty retreat down a side road. "Whoever falls asleep on the King's Highway is bound to lose either his hat or his head."

5

ONE SWELTERING SUMMER AFTERNOON, Nasruddin lay under the cool shade of his old mulberry tree, which provided ample shade. As he was gazing up at the leaves rustling the leaves overhead, he relaxed in his backyard and observed the day. He enjoyed the cooling breeze tousling the few remaining grey hairs on his head, since for a change, he had removed his turban. *There's not a single fool around to laugh at my old bald head,* he thought, *except for me,* and he chuckled to himself.

He had worked hard in his garden that year, and was quite pleased with the fruit of his labors. The season was especially great for growing fruit, and several heavy yellow-green watermelons ripening in the sunny far corner of the garden caught his eye.

As he lay there contemplating in the shade of his favorite mulberry tree, the wind rustled the leaves overhead and Nasruddin glanced up.

Nasruddin's thoughts turned to the intention of God's creation: "Lord, how is it that You have designed an immense and impressive tall tree like this mulberry to produce such puny, miniscule berries, yet chosen to design a weak, thin creeper to yield such a huge, juicy fruit like my melons?"

The breeze continued to waft across the Mullah's glistening brow as he considered the matter fully. The more he thought about the scheme of things, the more certain he became that God had made a colossal blunder in the current arrangement.

"If it had been me planning the matter," Nasruddin murmured to his attentive audience of berries and melons, "I would rather have placed the few very important melons waving proudly atop the strong branches of this formidable tree, and the numerous puny insignificant mulberries attached to the spineless vines laying so passively along the ground."

As the prone Mullah pondered the puzzle of this paradox, a strong gust blew up and swayed the branches of the tree above.

With an almost indistinguishable snap, a mulberry at the top of the tree broke off and fell, bounced down several branches, then finally landed with a plink on Nasruddin's forehead, right between the eyes. He jumped up, unhurt but quite startled.

"Ah Lord! Great indeed is Thy wisdom and mercy! Forgive me for mingling in Thy affairs!"

Nasruddin rewrapped the wet turban around his naked pate all the way down to his eyebrows, then settled back down for a nice long nap.

"I should have thought of that very reason earlier."

ONCE NASRUDDIN WAS HEADING to the woods near the forest to collect driftwood, for that is one of the things Nasruddin did for work, when he saw his neighbor Faik tending his grove of young olive trees.

"Tell me, Nasruddin," he inquired, "do you think my precious olive trees will bear fruit this year?"

"They will bear most certainly," replied Nasruddin, with an air of confidence. "God says and I say!" the Mullah declared, as he left to scour the lake banks for driftwood.

Several hours later, Nasruddin passed by Faik's olive trees on the way back, empty handed.

"Nasruddin," exclaimed Faik, "you are a man of peculiar perception! You predicted with absolute certainly the harvest of my olive trees, yet you cannot tell whether you will find driftwood on the lakeshore?"

"I always know what must be," Nasruddin said, shrugging his weary shoulders, "but what might be ... not so much."

ONE MARKET DAY, GRAPES were being sold at a very low price. However, Nasruddin's friend Faik asked to go to the market and buy grapes for him at an even lower price. Thus, the Mullah went to the market and negotiated with the sellers. After much persuasion, he bought some grapes for a very low price.

He returned to Faik and boasted: "I've done it! I had to haggle with the seller, and finally I told him all sorts of sob stories. In the end, he believed all my lies and let me have the grapes very cheap."

"That's great!" replied Faik effusively.

"I only did all that because you insisted," Nasruddin replied. "But now you most certainly must agree that I do deserve at least a little something!"

"Sure," replied Faik.

"Something for all my efforts and aggravation."

"Of course."

"Fine," said Nasruddin, "since I did all the work, now I am entitled to keep all the grapes for myself."

NASRUDDIN WAS CROSSING LAKE Akşehir on a sailboat, and a terrible storm blew up. The captain ordered all hands aloft to furl the sails and lash them to the masts.

Nasruddin ran up the deck to the captain, yelling, "What are you fools doing? Anyone can see that the ship moves from the bottom, but your men are trying to bind it up from above. If you are trying to keep the boat from rocking so wildly, then you must tie it up from below!"

ONCE NASRUDDIN WENT ON *hajj*, the pilgrimage to Mecca required of all faithful Muslims. As he reached the threshold, many people, including a black man, crowded to enter the *Kaaba*. Some of the pilgrims protested, crying: "O Lord! How can You admit to this holiest of holy sites, this black savage unbeliever?"

Nasruddin replied, "O sinners! Why do you insult this man here because of the dark color of his flesh? At least he is so open to show his transgressions outwardly on his skin. If we had the honesty and courage to reveal our many sins before everyone, then you and I would probably appear blacker than him."

ONCE NASRUDDIN WAS DELIVERING a sermon from the pulpit of the mosque. "Oh true believers," he exclaimed, "mark my words, for I am a prophet and the son of a prophet."

The worshipers sat staring at Nasruddin in slack-jawed disbelief at this dubious statement.

"In fact," said the Mullah, "I know precisely what you're thinking right now."

Berrak, from his seat in the congregation, spoke up. "Mullah, tell us what you think we are all thinking."

"Easy enough," Nasruddin replied, as he took a thoughtful pose and stroked his long grey beard. He rubbed his temples with his index fingers. He cleared his throat. "I can tell . . . that you are thinking . . . that I am a false prophet."

As a learned tribal elder and mullah of his town, Nasruddin was expected every Friday to give the sermon for the Muslim Sabbath. Every week he climbed the steps to the pulpit in his mosque to his congregation and would hold forth on many topics.

One Friday morning, however, even as he walked to the pulpit, nothing at all came to mind.

As he stood before the assembly, finally an idea surfaced. Assuming a fierce stance, Nasruddin announced in a severe voice, "O true believers! Do you know the topic about which I have come to speak to you?"

Puzzled glances were exchanged, and then the people answered in a hushed whisper, "No, not at all, we haven't a clue."

Nasruddin looked disparagingly at the congregation. "If you have no idea of the value of the message you are about to receive, then of what worth can be anything that I tell you?" And with that, he dismounted the pulpit and exited the mosque, free for the time being. Of course, the entire next week, Nasruddin's cryptic sermon was the talk of the village.

That Friday, again Nasruddin found himself about to address the expectant flock with nothing to say. Taking the pulpit, he announced in an even more fiery tone, "O true believers! Do you have any idea of what I have come here to speak about?"

This time, the group, as one person, rose and responded, "Yes, we do know."

Nasruddin replied, "Oh, so now you all know everything about the subject, do you? If it's so obvious, then why should I waste my breath explaining to you what you already know?" And he descended the pulpit, free for another week to do as he pleased, while everyone in town was abuzz all that week in anticipation of the next sermon from the inscrutable Mullah Nasruddin.

When Friday came around, as it inevitably does, once again Nasruddin found himself without a subject for his sermon. He slowly ascended the pulpit, then proclaimed in a furious roar that made every person in the mosque tremble with the fear of God, "O true believers! Do you know the topic about which I have come to speak to you today?"

As the group had agreed beforehand, half stood up and said, "Yes, we know," while the other half remained seated and said, "No, we don't."

Every head in the room leaned closer to hear what the great Mullah Nasruddin was going to say.

"The people who do know — and you know who you are! —" Nasruddin instructed sternly, "should teach those who don't know." And with that, he climbed down the pulpit and looking neither left nor right, scuffled out of the mosque, free and clear — until the next Friday, at least.

6

To CONCLUDE RAMADAN, DURING a scorching summer, Aslan, a wealthy merchant, invited Nasruddin and several of his friends to break the month of fasting. When everyone was seated, the first course was served. Normally this would be hot soup but, because of the heat, iced compote was the first dish. Nasruddin saw that while the host, as a joke, used a long-handled, large spoon almost like a ladle to serve himself, he had provided the guests with very short-handled shallow teaspoons, which barely gave them a taste of the compote.

Time and again the merchant dipped his spoon into the bowl of iced compote and brought it to his lips, slurping and exclaiming his delight, "Ooh! It's too delicious! I could die! So divine! To die for! Oh! I could just die!"

After several minutes of this display, during which the host tasted more compote than the rest of the guests combined, Nasruddin could no longer restrain himself and exclaimed, "Please, my dear sir! There is more soup in your beard than we have tasted with these baby spoons. Give us adult spoons like yours — let us die just a little, too!"

MEHMET, ONE OF NASRUDDIN's students, asked, "It is said that the hawk lives six months as a male, then six months as a female. Mullah, is that true?"

Nasruddin stroked his long white beard and replied, "In order to know, you must become a hawk for a year and a day."

BECAUSE NASRUDDIN WAS A holy man, he often walked from one town to another like a mendicant and spoke to people about the various prophets, saints, and great beings. He once described the life of Jesus in heaven. A curious woman was very interested to know what Jesus ate in heaven, and she asked the Mullah to tell her. But the Mullah had already been almost a whole month in this village without anyone having offered him any food. He replied, "Why in the Prophet's name do you want to know what Jesus eats in heaven, while right here on earth, you haven't even inquired of me if I've eaten even once for the past month?"

ONCE IN THE AKŞEHIR market, a poor man was passing the booth of Akram, a smoked meat vendor. The freshly smoked kabobs smelled so delicious to him, he could not resist wanting to taste some, but the poor man had only two small coppers to rub together. While Akram was distracted with other customers, the beggar got out from his bag a few stale crusts of bread and held them over the flaming meat so to absorb some of the delicious smoke.

The poor man had eaten one bread crust, and just as he was about to bring another to the aromatic smoke, Akram grabbed him roughly by the collar and demanded payment for the use of the smoke from his meats. The poor man naturally refused, and before things came to blows, the townsfolk, who had gathered as the conflict grew, brought the two men to the Mullah, who was sitting at the teahouse, to straighten matters out. Nasruddin listened attentively, stroking his beard, as each man told his side of the story. Finally when the vendor and the beggar had had their say, everyone turned to Nasruddin to see how he would settle the dispute.

Nasruddin requested that a money tray be brought, then instructed the vendor to hold the tray with both hands. Then Nasruddin asked the beggar if he had any money at all. Hesitantly the poor man produced the two copper coins that were his only wealth, and held them in the palm of his scrawny hand. Nasruddin noticed, as he instructed the poor man to drop the coins one at a time onto the tray the vendor held, how the vendor's eyes lit up with greedy anticipation. The pleasant clatter of the coins dropping onto the metal tray rang throughout the room.

Nasruddin asked Akram, "Did you hear the sound of the coins and see them drop onto the tray?"

Akram nodded vigorously, "Yes! Yes!" but just as he was about to move one hand from under the tray to take the coins, Nasruddin grabbed the tray out of his hands, then offered it back to the poor man and said, "Take your coins now and leave. The matter is settled, fair and square."

Akram was furious and demanded an explanation. Nasruddin replied with equanimity, "The sound and sight of the money that you have received is fair payment for the smell and taste of the smoke."

Nasruddin was invited by the town committee to interview for the position of local *cadi*. For years Nasruddin had waited and hoped for this chance to become the village judge, for that position become available just rarely, when one *qadi* died or moved.

More than anything, Nasruddin wanted to be seen as an important official, and as well, he longed to avail himself and his family of the benefits afforded the *qadi* by his community.

The morning of his appointment, Nasruddin arrived at the interview with a fishing net draped over him shoulders like a shawl. He stood before the committee with his head lowered and his eyes downcast.

Luqman, the head of the recruitment committee, asked the Mullah for an explanation for his odd attire. Nasruddin sighed deeply, then spoke with a slight trembling in his voice: "Oh, this old net? It is a moving and deeply personal story, but because you asked, I will tell you briefly about its significance. My beloved father was a fisherman, and this net was indeed the very last one he used before he died. So you see, I wear this net in his memory, to remind me of my humble roots."

The committee was so impressed with this show of humility and familial loyalty that they hired Nasruddin on the spot.

Months later, the committee decided to call on Nasruddin to see how he was doing in his position as qadi. He answered the door and invited the folks in.

As Nasruddin served the group cay, Luqman noticed something crumpled up in the corner. "Thank you for having us, Nasruddin. I could not help but notice — why do you no longer wear your father's fishing net? You made us believe this treasured memento of your father was so precious that it never left your back. And yet I do not recall seeing you with your dear father's netting since the day of the interview."

"Oh, that net?" replied the Mullah. He sat in his comfortable chair, picked up his teacup, and took a relaxed sip. "There is no need for the net," said Nasruddin with a sly smile, "once the fish has been caught."

⸎

"People are never satisfied with what they have at hand," observed Hamza one cold winter day in the teahouse. "They always have one complaint or the other. They grumble about the heat in the summertime and they grouse about the cold in the winter."

Nasruddin spoke up, "True, but have you ever heard anyone complain about springtime or autumn?"

⸎

One day a traveling musician came into the çay shop, and Wali, always one to dispute Nasruddin's boasting, borrowed the musician's mandolin and put it in Nasruddin's hands, telling him to play.

Nasruddin began strumming the strings. "I think you are supposed to press on the neck of the mandolin to make it sound different chords, Nasruddin."

"I knew that," said Nasruddin. "I was just warming up the instrument."

The Mullah grabbed the neck of the instrument like it was the throat of a turkey he was about to slaughter. He then began banging and twanging the strings, playing the same chord over and again.

"I have mastered this special chord," said Nasruddin, making a cacophony, "and I love to play it every chance I get."

"Nasruddin," said Wali, clasping his hands over his ears, "that is indeed quite a unique sound. Aren't you supposed to change the fingering every so often?"

"Not at all," sang Nasruddin, as he continued strumming on the same discord. "You see, most musicians have so little skill that they must constantly go from one note to another in search of this chord or that one. With the superior skill I acquired through continuous practice, I have perfected this one chord. Naturally, it is the only chord I choose to play."

While he twanged his one chord carelessly, Nasruddin sang one of his favorite pieces of advice:

> *Keep your feet warm*
> *and your head cool;*
> *watch what you eat,*
> *and don't brood as a rule.*

7

ONCE, NASRUDDIN WAS SERVING as *qadi* of Akşehir when the *bekche*, Luqman, led a near-naked man into the courtroom.

"Your Honor," said Luqman, "this man claims to have been ambushed and robbed by someone in our town."

"It's true," cried the disheveled and distraught man, "I have come here from Alexandria, and just outside the village two thugs took my cloak, my sword, and my horse. They even took my clothes and my boots. Someone from your village here must have done this, and I demand justice."

"Let me get this right. You claim that the thieves took your cloak, clothes, and boots, your sword, and your horse?"

"That is correct," the plaintiff replied.

"If the thieves left your underpants, they are most certainly not from here — our people are much more thorough than that. Therefore, the case is out of my jurisdiction. Case dismissed."

As EVERY RIGHTEOUS MUSLIM knows, Ramadan is the time when true believers fast from sunrise to sunset for a month. Once during Ramadan, Mullah Nasruddin was going from village to village in the vicinity, collecting alms and looking for work as an *imam*, a preacher in the mosque, for being a holy man was one of the things that Nasruddin did for work in those days. Sadly the Mullah met nothing but rejection all month, finding neither work nor charity, and as a result he had grown gaunt.

After the seventh episode of refusal from a village of Nasruddin's service, Nasruddin took his coat to Hussein the tailor to have it taken in, and asked how much it would cost. Hussein wanted nothing to do with the dirty, torn coat and named a price of four silver pieces to be rid of it.

"If I had four silver pieces to pay for the alteration of the coat," Nasruddin sighed, "I'd have the money to eat enough food to fit back into it."

WITH A GRIMACE, NASRUDDIN tightened his belt as much as he could, and left the tailor's shop, disheartened and hungry, ready to return home.

On his way, Nasruddin entered another village and came upon a crowd in the square arguing and shouting about something. As he approached the group he saw that they were standing around a captured fox.

One of the villagers told him, "This horrible fox that had killed many chickens, turkeys, and ducks, all around the village, eluding capture for months. Just that morning the fox fell into an ingenious trap, and now the town was about to decide what to do with the doomed beast. Some folks advocate torturing the fox, but I think that it ought to be put to death immediately and quickly."

Nasruddin raised his hand and announced, "Stand aside and let me in. I know how to handle this matter." The villagers, seeing the Mullah's white beard and hearing the confidence in his tone of voice, parted to let him through, all too glad to hand the fox's fate over to the preacher.

With a slight flourish, the Mullah took off his cloak and tied it around the fox's neck, then removed his scholar's turban, exposing his very bald pate, and placed it on the fox's head. Then he released the fox, and it scooted out under and between the legs of the people standing in the square before anyone even had time to grab it.

"What stupid thing have you done?" yelled the villagers at the Mullah, as they watched the fox, still wearing the turban and robe, slip back into the woods. "It took us months to capture that deadly creature! Why did you let it go, you bumbling booby?"

"Not to worry," replied Nasruddin calmly. "He won't last long. Anyone who sees the fox dressed up like that will mistake him for a holy man seeking charity or work, and without a doubt he will have starved to death before the week is out."

ONCE THE MULLAH WAS walking in an unfamiliar village, and sitting on a dirt pile by the side of the road were some urchins. For no reason, the punks started pelting him with stones.

"Stop it, children!" Nasruddin held up his cloak to protect himself.

The bully of the group stepped up and challenged the bony old Nasruddin, "Pay us a copper each or we won't let you go through."

Nasruddin protested, but the nasty kids responded with another volley of pebbles and dirt.

"Wait, wait — if you stop, I will tell you something of importance and great benefit."

They halted the assault. "Go ahead — but no philosophy," warned the boy.

"I happen to know that . . . that . . . that the mayor of the next village over is throwing a huge feast for everyone. Everyone is invited!" Nasruddin bluffed.

The bully was skeptical. "Yeah, is that so? Why's he having such a huge free feast, then, old man?"

"They mayor is having a feast . . . in honor of the wedding of his daughter, who is being married to a very fine young man—"

"What food is he serving?" the children demanded to know.

"Well, what food *isn't* he serving?" improvised Nasruddin, and as he described all the delicacies and fine sweets at the feast in elaborate mouthwatering detail, he convinced the little scoundrels — and almost himself — that there was a fabulous banquet to be had just down the road at the mayor's house. The delighted kids ran off in the direction from where Nasruddin had walked.

Nasruddin shook off the dust and resumed his journey, chuckling at his ingenuity. *Ah yes,* he thought, *I really am too clever for my own good. How gullible those kids were. What a fun ruse, and what a convincing actor I am! How I went on and on about the sweet hot bread smothered with honey, the spicy curried vegetables, the luscious kabobs, the fresh melon slices—*

Salivating profusely, Nasruddin stopped in his tracks. "What if," the Mullah mused aloud, "the mayor of the next village actually is holding a feast today? How could I miss out on such delicious food — and for free?" He slapped his bald forehead. "What kind of airhead am I?"

Nasruddin turned around, hiked up his baggy pants, and tore off after the children, his pointy shoes kicking up pebbles along the way. Seeing them in the distance, he ran, breathlessly yelling after them, "Wait for me!"

"After all," he panted, "the rumor might be true."

O<small>NE EVENING, JUST AS</small> Nasruddin was about to retire to bed, there was a knock at the gate. Tired and sleepy, Nasruddin put on his pointy slippers and shuffled out to see who was calling at that late hour.

Nasruddin discovered on his doorstep a bedraggled man who implored, "O Mullah! Have compassion and give me some alms." The beggar emitted a tubercular cough, and continued, extending his bony arm through the gate with his hand upturned. "Alms, please! And shelter, too, on this dreary night. You do not know me, but I speak the truth — I am the Prophet's son-in-law."

"You are the Prophet's own son-in-law?" Nasruddin said incredulously.

The beggar nodded earnestly. Still in his nightgown and slippers, Nasruddin stepped out from the gate and gently took the stranger's hand, then led him silently for several blocks until at last they stood before the arched entrance to the neighborhood mosque.

"Esteemed Son-in-law of the Prophet," Nasruddin said, facing the beggar and dropping his hand. "I am certain you will be more comfortable staying here, in your father-in-law's home, than you would at mine."

ONCE WHEN THE MULLAH was acting as *qadi*, or magistrate, for the village, for that is one of the many things that Nasruddin did for work in those days, a difficult case came before the court.

A boy, Jamal, was the plaintiff, who claimed that another boy, Ismail, had assaulted him by biting him on the ear. The accused child's main defense was that the plaintiff had actually bitten his own ear.

"Is the defendant a camel, that he could bite his own ear?" asked Nasruddin. "I declare, as there are no witnesses to the incident, there is a clear conflict of evidence," observed Nasruddin. "There is only one way to decide this — I must adjourn the court for half an hour."

Nasruddin went to the judges' chambers and tried without success to bite his own ear. Every time he snapped at his ear trying to gain purchase on it, he ended up twisting himself around, falling, and conking his head.

"*Vai, vai,*" he exclaimed. "Big head, big headache."

When court resumed, the bashed and black-and-blue Nasruddin declared, "I have found the answer. Clerk, examine the head of the plaintiff. If it is bruised and cut, the plaintiff bit his own ear, and I find for the defendant. If, on the other hand, there are no bruises on his head, the other boy bit his ear, and that is clearly a case of assault."

A WIDOW CAME TO THE Mullah in court with her child. She said, "I am very poor. My young son eats a great amount of sugar — in fact he is addicted to it. He eats so much sugar that I cannot afford enough food for his brothers and sisters. Would you, as the local mullah, please force him to quit his sugar habit, as neither his father nor I have been able to control him?"

"Madam," Nasruddin said, stroking his long white beard, "the matter is not as easy as it seems. Please return next week, after I have considered the case fully."

A week later, the woman again came to Nasruddin's court and requested enforcement of her request.

"I am sorry," he said, "but there will be another adjournment of this very tricky case until next week."

The woman returned the following two weeks but was turned away by the *bekche,* who told her, " The Mullah is still taking your matter under primary consideration. Please appear in court again next week.

Finally Nasruddin announced, "The Court will now give its injunction. Call the mother and the boy."

They were brought in the courtroom, and the boy was ordered to stand before the stern-looking Nasruddin.

"Boy!" thundered the Mullah at the woman's trembling son. "You are now hereby commanded to give up your habit of eating sugar! You are expressly forbidden to eat sugar, except for one tablespoon per day!"

The child, naturally, was terrified, and agreed to change his sugar-addicted ways. The woman offered her profuse thanks to Nasruddin and was about to leave the court with her newly reformed son when she turned around and asked, "Your Honor, I am mystified as to why you could not forbid the child to eat sugar at one of the earlier hearings."

"Madam," replied Nasruddin, "surely you can understand that before I could very well tell the boy to stop eating sugar, it was first necessary for me to quit my own sugar addiction. How could I have possibly known beforehand that giving up sweets would take me so long?"

PART SIX

COURTLY SAGE

1

NASRUDDIN BOASTED THAT HE was a saint with supernatural powers. One day Ali, the teahouse keeper, challenged him to perform a miracle.

"What kind of miracle do you prefer?" asked the Mullah.

Ali pointed to a large tree. "Make that tree standing over there across the river get up and move to where we are here."

Nasruddin stuck his arms out toward the tree and bellowed at the top of his lungs, "Come to *meeeeee*, great old *treeeeee!*" three times.

After a pause, Ali exclaimed, "Mullah, the tree didn't budge an inch!" Arms still outstretched, Nasruddin started wading into the river toward the tree. "Mullah, why are you moving, instead of the tree?"

"I am a very modest and humble man, and the venerable tree is much older and prouder than me. Since obviously the tree is too egotistical to come to me, I will gladly go to the tree in order to avoid embarrassing it."

THE MULLAH WAS ABOUT to start repairing the roof of his house when an old, bedraggled beggar knocked at the front gate. From the roof Nasruddin could see a raggedly dressed man gesturing wildly at him, calling out, "Excuse me, sir! Hello there. Please come down."

Nasruddin waved back and yelled down to the man, "What do you want?"

"Please come down, I beg of you, kind sir. I have something important to ask."

"I'm listening. Shout it up to me."

"Have some respect for a poor old man. What I must say I cannot yell to you from here. In the compassionate name of the Prophet, I beg you, come down here."

Nasruddin put down his hammer, climbed down the ladder, opened the gate, and stood in front of the man. "Now tell me what you want."

"Alms! Give me alms! I am a poor cripple, can't you see?" beseeched the beggar.

"Of course I support the disabled," said Nasruddin. "But tell me, why could you not ask me this when you could plainly see that I was about to start working on my roof?"

"I was ashamed. I am yet ashamed. I will ever hence live in this shame. Now give me alms."

"Please, do not have false pride. Come up to the roof with me."

"Impossible!" screeched the beggar. I cannot climb to your roof. Give me *baksheesh* here, now."

"I will be happy to give you my answer up there," replied Nasruddin over his shoulder as he walked away. He went to the house and climbed the ladder, and the feeble old man managed to follow him up and onto the roof. As Nasruddin resumed his roof repair, he raised his hammer again and said, "My answer is: No!" and brought the hammer down to drive a nail into a shingle.

The beggar was distraught. "Why couldn't you have told me when I was downstairs?"

"For the same reason you couldn't ask me when I was up." said Nasruddin, as he brought down his hammer on the next nail.

ONE OF NASRUDDIN'S FARAWAY disciples, Firat, came to spend time at the master's feet. Complaining of a lack of apparent progress, the student implored the Mullah, "Tell me a mystical secret, as I have heard you have done with others."

Nasruddin said, "When you are ready for the teaching, I will impart it."

Firat acquiesced and returned home. Every year, he returned to be with Nasruddin, and this scenario was repeated each time.

At long last Nasruddin responded to the student's request, "My child, can you keep a secret?"

"I would never impart it to anyone," avowed Firat.

"You know that one cannot expect others to act as one's storehouse of truth?" asked Nasruddin.

The student persisted, "True, but still, I have come here so many years and I wish to hear your secret mystical teaching."

"So I've noticed. Are you aware that your need is to emulate me?"

"Yes."

Nasruddin beckoned Firat to lean forward. "Then you must carefully observe," the Mullah whispered, "that I can keep a secret as well as you can."

❦

Hussein asked Nasruddin, "To which side should one turn, when doing ablutions in the river?"

Nasruddin replied, "You should always turn to the side of the river where you left your clothes."

❦

Late one evening, Nasruddin and his young son, Ahmet, were walking down a road in town. They saw two thieves trying to break into a business, making a lot of noise by filing the front door lock. Nasruddin tried to get past the danger without making more trouble for himself but then the inquisitive boy said loudly, "Father! Who are those men in front of the store?"

"You hush — me hush!" whispered Nasruddin. "The men are *rebab* musicians."

"But Father! What are they doing?"

"Shhh! They're playing a special sort of song," said Nasruddin.

"What sort of music are they playing? ... Father! I can't hear the *rebab* music," whined Ahmet.

"Be quiet!" Nasruddin hushed his son, desperate to avoid attracting the thieves' attention. "They're playing a song, all right — but you won't hear the music until tomorrow."

❦

One Friday, while the Mullah was delivering a sermon on avarice, he declared, "O people! I have these words of wisdom for you."

Everyone leaned in closer to listen.

"Do you want to know how to get rich without working, attain prosperity without the least bit of forethought, and live like a sultan without a worry?"

"Yes! Yes! Of course!" the crowd shouted.

"Well," proclaimed Nasruddin, "so do I!"

❦

Nasruddin was very wise when it came to helping others with their problems, but not always so insightful as to his own worries or concerns.

A certain business conflict arose that made Nasruddin pensive and unsure. "Big head, big headache," he complained to his friend Hussein one day. "What in the Prophet's name am I to do about this matter?"

Hussein advised him to take his troubles right to the top: "Go to the largest mosque you can find and offer your obeisance to God there. *Insh'allah*, your prayers will be answered there."

Nasruddin thanked Hussein and continued on his way. He knew that Allah always answers the prayers of the faithful, so the next day he threw his leg over his little grey donkey's back, adjusted his flowing robes and turban, and rode to the Great Mosque in the capital city.

The Great Mosque of the Shah was magnificent indeed, with its tall minarets, its splendid high dome inlaid with turquoise, lapis lazuli, and gold, its intricate latticework and tile mosaics, and its thick Persian carpets.

For thirty days Nasruddin prayed pleasantly under the huge dome, yet no clear answer to his problem arose.

Nasruddin returned home, and the next day he ran into his brother Selim, who was conciliatory when he learned of Nasruddin's further worries. Selim advised him to try a local place of worship: "Just go to the next town over, to the *takkia* of Sheikh Ahan, the Sufi mystic, and offer your obeisance to God there. It is an oratory, like a tiny mosque, attached to the Sufi's house, and is said to confer blessings on all true believers. *Insh'allah*, your prayers will be answered there."

Nasruddin thanked Selim profusely. The next day, the Mullah threw his leg over the back of his little grey donkey, Karakacan, and rode to the Sufi master's *takkia*, a run-down one-room wood hut with a low ceiling and a window less than a foot wide. This *takkia* looked humble indeed. Still Nasruddin bowed his head as he stepped inside the small, unadorned room, unrolled his prayer rug on the dirt floor, and prayed devoutly.

The next morning, Nasruddin awoke with the solution to his problem. His prayers were answered, finally!

First thing the following day, Nasruddin rode back to the Great Mosque in the capital city. He quietly entered the magnificent Great Mosque of the Shah, with its high minarets, and its exquisite dome ornamented with turquoise, lapis lazuli, and gold, and he stood in the holy spot of echoes.

He took a deep breath and intoned loudly, so that his words would be repeated over and again under the vaulted ceiling, "Shame, shame, shame on you, you great big fancy mosque! To think that a simple baby mosquelet called a *takkia* could do what you were unable to accomplish!"

2

I N THE VILLAGE, THERE was a group of older boys liked to play jokes on their beloved teacher, Mullah Nasruddin, or at least they tried to pull a fast one on him. Like all kids, and like plenty of adults, Nasruddin loved a good prank, and the boys knew that the Mullah was more than likely to discern their hidden intents and turn the trick upside down on them, and so everyone had a good time.

Nasruddin made a point of visiting the *hammam* every Thursday morning. It was a sociable habit of his to spend this special time at the Turkish baths steaming, sudsing, and soaping, and relaxing on the *sadir,* the high board couch, as the *hammamji* brought bowl after bowl of steaming hot water for his tub.

So the young men hatched what they hoped would be a foolproof scheme to trick Nasruddin into paying for all of them. Each of the boys brought an egg secretly into the *hammam,* and hid it between his legs under the towels as they sat down in the steamroom.

After Nasruddin paid his fee and changed into his towel, he walked to the main basin, and was surprised that instead of the noisy boys Nasruddin expected, they were all sitting together on one *sadir,* conspicuously quiet and cross-legged.

Nasruddin settled into his usual seat and relaxed. He knew his voice sounded full and rich in the *hammam,* and he hummed a little, testing the sound. He was glad the children were being quiet so that he could hear his marvelous voice better, and he drifted into a humming reverie.

Nasruddin's meditation in the baths was interrupted by one of the boys, Mehmet, who said, "I have an idea, Mullah! Let's imagine that we are all fowls, and can lay eggs. The chicken who fails to lay an egg will have to pay the bath for us all!" The boys quickly agreed and cajoled Nasruddin to join the dare. After some persuasive bragging and nagging, Nasruddin eventually agreed to the wager.

After a moment, Mehmet cackled nervously, flapped his arms a few times, sat up, reached under his towel, and held out an egg. After six eggs were incubated in this manner for all six boys, they taunted Nasruddin, "Your turn now, Nasruddin *effendi*! You must show us your contribution to the poultry flock." The boys were making every effort to restrain from giggling, but when Mehmet blurted, "The Mullah lays — or the Mullah pays!" they all broke out into hilarity.

The Mullah laughed with the boys for a minute, and then suddenly he threw his head back, and crowed loud, his voice reverberating through the *hammam.* The boys were taken aback, dumbstruck as Nasruddin flapped his arms, clucking and crowing! The boys watched as he slowly stood.

Nasruddin flailed and bobbed and pumped his legs, eventually letting his old ragged towel drop to the floor. The boys squealed and pretended to look away, as Nasruddin scuttled around in his underwear, still doing a very convincing rooster imitation, then pretended to suddenly notice that his towel had fallen. "Here are two large, hairy eggs — twice as many and double the size what any of you young chicks could produce from between your legs." He retrieved his towel and redraped himself modestly as he sat back down, sporting a huge smile. "And besides, among all these small hens, shouldn't there be at least one large, mature cock as well?"

The boys clucked and good-naturedly paid their own bath fees, and everyone had a good steam and a hearty laugh.

❦

Once Nasruddin was on his way to market, one of the little village boys, Ismail, ran up to Nasruddin and asked if he would buy him a whistle. The rest of the kids clamored around Nasruddin and implored him to buy them whistles too, but only Ismail actually had the coins, which he gave to Nasruddin.

As Nasruddin returned to town, the boys swarmed him, each tugging at his worn white robes and demanding a whistle. Finally Nasruddin held up the one whistle he had bought, and cried, "Enough! This whistle is for Ismail, and Ismail alone." The boys groaned in protest as Nasruddin handed Ismail his shiny new toy. "This is how it works, kids: whoever pays, gets to blow the whistle."

❦

Nasruddin had become old and was having a rough time financially. Once, while walking up the steep hill to the schoolhouse with Mehmet following, his student asked, "Why did God invent humankind?"

"To climb up hills," gasped Nasruddin, "and to pay his debts."

❦

Looking for a psychic to serve their village, the *imam* of Akşehir interviewed Nasruddin, "Is it true that you can communicate with the dead?"

Nasruddin answered, "Yes! In fact, just last week I spoke with a dear friend for more than seven hours after he passed on."

The cleric, duly impressed, said, "Miraculous! How did you communicate with your beloved friend in the afterlife?"

"Oh, it was easy enough to communicate to him. I talked," Nasruddin replied, "and he listened, but didn't answer."

ONCE NASRUDDIN WAS IN the teahouse when Abdul's boy Ismail ran in, clearly panicked. "Father cannot come down from the roof — please come now and help!" the boy cried. The Mullah and the men immediately left and followed Ismail, who explained what happened as they ran: "Father was repairing our roof, and had just finished applying a fresh coat of clay across the entire rooftop when he realized he had backed himself to the edge of the roof opposite to that of the stairs."

Nasruddin arrived to find Abdul standing forlornly on the corner of the roof of his house.

Nobody had a ladder that tall, and now Abdul was stuck: either he could jump, which would surely injure him; he could walk back across the roof to the stairs, leaving deep impressions in the clay; he could stay there until the clay dried, which might take an entire day; or perhaps somehow the Mullah could figure out how to get Abdul down.

Nasruddin stroked his white beard and said, "Well, I'm considering a course of action that worked well in another situation — I was able to save three men then, but I'm not so sure this method would work. Still, I must do everything I can to try to rescue him."

Nasruddin told Ismail, "Bring me a long rope."

While the boy ran to get the rope, the Mullah yelled up to Abdul, "Hang in there — I believe we may have a solution at hand!"

"Thank you," called out Abdul. "I'm starting to feel a bit dizzy."

When Ismail returned, the Mullah directed the menfolk, "Come and line up behind me, holding onto the rope." The men arranged themselves and Nasruddin tossed the other end of the rope to Abdul.

He said, "Tie the rope securely around your waist and make sure it's knotted tightly." Abdul did as the Mullah instructed. Then Nasruddin spoke to the men who were lined up behind him, holding the rope, "All right, grab the rope firmly, and on the count of three, pull together!"

Abdul said, "Wait! Are you quite certain this will work?"

"I have used almost the exact same technique to rescue three men before. Please, you must trust me."

Nasruddin checked the line of men behind him, braced himself, and called out, "One! Two! Three!"

Nasruddin and all the men jerked the rope hard and, finding no resistance at the other end of the rope, tumbled backward onto each other in a pile on the ground. Abdul was yanked off the roof, briefly seeming as if he were flying, but shortly his body plummeted straight down. His fall was broken by a small shrubbery, but from the crunch of his impact and his wails of pain immediately after, it was certain that his landing had cracked at least some of his bones.

"*Ai vai!* Big ass, big pain in the ass," Nasruddin said, as he rubbed his bruised backside. "Something went wrong. Virtually the same method had worked perfectly when I saved three guys who were stuck."

"What happened then?" whispered the injured Abdul. "Where in the world did you save these people from, using this way of counting to three and pulling?"

"Well," Nasruddin replied sheepishly, "They had fallen in wells."

NASRUDDIN WENT TO AGHA the barber, who shaved his head with a dull razor and a clumsy hand. The aged Agha, whose feeble fingers were not as steady as they used to be, nicked Nasruddin's ear, clucked his tongue, daubed the spot with styptic, and pressed a small tuft of cotton on the cut to stanch the bleeding. Then Agha cut Nasruddin's forehead, clucked his tongue, hit the spot with styptic, and pressed a cotton ball on the nick. This procedure continued as they talked.

By the time that Agha had finished shaving one half of Nasruddin's head, there were at least a dozen wisps of slightly bloody cotton perched on that side of his skin.

The barber was about to start in on the other side of his head when the Mullah caught his reflection in the barber's mirror. Nasruddin jumped up, threw off the barber gown, grabbed his turban, and headed for the door.

"But Nasruddin, wait — I have not finished your shave!"

"Thank you kindly, Agha, but never mind," replied Nasruddin. "Since I see now that you have decided to seed cotton on one side on my face, I have decided to grow barley on the other."

NASRUDDIN COMMENTED ONE DAY to Agha the barber as he was about to get a haircut, "I might not have much hair on the top of my head nowadays, but I used to have to shave thirty times a day."

Agha nearly dropped his razor. "That's freakish," he said.

"Oh, not really," replied Nasruddin, "you see, I used to work at a barbershop myself."

3

L ATE ONE AFTERNOON, MULLAH's friend and neighbor Hussein came to Nasruddin's door and greeted the Mullah. "*Salaam*," they both said. The Mullah noticed immediately that Hussein was walking with a slight limp.

"Why are you barefoot today?" asked the Mullah.

"Because I lost my shoes, dear friend. Someone swiped them while I was at a tea party at Jafar's house," said Hussein. "I got there last. There were nine other men there when I arrived, who had already removed their shoes and placed them neatly outside the door. Nine pairs of shoes neatly lined up, and I noticed that none of the shoes were as new as mine. I left my shoes outside with the others and went inside to gossip and drink tea."

The Mullah, used to hearing the complaints of all his neighbors and friends, stroked his beard thoughtfully and nodded for Hussein to continue.

"The men all filed out, one by one, until I was the last left. So, when I got outside afterward, what did I find?"

"You found that someone was playing a trick on you by taking your shoes," said the Mullah.

"Indeed, my friend, you understand," said Hussein. "But which one?"

The two sat and considered the matter. Nasruddin stroked his thick white beard to help him think. Fatima brought cups of hot sweet tea to assist in the thinking. After a while, Nasruddin's eyes widened and he snapped his fingers. "One ties up a donkey by its feet, and a person by their tongue. I know how we can catch the trickster. Hussein, tell all nine men to come to my house tomorrow morning, and we will find out which one of them took your shoes."

The next morning, Nasruddin was up early in his garden, picking something green from his beds, then doing something in his donkey's stable. Shortly ten pairs of shoes arrived at Nasruddin's doorstep. Two by two, the feet belonging to the shoes entered and were led back outside to the yard.

After the *salaams* of greeting were exchanged, the Mullah spoke. "I understand that one of you has played a trick on our friend Hussein here by snatching his shoes on the way exiting the tea party." Each man put on his best who-me face.

"It would save time if the culprit would return Hussein's shoes now." The men regarded each other with a you-do-it expression.

"It will be easy to reveal who stole Hussein's shoes. Even my donkey can do it." The Mullah surveyed the men's faces to see might seem worried or nervous.

"Follow me," Nasruddin said, leading the group to his stable. "One by one, go into the stable and close the door behind you so nobody can see you. Then you are to lightly grasp the tufted end of my donkey's tail and pull — very gently, of course. When the thief pulls the tail, my donkey will bray."

The men complied and one by one went into the stable and closed the door behind him, then shortly emerged quietly with a relieved expression. Not one bray was heard.

"Your test has failed," said Hussein dejectedly. "I was so certain you could find the shoe thief, Nasruddin."

"My test has just begun," replied the Mullah. "Now I want each of you to pass by me and touch my nose and beard — first with your right hand and then with your left."

The men filed past Nasruddin, touching his nose as beard as he had instructed. Nuri, who had been a student of the Mullah's in the *madrasa,* could not resist the urge to tweak the Mullah's nose and tug his beard just a bit. Hussein was dubious that this test was any better than the first. Only after the nine men had complied and stepped back together did the Mullah speak.

He pointed an accusing finger at Musa, the camel seller. "You took the shoes, Musa, and I can prove it."

"It was just a joke," Musa admitted sheepishly, cowering as the other men glared at him. "They're in my donkey's saddlebag, by your gate. But how did you know?"

"It was simple," the Mullah chuckled. "Just smell your hands, Musa."

Musa sniffed and found nothing but the usual smells of his donkey, saddlebag leather, wood and lacquer, and the last meal he ate.

"Now smell the hands of any other man," Nasruddin told Musa.

Musa sniffed at the hands of the men as they reached them out before him. "Spearmint!" he exclaimed. "They all smell of the spearmint that grows in your garden."

Just then there was a friendly bray and Karakacan, Nasruddin's little grey donkey, trotted out of the stable, evidently feeling she'd been left alone long enough and wanting also to find out who had taken Hussein's shoes.

"Smell my donkey's tail," Nasruddin ordered Musa. "Go ahead and smell the tufted end where you alone were afraid to pull, for fear of being betrayed by my donkey braying."

Musa caught the end of the donkey's flickering tail, and gave it a whiff. It was indeed spearmint that he detected, and he realized how the Mullah had tricked him into *not* touching the tail when it was his turn. And because it was such a clever test of the Mullah, Musa couldn't help but laugh along with the other men as they went out to his donkey's saddlebag to fetch Hussein's shoes.

ONCE NASRUDDIN'S FRIEND, HUSSEIN, brought him a nice juicy quail. The Mullah wanted to roast the bird, which he mistakenly thought was a chicken, so he prepared the fowl and put it over a low fire to cook slowly, before heading downtown to hang out at the teahouse and invite his friends over for a delectable dinner, wishing to qualm the doubts of those who would question his skill as a cook.

Akram, along with the other wags, wanted to play a trick that day on the Mullah. While the wags listened to Nasruddin talk about his delicious roast chicken (actually a quail), Akram slipped out of the teahouse and ran to the Mullah's house. He sneaked in the back door to the kitchen, put out the cooking fire, removed the semi-cooked quail in its roasting pan, and let the oven cool. Then he substituted a live chicken for the cooked one, and closed the oven door.

When Nasruddin returned home later that afternoon with his friends, he was shocked to see Akram outside his door, dancing and singing and praising Nasruddin's chicken.

"Mullah," exclaimed Akram, "It is a miracle! Your roasted bird has come back to life!"

Nasruddin opened the oven door and was shocked to find a live chicken — looking not at all like the quail that he was originally given — squawking and flapping its wings on its way out the window. The Mullah peered inside the otherwise empty oven, then turned to face Akram and the rest of the men, all of who were grinning wickedly.

"The miracle of changing the fowl I prepared is all very well, but there is the matter of certain details," the Mullah said suspiciously. "For example, where are the butter, salt and pepper, and all the spices? What happened to the pot and the lid? What accounts for the missing firewood? Worst of all, it appears that this 'miracle' has caused my effort in preparing the delicious bird to have disappeared."

AN ANCIENT, FRAGILE, AND valuable vase was discovered by the villagers, and there was a dispute at the teahouse as to the exact volume of its capacity. When the Mullah arrived, they implored him for a solution to the problem.

"The answer is quite apparent, my friends," the Mullah assured the group. "Bring the vase, and a volume of sand."

The teahouse wags did as Nasruddin instructed. The Mullah then proceeded to have them fill the vase, layer after layer, tamping it down with the bottom of his teacup. Ultimately it burst.

"There you are," the Mullah said triumphantly. "We have reached the maximum capacity. Now just remove one grain of sand, count the remaining grains, and you will know the exact amount needed to fill a container like this."

NASRUDDIN AND HIS FRIEND Abdul were visiting a nearby town together when they became thirsty. They stopped at a café and found they could afford only a single glass of milk, which they ordered.

"You go ahead and drink your share first," said Abdul. "Let me drink my part with this packet of sugar."

"Why not add it now? I will drink only my half."

"Certainly not, Nasruddin! There is only enough sugar to sweeten half a glass of milk!"

Nasruddin went to the café owner and returned with a saltshaker. "No problem," he said, "I'll drink my half first. But then you won't mind if I flavor mine with salt, will you?"

NASRUDDIN, WHO HAD A great many occupations, once ran a lecture bureau, and got an urgent request for a scholar to address a scientific topic at a public forum. Try as he may to locate a true scientist to fill the bill, Nasruddin could only find two mediocre speakers.

Nonetheless, the Mullah went ahead and completed all the arrangements for the lecture, then sent ahead a message to his client: "Full wit unavailable. Sending two half-wits."

HUSSEIN ONCE COMPLAINED TO the Mullah, "I have terrible pain in my right eye. What do you advise?"

Nasruddin thought for a moment, then said, "Pull it out."

Hussein said, "Nasruddin, you dolt, you can't be serious."

The Mullah replied, "Well, last month my tooth hurt horrifically for weeks, until I couldn't bear the pain any more. So finally I had the tooth pulled — and then I felt much better. So if it worked for my tooth, it should work for your eye too, shouldn't it?"

ONCE FIRAT CAME ACROSS Nasruddin standing silently at a nondescript crossroads, casually observing the lack of traffic, and asked what he was doing there.

"Someday, it is possible," Nasruddin responded, "that something of great historical importance will happen right here, and no doubt a crowd will gather. I want to be sure to get a good view of the event, so I have come early before all the others to stake out a spot."

4

WHEN NASRUDDIN WAS IN between jobs, he took to the street, where he was ridiculed as a beggar and a fool. No matter how often someone offered the Mullah the choice between a large coin and a small one, he always picked the smaller piece.

One day Faruk commented to him, "Mullah, why do you not take the bigger coin? That way, you will eventually acquire some funds and people will no longer make fun of you."

"I suppose you are correct," said Nasruddin, "but if I always took the larger coin and saved them, then people would stop offering me money altogether to prove that I am more of a moron than they are. Then I would receive absolutely no money at all. That is why I always choose the smaller coin."

ONCE WHILE THE MULLAH was exiting the mosque, a beggar in the street pleaded with him for alms. "Kindly have mercy upon an old, devout mendicant and give me *baksheesh.*"

Nasruddin asked the man, "Tell me first, are you extravagant?"

The beggar replied in the affirmative.

"Do you like to chill at the café, drinking coffee and smoking?"

The beggar nodded and said yes.

"Do you care to lounge around in the baths every day?"

"Most certainly."

"And do you enjoy yourself by going out to nightclubs to drink alcohol and smoke hashish?"

"Yes, Mullah, all these activities give me great pleasure."

Mullah clucked his tongue at the man and handed him a gold piece.

A few yards away sat another pious beggar who witnessed the conversation and supplicated Nasruddin for a handout.

The Mullah asked him, "Are you extravagant?"

"No, Mullah, I have taken a vow of poverty."

"Do you like to chill at the café, drinking coffee and smoking?"

"No, of course I don't engage in such activities."

"Do you care to lounge around in the baths every day?"

"No, I never do that. I am constantly at the mosque, saying my prayers and meditating on the Almighty Within."

"And do you take pleasure in alcohol, hash, or other drugs?"

"Not at all, *effendi*. I have devoted my entire life to purity, abstinence, and service."

The Mullah handed him a small copper coin.

"Why in the Prophet's name," cried the second beggar, "do you hand me, a thrifty and pious man, a copper, when you gave that no-good spendthrift fellow a gold piece?"

"Well, clearly, my good man," said Nasruddin, "his economic needs are greater than yours."

ONCE NASRUDDIN APPEARED AT the doorstep of his neighbor, Aslan, with his palms folded. "Forgive the intrusion, *effendi*, but I am collecting funds to pay the debt of a poor man who cannot meet his obligations."

"What is his situation?" asked Aslan.

"The creditor cannot wait another day," said the Mullah.

"Oh my, that sounds dire. Quite commendable of you," said Aslan, as he handed the Mullah a coin. "By the way, who is this most unfortunate person?"

"Me," he replied, before he hurried away.

A few weeks later, Nasruddin knocked at Aslan's door again.

"I suppose you are calling about someone's debt," the man said.

Nasruddin stood placidly and replied, "I am."

"Wait — don't tell me. My guess is that this someone cannot pay a debt, and you want *baksheesh* to help the poor fellow out," the neighbor said.

"That is true," said Nasruddin.

"And I suppose it is you who owes the money," said Aslan.

"Not this time."

"Glad to hear it. Here, take a contribution."

Nasruddin pocketed the coin, bowed, and turned to leave.

"Hold on, Mullah. May I ask, who is the beneficiary of your charity this time?"

"Ah, you see . . . I am now the creditor."

Hakim, a poor man, was traveling and arrived in Akşehir famished. Seating himself at a local café, he boldly ordered boiled eggs, then slipped away without paying. Eventually Hakim found work in a nearby village, and within a year returned to pay his debt, offering the restaurateur a silver piece, which was quite generous, given the value of the meal served before. The restaurateur gave him an exorbitant bill for four silver pieces.

When Hakim protested the price, the restaurateur said, "Look, if instead of feeding you those eggs, I had kept them and the hen had hatched them, they would have become chickens. Their offspring, and theirs, and theirs, would have produced many thousands more eggs — worth far more than four silver pieces. In fact, you got them cheap." Neither man would compromise, so they agreed to arbitration.

As the local judge, Nasruddin was always being called to settle disputes like this. After he arrived at the scene and the two men told their arguments, the Mullah stood and stroked his beard for a minute contemplating.

Then he asked the restaurateur to boil some water in a small pot and bring him a handful of corn. When the water was at a full boil, he threw in the corn and waited ten minutes, then asked that the berries be strained out of the water. When they had cooled a bit, Nasruddin took them and proceeded to dig a small hole in the earth nearby, wherein he dropped the corn and began to cover them up.

"What are you doing, Nasruddin? Why did you waste my corn like that?" cried the restaurateur.

"Planting corn, so that it will multiply."

"Since when could something that was boiled possibly multiply like that?"

"Exactly my point," said Nasruddin. "This case is dismissed. Good day to you both."

Nasruddin came across a bereft traveler at a crossroads, sitting disconsolately on the roadside with his baggage, and asked the sorry-looking soul what was bothering him.

"Brother," sighed the man, "there is not a single thing in life left for me. I have enough money to live comfortably, and I am traveling only because there is nothing of sufficient interest compelling me to stay home. I realize I seek happiness, but thus far in my long journey I have not found it."

"Happiness is not where you seek it, but where you find it," observed Nasruddin.

"Whatever do you mean?" asked the stranger.

Without a word or change of expression, Nasruddin seized the traveler's belongings and hightailed it down the road, with the man trailing behind screaming at him to stop. Nasruddin outpaced him and, since he knew the shortcuts, was able to double back behind the man. As the Mullah approached, he saw the traveler was once again sitting on the side of the road, his head in his hands, crying even more pitifully, more unhappy than before because of the loss of his luggage.

Silently he crept up behind the traveler and placed the bags near him, then moved to a concealed spot to observe. When the miserable man finished weeping and looked around, he couldn't believe his eyes: there was his baggage, waiting for him. Overjoyed, he ran to his property and grabbed the bags, embracing them to his chest. As the traveler danced and spun around, praising God for the return of his things, it seemed to Nasruddin, he looked like an ecstatic dervish, whirling with a bag of laundry in each hand.

"At least," thought Nasruddin, satisfied with the outcome, "he has discovered one way of producing happiness."

A farmer had a goat that came down with a bad case of mange. In those days, people treated mange by applying a coat of tar to the scabrous parts of the animal's skin. The man was very pure and simple, however, so instead he brought the sick goat to Nasruddin and said, "Mullah, I know you are a very pious and holy man. Please just breathe on the goat and I am certain that it will be healed."

After a slight pause, Nasruddin said, "Alright, I'll breathe on your goat if you so wish. If I were you, though, I wouldn't hesitate to mix some tar with my breath and apply that to the goat's scabs as well."

❦

NASRUDDIN WAS TRAVELING HOME from his long pilgrimage to holy sites in India along an unfamiliar road, and he became very thirsty. He thought he'd very much like to find a fruit stand of some sort. No sooner did he think these thoughts than did he come across a friendly looking man sitting in the shade of a tree with a large basket full of bright shiny red fruits before him.

"Just what I was looking for! Those look delicious, my good fellow," said Nasruddin, taking two coppers from the knot at the end of his turban and handing them to the man. The man took the money and handed Nasruddin the whole basket of fruit, for this sort of fruit is quite cheap in India, and people usually buy it in much smaller quantities.

Nasruddin sat down to eat in the shady spot the fruit-seller had abandoned, and started to nibble on the shiny fruit. Within seconds, his mouth and throat burned, tears coursed down his cheeks, sweat poured from atop his bald head, and he was gasping for breath. Still he kept eating the awful fruit, moaning in pain at the fire in his mouth and throat.

Fortunately, Nasruddin's friend from Konya, Jalal, who happened to be also traveling on pilgrimage, came across Nasruddin sitting by the road. Nasruddin recognized his compatriot and called out to him, "Oh Jalal! These horrid infidel fruits must be the toenail clippings of Satan!"

"Nasruddin, you fool! Haven't you ever heard of the red demon chilies of Hindustan? Stop eating them at once, or Death will claim a victim before the sun has set!"

"*Aman aman!* I cannot move from here," gasped the crimson-faced Nasruddin, "until I have finished the whole basketful."

"Lunatic!" cried Jalal. "Nasruddin, those 'fruits' belong in curry. Throw them away at once before you kill yourself!"

"*Ai vai!* Allah save me!" lamented Nasruddin, still bravely munching chilies. "I am no longer eating the fruit — now I am eating my money."

5

ONE EVENING, NASRUDDIN WAS walking along an alleyway when a man fell from a roof and landed on his head, breaking his fall. The man was unhurt, but the Mullah was taken away in a stretcher to Berrak the doctor.

When the Mullah's students arrived at his bedside, Hussein asked, "Teacher, how did this accident happen? Do you have any words of wisdom about the incident?"

"Never hold any belief in the inevitability of cause and effect! That fellow falls off the roof — and yet I am the one who is injured. Shun reliance upon theoretical questions such as 'If a man falls off the roof, will his neck be broken?'"

ᴏᴏ

ONCE NASRUDDIN WAS TRAVELING when he came upon a village that at first glance seemed rather destitute but which, upon closer examination, had all its residents outside in the town green, drinking, eating, playing music and dancing in joyful rhythms.

"How extraordinary! What a blessed place this must be," Nasruddin exclaimed to several of the villagers. "Where I come from the people are nearly starving."

"Actually," spoke up one of the town elders, "it's quite like that here, but today is a special feast day."

Another spoke up, "Yes, everyone in our village has saved and prepared something for this day. That is why there is so much food and drink and merriment."

Nasruddin considered the matter for a moment, then remarked, "If only every day were declared a feast day, then everyone would be always as happy as they are today — and nobody would ever go hungry!"

ᴏᴏ

NASRUDDIN WALKED INTO THE teahouse and declared, "I haven't been able to eat anything for three days."

"Goodness," said Ali, "you must have been quite ill, considering your appetite. Are you feeling better now?"

"I wasn't sick," answered Nasruddin. "I was broke, and nobody asked me to join them for a meal."

ᴏᴏ

HUSSEIN COMPLAINED TO NASRUDDIN, "My house doesn't get enough sunlight."

Nasruddin asked, "Do you get sunshine in your garden?"

"Yes, actually, we do."

"There's your solution: move your house into your garden."

ONCE MULLAH NASRUDDIN WAS traveling aboard a ship when a fierce storm blew up fast. The boat was tossed to and fro and the topsail tore. The captain ordered all hands to furl the sails and lash them to the masts. One sailor rushed up the mast to tie up the torn sail when Nasruddin shouted, "You fool! What are you doing? If you want to keep the boat from rocking so, you must tie it down from below, not from the top!"

NASRUDDIN REMOVED HIS TURBAN, threw it high into the air, and declared, "Between its going up and coming down, there will be one thousand hopes."

DESPITE FATIMA'S COMPLAINTS AND pleas, Nasruddin was too busy with his mullah work to keep up his property, so the house got quite dilapidated. The shutters were stuck shut, the windows didn't close or open properly and were drafty, the cellar was cluttered with junk, and the back door had almost fallen off its hinges.

One day Nasruddin was walking back home from Konya when he saw a large funeral procession. Several men carried the coffin, followed by mourners in black, and one grey-haired lady, supported by a man and a woman at each side, wailed inconsolably in grief. Carrying a candle, the *imam* walked in front and intoned,

> *Vai!* The beloved is going where there is no light,
> *Vai!* The beloved is going where there is no heat,
> *Vai!* The beloved is going where there is no water,
> *Vai!* The beloved is going where there is no air,
> *Vai!* The beloved is going where there is no space at all . . .

Terrified, Nasruddin took off through a shortcut back to his run-down old house and arrived breathless from running. He chained and padlocked the front gate behind him, then dashed into the house and frantically began to move furniture around to block the front door.

Fatima asked, "What in the world are you doing, Nasruddin?"

The Mullah gasped to Fatima, "Hurry — go now and bolt and barricade the back door! There is a funeral coming — and they are going to bury a dead man in our house!"

6

ONCE NASRUDDIN WAS TRAVELING with his old friend Hussein, and night fell. They stopped at a crossroads and, hoping to spend the night alone, Nasruddin told Hussein that he planned to spend the night under the starry sky, but Hussein agreed to sleep there as well, rather than go home.

"Have you appointed someone to protect your wife's virtue in your absence?" Nasruddin asked.

"Yes, Mullah," said Hussein, "I requested my good friend and neighbor Hamza to look after my wife, Setare, while I'm away."

"And whom, may I ask," inquired Nasruddin, "have you appointed to look after the virtue of your good friend and neighbor Hamza?"

ONE MORNING, NASRUDDIN ENTERED the mosque and, as is customary, he left his pointy shoes outside, went inside, and sat down cross-legged in a row in the middle of the main floor.

As the mosque filled, Hussein was seated in the row behind him. As they bowed in unison during the *namaz*, Hussein couldn't help but notice that Nasruddin's shirttail was rather short and exposed his thighs. The man, thinking it looked unseemly, was affronted.

I did not come here to the mosque to pray, Hussein thought, *for a vision of this idiot's hairy backside,* and he tugged Nasruddin's shirt down before proceeding with his namaz.

Immediately Nasruddin yanked hard on the shirttail of the man in front of him, Berrak, the village doctor, who was already immersed in prayer and was startled.

Berrak turned around and said, "What, in the name of the Prophet, are you doing?"

Nasruddin shrugged and pointed his thumb back, as if to say, "Don't ask me — ask the fellow behind me — he started it."

Hussein looked up and said, "Berrak, you have broken the silence and negated the prayer."

"So have you," replied Berrak. "Now we will both have to repeat it all over from the start."

"Praise Allah," whispered Nasruddin, "I am the only one who has not broken his silence."

"O YE TRUE BELIEVERS!" THE Mullah preached one Friday during his sermon. "The organization of Nature is indeed magnificent, and it is marvelous and astounding how everything upon this earth is arranged somehow for the advantage and advancement of Mankind!"

Hussein, in the congregation, called out, "Mullah, please give us an example of the human benefit of this cosmic arrangement."

"For instance, you may have observed that, by the mercy of God, the camel has no wings."

"And that benefits us ... how, exactly?" questioned Hussein.

"Obviously, if camels had wings," explained Nasruddin, "they might roost on rooftops, crash through our ceilings when they landed — to say nothing of the noise and the smell — let alone the constant chewing and spitting their cud."

ONE DAY, HUSSEIN ASKED Nasruddin, "Mullah, the world is strange, with some people going this way and others going in the exact opposite direction, everyone else going in all different ways, all at the same time. Wouldn't it be better if everyone in the world walked in the same direction?"

Nasruddin replied, "If everyone in the world walked the same way all at once, the Earth would tilt and lose its balance, then wobble upside-down like a turtle turned over onto its back."

ONCE NASRUDDIN WAS SENT with the Turkish ambassador and an interpreter on an important and delicate diplomatic mission to the Kurdish people. He was instructed not to speak under any circumstances without the official interpreter.

They traveled several days, and when they arrived in Kurdistan, they were informed that the Kurdish leaders had prepared a lavish state dinner with many guests from around Kurdistan in the diplomatic delegation's honor.

The delegates put on their finery and proceeded to the vast dining hall where, using the translator, they were introduced to all the many dignitaries in attendance. At long last, everyone was seated for the elegant feast, with the Turkish delegation on the right side of the head table.

Everything was going well, but in an extended silent pause, just as the Kurdish leader was about to propose a toast, Nasruddin suddenly broke wind, loud and long.

The crimson-faced Turkish diplomat leaned over to the Mullah and hissed, "You farted, Nasruddin, and have thus brought shame on Turkey!"

Nasruddin simply smiled and replied: "But these are all Kurds here! How in the world could they possibly understand a Turkish fart?"

✍

ONCE AT THE TEAHOUSE when he encountered his doctor, Berrak, Nasruddin confessed to nearly constant amnesia. "My worse fault is that I cannot remember anything."

Berrak asked, "Tell me, Nasruddin, when did this start?"

"When did *what* start?" said the Mullah.

"When did your amnesia start?" answered Berrak.

"I had amnesia?"

"Nasruddin," chimed in Ali, "didn't you tell us you took a memory-improvement correspondence course last month? How did that go?"

"I'm definitely improving. Now I can usually remember that I have forgotten ... something."

✍

ONCE NASRUDDIN WAS LEAVING his home leading his little grey donkey, Karakacan, when his neighbor Faik asked, "Where are you going, Mullah?"

"I am going to ride to the capital and take the King's Highway."

"Eh?" Faik raised an eyebrow. "Well, you might best leave your donkey at home. There are robbers on that road, the *Shah-Rah*, and they might steal your ass out from underneath your seat."

Nasruddin considered the matter and replied, "There are likely as many bandits around my house who would steal it from my stable as there are on the road, so I think it's best to take my donkey with me."

Faik, concerned for Nasruddin's safety, gave him a good sword with which to protect himself. He said, "Do not hesitate to use it to save yourself."

On a desolate stretch of the *Shah-Rah*, a burly, scruffy, scraggly fellow approached, and Nasruddin thought, "This fellow is undoubtedly a ruffian, and I'd best find some way to placate him before he attacks me and steals my donkey."

The traveler, who was nothing more than a gentle, ragged mendicant returning home from a lengthy pilgrimage, had raised his hand and was about to offer a friendly greeting when Nasruddin shrieked in fear, "*Please!* Just take this sword and leave my donkey and me in peace!"

The fellow, surprised and delighted with his good fortune, agreeably took the sword and continued along his way.

"That was a close one," said the Mullah, as he continued on his trip.

When Nasruddin returned home, Faik inquired how the journey went.

"I was dubious," Nasruddin replied, "about your claims regarding the efficacy of your sword, but you were quite right."

"What do you mean about my sword?" asked Faik.

"Yours saved my ass from being stolen."

7

O NCE NASRUDDIN WAS WALKING to a particular destination when he met a well-heeled traveler at a crossroads who asked, "Pardon me, Mullah, but can you tell me which of these turnings do I take to get to the capital?"

"How could you tell that I was a Mullah?"

The stranger had just made a good guess, but still, he wanted to score off this bumpkin. "As it so happens, I am a seer and psychic. I can read others' minds," he said smugly.

Nasruddin said, "If you are such a great psychic, then read the directions to Konya from my mind."

The traveler asked, "Can you just tell me what day is it?"

Nasruddin replied, "Sorry, but I'm not from here. I have no idea of the names for things in this part of the world. You're better off asking one of the locals what they call the days of the week."

THE TRAVELER BERATED NASRUDDIN, "Never mind, you peabrain — just tell me how long will it take me to reach Konya."

Nasruddin stood and regarded the man impassively but said nothing. Puzzled, the man wondered what was wrong with Nasruddin, who suddenly acted as if he were hard of hearing or altogether deaf.

"Pardon me for the bother, O great mullah," he said, shouting and gesturing in a makeshift sign language, "but can you just tell me how long will it take me to reach Konya?"

Still Nasruddin did nothing but stare at the traveler, who grew quite angry and yelled in Nasruddin's face, "What is your problem? I'm just asking a simple question! You are not just a fool — you're an imbecile!" And with that, the furious traveler turned on his heels and started striding away from Nasruddin.

"My friend," Nasruddin called out to the man after he watched him walk for about half a minute, "it will take you two hours at the most."

Irritated, the man swung around and faced Nasruddin. "You idiot!" the man yelled from the distance. "Why could you not tell me that when I was standing in front of you?"

"Because," Nasruddin hollered back, "I could not estimate how long it would take you to traverse the distance until I saw how fast you were actually walking."

As Nasruddin returned to the highway, he thought it a fine afternoon to take a shortcut through the woods. He wondered why nobody went through the awe-inspiring forest to save time getting home. "Why should I plod along a dusty old road," he contemplated aloud, "when I could be communing with Nature, listening to birdsong, and smelling the fragrant flowers? This is indeed a day for fortunate pursuits."

So thinking such thoughts, Nasruddin launched himself into the greenery. He hadn't gotten too far on his nature sojourn, however, before he tripped on an overgrown tree root, fell into a deep pit, and twisted his ankle. As he lay in the bottom of the ditch, he reflected on his circumstance.

Although in much pain, Nasruddin's attitude remained positive. "Today is indeed a lucky day, after all," he said. "It's a good thing that when I hurt myself, I fell into this lovely, quiet, remote pit — just imagine how embarrassed I'd be if the same thing had happened on that nasty, noisy highway!"

The next time Nasruddin was traveling on the *Shah-Rah*, the King's Highway, and decided to take a shortcut home, he managed to avoid the tree roots and deep trenches; however, before too long he found himself in a boggy marsh. The ground was wet and soft, and the going was soggy. After not very far, when he pulled out one foot, his pointy shoe came off from his foot, sucked under by the mud. Nasruddin said, "Now I know why nobody comes *this* way. Okay, marsh — now give me back my shoe." The mud had no reply.

Nasruddin retraced his steps to the road and walked backward for several minutes, then returned, walking facing forward to the marsh. "Marsh, O marsh!"

he said, "I have given back the stolen time and effort to the shortcut; now give me back my shoe."

Still the mud remained silent and passive, so the Mullah reached down into the muck and with much effort managed to retrieve his shoe and pull it out.

"This marsh," said Nasruddin as he made his muddy way back to the road, "must be inhabited by a *djinn*! It obviously intends to make me pay for my mistakes by stealing my time and slippers. But although he acts like a proper arbiter of public conscience, he is a hypocrite! He pretended to take so much interest in my shoe by making me struggle so much, but he has released it back to me only after mucking it up."

ONCE ALI HAD TO leave the teahouse for almost an hour because he ran out of tea, of all things, and he had to bring more from its storage place. In his absence, everyone criticized him. Hamza cracked, "That Ali is as useless as a cabbage."

Nasruddin said, "Not true, my friend. Even a cabbage can be cooked and eaten. But what useful object can Ali be turned into?"

ONE FINE MORNING IN the teahouse, the men were chatting when Nasruddin remarked, "Wouldn't this be a perfect day for a picnic?"

"Mullah, that's an excellent idea," said Faik. "I will bring some baba ghanoush and pita bread."

"Delightful," piped in Hamza, "I can bring a chicken to roast."

Hussein said, "I'll bring some cheeses and fresh fruit."

"My wife made the most delicious stuffed grape leaves yesterday," said Ali, "and there was plenty left over. I can bring that."

"If all of us are going," said Ali, the teahouse owner. "I'll just close up shop early today and come with. And I have a tray of baklava to share."

Everyone in the room offered to contribute something to the impromptu picnic potluck — except for Nasruddin, who smacked his lips and clapped his hands in anticipation of so much good food.

"Do tell, Nasruddin," said Faik, "what do you have to offer?"

"I offer this, my most solemn vow: May the curses of Muhammad, the Prophets, and the angels descend upon me in vengeful retribution if I leave this picnic for one minute — even if should last for weeks!"

∾

ONCE THE MULLAH WAS nodding off in a peaceful dream as he rode his faithful donkey Karakacan (backward as usual) past the brook, where the local boys swimming in the water had decided to try to play another one of their pranks on Nasruddin. The Mullah's students were always thinking up ways to fool their beloved teacher, despite the fact that nine out of ten of their tricks ended up backfiring on them. Still, loving fresh mischief just as much as kids nowadays, the boys delighted in coming up with new antics. Quickly they huddled together waist-deep in the shallow water of the brook, legs locked and stiff, as if their feet had taken root in the muddy bottom of the brook.

They heard the steady, familiar clip-clop of the little grey donkey's hooves on the ground as the Mullah approached.

"Should we call out to him?" whispered Mehmet.

"He always addresses us first," hissed back Ishmail, who had his back turned to the bank. "If we wait for him to speak first, he won't suspect anything."

The sound of donkey hooves slowed, then stopped close to the boys.

"Good morning, children!" said Nasruddin. "What do you see in that dark water that makes you stand together like young bamboo trees in the brook?"

"Mullah, Allah be praised that you have heard our prayers!" called out Ishmail over his shoulder. "*Ai vai!* Help us! We are stuck!"

"What seems to be the problem, children?"

"When we arrived here at the brook, each boy had his own legs," whined Mehmet. The boys seemed to strain at pulling their legs out of the water, and indeed they appeared to be stuck in the mud. "But we have been swimming so long now that all our legs are mixed up. Please — you must help us sort out which legs are which!"

"Which legs are whose," replied Nasruddin, ever the pedant, drowsily dismounting his donkey.

The situation indeed seemed dire. Mehmet's right leg was paired up with Ishmail's left leg and Mehmet's right foot. Ishmail's right leg and Sedat's right leg had somehow joined together with Nuri's torso. Nuri's right leg was still unaccounted for.

As the boys implored Nasruddin to come in — they were just six or seven feet from the water's edge — and save them from their horrible fate, he stroked his long white beard.

He clucked his tongue as if he might be very sorry for the boys — or it may have meant something else entirely.

After considering the situation, he went to the saddlebag on his donkey and pulled out a huge knife, with which he cut off a supple switch from a nearby tree about nine feet long.

"Here, this should fix your dilemma," said Nasruddin, returning to the shore with the switch, which he started to wield most effectively on the arms and shoulders of the boys.

The boys who could see Nasruddin were able to duck most of the lashes, but Ishmael, being closest with his back to Nasruddin, ended up getting the brunt of Nasruddin's remedy for mixed-up legs. Finally Ishmael could stand the abuse no more and jumped up howling, scattering the circle of boys.

"There you go," said Nasruddin, "you found your own legs, after all, without my help."

Nasruddin threw the switch in the water, then mounted his donkey, not a stitch of his clothing wet. As he rode away backward, facing the boys as they scrambled up to the bank to inspect their welts, he called out, "You better hang onto that stick — just in case your legs should happen to get all mixed up again."

— ∞ —

PART SEVEN

WISE OLD FOOL

1

ONCE NASRUDDIN WAS IN the *hammam* all by himself, and he began to sing loudly in his throaty voice. Greatly impressed with the acoustics of the old bathhouse, he was so pleased with the sound of his voice that as soon as he exited the *hammam,* he climbed up to top of the nearest minaret and began the midday call to prayer.

The townsfolk in the square below were alarmed by the sound of Nasruddin's warbling, and one man cried out to him, "Hey Nasruddin, what are you doing up there? It's not your job to make the call to prayer — it's not even the right time for it. Besides, you sound like a dying buzzard!"

Nasruddin leaned out from the minaret, shook his finger, and shouted defiantly, "You should build a *hammam* with marble walls up here, and then you'll hear what a fine voice I have!"

AS SOON AS HE finished intoning the prayer from atop the minaret, Nasruddin rushed down the stairs and out the mosque. He threw his leg around Karakacan's back and urged the little burro to hurry.

Nasruddin's student, Nuri, saw them passing out of town at top donkey power, and called out, "Mullah, where are you going in such a big rush?"

He yelled back to the boy, "That was absolutely the most resonant, penetrating, and convincing call I have ever given. I must hurry to see how far my voice carried." And on he rode . . .

ONE SUMMER DAY, NASRUDDIN was tending his garden barefoot when he stepped on a huge thorn and gashed himself. "O praise Allah! Praise Allah!" he shouted, hopping on one foot while holding the other, trying to stanch the blood flow.

Faik, his neighbor, who was walking nearby, heard the Mullah's cries of agony and asked him, "Nasruddin, you're bleeding like a stuck pig. Why do you praise Allah after you have maimed yourself so?"

"Because, thank Allah," said Nasruddin, grimacing and hopping around on one foot, "I was not wearing the brand new sandals I bought yesterday. Surely I would have ruined them."

ONCE AKRAM, THE BUTCHER, a very beefy, intimidating fellow, approached Mullah Nasruddin and said, "You are a learned scholar, and I am illiterate. I beseech you, please write a letter for me to my distant aunt."

After stroking his long beard for a minute, Nasruddin declined, saying, "I'm sorry but I can't today. Come back next week."

"Why can't you do it now?"

"Because today I have injured my foot."

"But you don't write with your foot!" protested Akram. "Why should a sore foot prevent you from writing my letter?"

"Since my handwriting is so terrible, no one can read it," the Mullah answered. So it's more than just writing the letter that is involved here. I'll have to travel to interpret the letter. And as I said, my foot is sore and I cannot walk on it. So there's no real point in my writing the letter now, is there?"

LATER WHEN AKRAM'S AUNT returned the letter, the illiterate butcher went to Nasruddin and asked him to read it to him.

"As much as I wish I could help you, you must find someone else to read it," the Mullah stated.

"Why cannot you read this letter to me?" You wrote the letter she is answering!"

"Well, it's from Aleppo, at the end of the Silk Road. That is just too far away: if the letter had been from someplace closer, maybe I could read it. And the handwriting is even worse than mine," said Nasruddin, handing back the letter.

When Nasruddin refused to read Akram's letter to him, the huge butcher grabbed the Mullah's turban and began to beat him about the head with it. "You wear the turban of a learned man, yet you cannot even read a simple letter! You should be ashamed to be wearing the turban of wisdom."

Nasruddin stood up to leave. "Fine! If you think it's the turban that knows how to read, put it on your own head and read the letter yourself."

ANOTHER TIME, AKRAM ASKED Nasruddin to write a letter for him to his brother. After he finished dictating the note to Nasruddin, he said, "Now read it back to me, to make sure I have left out nothing."

Mullah peered at the scrawl but couldn't make it out in the least. He got as far as "My dear Brother—" then sputtered, "I am not sure if the next word is "know," "now," or "work.""

"This script is illegible. Who in the world is going to be able to read your handwriting if even you can't?"

"Let me remind you, *effendi*," said Nasruddin, "at present it is not my job to read the letter, just to write the thing."

"Oh. Well, that makes uncommon sense, Mullah," agreed Akram, quite convinced. "Besides, the note is not addressed to you in the first place, is it, now?"

ONCE NASRUDDIN WAS PERFORMING his ablutions — his ritual prayers while bathing — on the shores of Akşehir River. As he was washing his left foot, he noticed his shoe floating away. He lunged forward to catch it, but it was too late. His pointy shoe was heading downstream in a hurry.

At first he did not know what to do, but then Nasruddin was so enraged at the brook for taking his shoe that he turned his back to it and loudly broke wind. Of course, in Islamic religious culture, passing wind while performing a sacred rite of prayer is a vile act that invalidates the ritual.

Nasruddin then stood upright, faced the brook, and shouted, "O brook! I gave you back your ablution! Now — give me back my shoe!"

2

ONE SWELTERING AFTERNOON, NASRUDDIN and some friends went to bathe in the cool fresh water of Lake Akşehir. They were just starting to disrobe when they heard a loud splash nearby, followed by an ominous silence. Then they heard the voices of some young boys shrieking from the dock. The men, led by Luqman, the *bekche*, the town watchman, ran out to find out why the boys were yelling.

"That boy's father," said one of the three boys shouting and pointing at the end of the dock, "the last new tax collector, came out here to get his son, and he fell in — but he can't swim!"

The men could see that Eren, the former tax collector, who was rather portly, was flailing and going down fast. Luqman took charge and leaned over the water, reaching out to grab the hand of the taxman, yelling, "Give me your hand and I will save you! Give me your hand!"

Eren blubbered and thrashed and went down again for a bit longer.

When Eren's head came back out of the water Luqman yelled, "Give me your hand, Eren, and I will pull you out! Give me your hand!"

The sinking man double-blubbered and gasp-thrashed and went down once again for even longer.

Nasruddin knew there was one last chance to save him.

Finally Nasruddin said, "Let me try," and instructed Luqman to hold his waist while he leaned out over the water. As the tax collector surfaced for the last time, Nasruddin stretched his hand out toward him as far as he could and yelled, "Eren! *Take* my hand! *Take* it now!"

The big man immediately responded by grabbing Nasruddin's wrist as the bekche pulled Nasruddin back onto the dock. Everyone helped haul Eren out of the water safely, and was panting at the exertion.

After everyone recovered and caught their breath, Luqman asked Nasruddin, "How were you able to entice Eren to come out of the water when I could not?"

"It's all in knowing how to phrase the imperative," said Nasruddin, "in the appropriate way. A tax collector is not oriented to *give* anybody anything, let alone his hand and his body. So I knew when I told him to *take* something from me, he would naturally understand and let us save him."

NASRUDDIN CALLED ON HIS rich friend Aslan, and quietly asked to borrow a thousand dinars.

"What do you need a thousand dinars for, Nasruddin?"

"I want to buy an elephant."

"Why in the world do you want to buy an elephant?" asked Aslan.

"I want to breed elephants."

"But, Nasruddin, surely you realize that you need at least two to breed elephants. And if you don't have money to buy one elephant, you don't have the money to buy two, let alone cover the expense to feed and maintain them, and then a third, and then—"

"My dear Aslan," Nasruddin interrupted, "as much as I appreciate your business acumen, I came here to get a thousand dinars, not advice about breeding elephants."

ONCE NASRUDDIN NEEDED A new shirt made for him to wear at official services, so he went to the tailor, Hussein, to be measured for the garment. When Nasruddin asked how much time it would require to finish the shirt, Hussein said, "Two weeks, *Insh'allah.*"

Two weeks later, Nasruddin returned to the tailor's shop to find out the shirt was not ready. "Come back in a week and, *Insh'allah,* your new shirt will be ready for you."

When Nasruddin returned the next week, Hussein still had not finished the job. "Come back in one more week more and, *Insh—*"

"How long will it take," the exasperated Nasruddin interrupted the tailor, "if you leave Allah out of it?"

WHEN NASRUDDIN'S NEW SHIRT was finally ready, he went to Hussein at the tailor's shop to pick it up. He paid for the shirt, then decided to shop for some new trousers. He chose a nice pair of baggy pants and tried them on, and the two bargained and agreed on a price. After a minute, Nasruddin changed his mind, took off the pants and returned them to Hussein. Then, he picked out a cloak that the tailor informed him was the same price as the pants.

He picked up his shirt and the cloak, gave Hussein his thanks, and began to leave the store. Hussein stopped him saying, "But Nasruddin! You have not paid me for that cloak."

"But I paid you for the shirt, and left you the pants," the Mullah explained patiently, "which you told me cost exactly the same as the cloak."

"Yes, but you didn't buy the trousers."

"Of course I didn't pay you for the pants," Nasruddin rebuffed Hussein, "why in the Prophet's name would you expect me to pay for something I didn't buy in the first place?"

WHILE THE MULLAH WAS an eggseller, which is yet another of the things he did for work, he used to buy nine eggs for two coppers, the going rate. Then he would sell at a considerable discount, six eggs for one copper. This naturally made his egg business very popular with customers. Jafar, a local merchant, asked how he could conduct business this way.

"It is more important to be popular than to make too much money," replied Nasruddin. "The truth is, people don't care if you are making a lot of cash, but they do like to see that I have so many satisfied customers. And surely you don't want me to seem a profiteer!"

✍

HUSSEIN ASKED NASRUDDIN FOR a loan on credit, according to certain terms. Nasruddin replied, "I have neither money to loan you nor credit to offer you, but help yourself to whatever terms you like, and by all means — take as much of that as you need."

✍

NASRUDDIN WENT TO THE town market, where he proceeded to buy too much for a scrawny buzzard like himself to schlep all the way back home, so he looked around for a porter. "You," called Nasruddin to the first one he saw, a burly, bearded man with several tattoos peeking through the thick hair on his forearms, "I will hire you to take this sack and lug it back to my house for me."

"May I be your sacrifice, *effendi*. Where is your residence, exactly, sir?"

"Not so fast, big guy," Nasruddin said dubiously. "I don't know you from Adam. For all I know, you may be an ex-con, or even a murderer. Do you really take me to be so naïve that I'm going to trust you with the address?"

The porter bowed slightly and said, " Kind *sheikh,* my name indeed is Kaba Adam, and I am most pleased to serve you."

"Enough with the introductions. Just grab the bag and follow me."

"As you wish, my kind sir."

The bearish porter hefted the sack upon his back and dutifully followed. The Mullah was walking quickly as he slipped through the bazaar throngs, expecting the huge fellow carrying his heavy load somehow to keep up with him.

Within minutes, though, Nasruddin became separated from the porter. Quickly he retraced his steps, but try as he might Naruddin could not locate the fellow, or his purchases. He returned home empty handed.

The following week, Nasruddin was walking with his brother in the bazaar when Selim pointed out a brawny, hairy porter. "Isn't that the man you described, who carried your sack last week from the market?"

Nasruddin nodded silently to confirm that this was indeed that porter, Kaba Adam. He took a few steps back, turned on his heels, and started off in the opposite direction heading out of the bazaar. Selim followed, calling to him, "Nasruddin, where are you running? Why are you hiding? Isn't this the man you were looking for all week long? Aren't you going to confront him now and get your sack and everything in it that you bought?"

Nasruddin paused long enough to call back, "No way! I have to hide from him. If he sees me now, no doubt he'll want to charge me for carrying my things for the whole week — plus interest!"

3

NASRUDDIN HEARD AN IMAM say that anyone who fasts on the holy day of Ashura will undoubtedly attain the full equivalent religious merit of fasting for a whole year.

So on the holiday, the Mullah fasted until midday, then he broke the fast by eating a large and sumptuous lunch. When asked, he replied: "I've already earned enough merit from observing Lent to last me through the rest of the year!"

FAIK AND SEVERAL OTHER townsfolk considered themselves, at least for a while, to be Nasruddin's enemies. They wanted to get rid of him once and for all and so they devised a plot to track him down and lynch him. Nasruddin overheard the men plotting, however, and learned that they planned to come in a few hours to his house.

Nasruddin calmly went in his backyard and dug a narrow grave in the garden. Then he told Fatima, "When my enemies come looking for me, tell them that I died from a heart attack. When they ask for proof, tell them if they want to pay their respects that my grave is in the garden, and that you will lead them out back and show it to them, one at a time."

The Mullah took his old family branding iron and a small charcoal cooker and lay down in the grave, then he covered the pit with an old board that had a knothole about the size of a fist in the middle.

Soon, Faik and the band of Nasruddin's adversaries arrived and asked Fatima where her husband was.

"My poor husband is dead!" sobbed Fatima, and offered to show them the grave, one by one. The men were all secretly delighted that God had already accomplished what they had been scheming for so long. Faik suggested to the group, "Let's all take a dump on him!" The rest of the group agreed that was a very good idea.

So Fatima showed Faik out to the backyard, then went back into the house. Faik approached the grave, then pulled down his pants and squatted on Nasruddin's grave over the open hole.

Nasruddin, hidden in the covered grave, had heated the branding seal in the charcoal fire until it was blazing hot. When Faik hovered over the hole, the Mullah stuck the red-hot branding iron through the hole and burned Faik's rump with it, leaving an impression of the family seal.

Although Faik wanted to yell out in pain, he controlled himself, not because he realized the Mullah had tricked him — but because he was hoping the same fate would eventually befall each of his accomplices. So Faik simply stood up, adjusted his trousers, and walked back in the house, where he told the next fellow that it was now his turn. One by one, they each came to be branded on their backsides, and the Nasruddin family seal marked them all.

Furious later that the Mullah had hoodwinked them yet once again, Faik and the group went to the sultan, and complained that the Mullah had played a cruel hoax on them. Tamerlane sent for the Mullah, and asked him to explain how he came have such a bad reputation among these men.

Nasruddin explained to the sultan, "Everything that these men accuse me of is all lies and deception, Your Majesty! It is true, however, that these people who accuse me, every single one of them, are slaves of my father. If you do not believe me, you can inspect for yourself and see that each one of them has the family seal branded on his ass."

The sultan made the men expose themselves. Of course, they discovered that Nasruddin's assertion was correct, and the sultan decreed that his enemies were sentenced to serve him for the rest of their lives.

ONE NIGHT, WHILE HE was sleeping, Nasruddin accidentally pissed the bed. Of course this awakened him, and he realized what he'd done, but was not sure how to tell his wife, Fatima, snoring fast asleep next to him.

So he arranged his blanket partly over the damp spot and then lay back down, pretending to be asleep.

Then Nasruddin sat up in bed with a shout, "Arghhh! Dear Allah, save me!"

Fatima awoke and turned her head to look at her husband. "What's the matter, Nasruddin?"

The trembling and visibly shaken Mullah replied, "Wife, you have no idea what sort of horrifying nightmare I've just had!"

She asked, "What did you dream?"

"I saw three tall minarets, one set right above the next, and atop the third minaret was an egg, and on that egg was a needle, and on that needle balanced a covered table, and at that table I had to eat my dinner!"

Fatima was shocked and gasped, "God! How terrifying! What a predicament! My poor husband!"

Nasruddin replied calmly, "You can't imagine how shocked I was!"

Fatima sympathized, "I can only imagine. You must have been frightened beyond belief. Out of sheer fear, I would have wet the bed, or worse!"

"Indeed," Nasruddin agreed. "That is *exactly* what I would've done too!"

ONE DAY, NASRUDDIN WENT out hunting and shot two quails. He brought them to his wife and told her to prepare the fowls, because he wanted to invite his wealthy friend Aslan to dinner to impress him.

So Fatima took the birds, and she plucked and prepared them. As she was roasting the quails, the smell was irresistibly delicious. Since Fatima had very little self-control, she could not stop herself from tasting the quail to make sure it was just as delectable as it smelled — just a little piece, so that Nasruddin would never notice. So she tasted the quail, and tasted it again, and again, until she finally had eaten both quails. When she realized what she had done, she became very upset and did not know at first what she should do.

At noon, when Nasruddin and Aslan arrived, she gave her husband a knife and asked him to grind it so that it could cut the bread. Then she went to the Mullah's friend and said to him, "My husband has a very bad habit. Every time he invites someone to dinner, he cuts off the ears of the guest. Can't you see how keenly he sharpens his knife over there?"

"God save me!" Aslan yelped with fear and quickly ran out the door.

Fatima immediately called out to her husband, "Hey, your friend has taken the two quails and gone!"

Immediately the Mullah ran out into the street after his friend brandishing the knife in his hand, crying out, 'Please, please, my friend, be fair: just let me have at least one of them!"

Aslan looked back, saw the huge knife in Nasruddin's hand, and then he ran even faster away, shouting back, "If you can catch me, then you can have both!"

One afternoon in the teashop, Hussein asked Nasruddin, "Who do you think are more despicable: those people who have been married before you, or those who had married after you did?"

The Mullah said, "Both are despicable!"

Hussein asked, "What makes you say that?"

The Mullah replied: "I despise the people who got married before me, because they poorly advised me to get married. And I am angry at those who have married after me, because they have not followed my advice!"

When Hussein, one of Nasruddin's oldest and dearest friends, passed away, the Mullah was inconsolable. He slowly followed the funeral procession, constantly sobbing and pounding his chest in great sorrow: "Who will now take an oath to me, if I should lie! Who will now urge me to drink wine, even if I should feel remorse! And who will now pay for me in a brothel, if I have no money!

The Mullah cried, "May Allah, after my dear friend's death, never mislead me! *Ai vai!* If only He had not deprived me of my friend's support!"

One day while on pilgrimage, Nasruddin met on the road to Konya some affable fellows, seven or eight comrades who rather reminded him of himself. They seemed to be quite friendly folks, and interested in the Mullah's teachings, so they traveled together for a while.

After a few hours, the group of men got hungry. As the hour was late, their hunger began to gnaw at them, and one of the Mullah's new disciples asked, "Nasruddin, you are our leader on this journey, but what shall we feed ourselves? There is nothing here that we can eat!"

The Mullah replied, "Wait a moment! First, we ought to collect some firewood, then we will find something like a hare or something we can roast over the fire and then eat."

They were out in the country, and his new friends asked him, "Really? You think we can catch a rabbit?"

To which he replied, "Sure, just a rabbit, a bird, a chicken. We will hunt it down or as a last resort we shall steal it from somewhere. But first let us gather kindling and wood together for the fire."

The friends thought to themselves: "Well, let's first wait and collect the wood." They had no axes or other tools to help in the process, and so the men had to collect the wood by hand.

Eventually the Mullah directed everyone to climb into a very old, tall oak tree. He climbed up in the tree to the top branch and shouted to one of his friends to hang onto his feet. Then he shouted to another man to hang on to the feet of the second, and to the next man to do the same, and so on. Finally, after they all had formed a chain so, Nasruddin called down to the men from the uppermost branch: "Well, guys — are you all ready?"

When they answered in the affirmative, the Mullah said, "Hold on one second, fellows, I just want to just spit in my hands to get a better grip!" He let go of the branch, and all the men fell to the ground one atop another in a pile.

Down on the ground, only Nasruddin and the fellow right below him were unhurt; all of the others were either maimed or wounded. So since only these two could walk, they went on their way again.

Finally they arrived in a town where they saw someone selling seeds in a bag, and Nasruddin asked him, "What are you vending in that bag?"

The seller replied, "These are nail seedlings."

"What? Nail seedlings? I've never heard of such a marvelous thing!" Nasruddin turned to his companion and asked, "Shall we buy some?"

"Yes," the man agreed, "let us buy some and plant them!"

The Mullah turned back to the vendor and asked, "Will you kindly sell us some of your precious seedlings?"

"Yes, certainly. I will be only too happy to sell some to you!"

So they bought some of these nail seedlings.

The seller warned the men, "Do take extra care when you plant the seedlings, that the insects do not eat them!"

And they assured him: "Don't worry! That's our concern, not yours."

They both went back to the land and planted the seedlings. Then they both kept a vigil, one on either side, to guard the seedlings.

Now there were some grasshoppers around who liked to eat these kind of seeds. As the two men stood guard, side by side, rifle in hand, suddenly, a grasshopper jumped right onto the other fellow's forehead. The fellow quietly whistled to Nasruddin and showed him that the grasshopper had landed on his forehead. Nasruddin watched, nodded, then carefully took his rifle and fired: bang! He killed the locust, but of course also his friend. So he remarked to the grasshopper, "Fair enough. One of our men, and one of yours."

4

ONE OF NASRUDDIN'S CREDITORS, Aslan, had become impatient with him, and started to harass him for the money.

"Listen," said the Mullah to his irate neighbor, "last night Fatima and I came up with a fantastic plan to repay the debt."

"Is that so?" asked Aslan. "This I have to hear."

"You bet," enthused Nasruddin. "Here's how it's going to work: We have hedges planted behind the house. In the spring, they will grow up to be full and bushy. When sheep walk by the yard, their wool will catch on the low branches. Fatima will collect the wool and spin it into thread, which we will then dye and weave into clothes. We will sell the clothes at a handsome profit, which will easily pay off every last coin we owe you."

When Aslan understood Nasruddin's scheme, he guffawed uproariously.

"No doubt," said Nasruddin confidently, "you can already hear the clink of the coins in your hand, and that's why you are laughing with joy."

NASRUDDIN WENT TO KONYA on business but unexpectedly ran out of money. He was famished and walked through the bazaar, but all he could do is wander from booth to booth. Finally, salivating at the many delicacies, none of which he could afford, he came across a *halvah* vendor. When Nasruddin saw the mouthwatering display of halvah, he went up to one shelf mounded with the sweetmeats. Without hesitating, he started grabbing large pieces of every kind of delicious halvah and wolfing them down.

The shop owner, incensed that this customer would eat his fine halvah before asking or paying for it, grabbed a large wooden paddle he used for stirring pots and began to beat Nasruddin about the head with it.

Nasruddin called out to the customers nearby, between bites, "The merchants of Konya . . . are so nice . . . they beat you . . . to make you eat . . . their delicious halvah."

The vendor yelled, "All these pieces of delicious halvah that you are helping yourself to — they are mine!"

Trying to fend off the paddling, Nasruddin said, "Are you sure they're yours?"

"Of course I'm sure! I make all the halvah here with my own two hands!"

"But if they are all yours, why aren't you eating them? Go ahead, eat them already! What's keeping you?"

"One thing is for certain, they are not yours!" exclaimed the halvah wallah.

"Wait just a minute!" Nasruddin said in his defense. "Did you see me walk into your shop?"

"Yes."

"Have you seen me before — ever, in your entire life?"

"No."

"Are you sure?" asked Nasruddin.

"I swear to God — never before in my life I have seen the likes of you."

Nasruddin asked coyly, "Then how do you know it's *me?*"

WHILE NASRUDDIN WAS IN the *halvah* shop, gobbling all the pastries he could get his hands on, the halvah vendor collared the Mullah and said, "So then — introduce yourself to me, so I can meet the dunce who thinks he can get away with eating my halvah without paying for it."

"Gladly, I will identify myself," said Nasruddin, "except first I must check one thing in your storefront window." The vendor loosened his grip, and Nasruddin stepped back out onto the street, adjusting his turban in the window glass reflection. Then, peering past his reflection into the store, Nasruddin smiled and waved at the halvah vendor, and said, "Yep — it's me all right!"

Nasruddin dashed back into the crowd and through several alleyways into an unfamiliar neighborhood, where he promptly became lost. He wandered the streets and wondered, "How do people manage to keep track of themselves, here in the big city, with all this bustle and distraction? I can't tell where I am. What's to keep me from losing myself completely among the crowds? I better be alert and remember myself well, lest I misplace myself in all this chaos."

Toward the end of the day, Nasruddin drifted to the edge of the city, where he encountered a caravan, which would provide him a cot for the night among others. The old geezer in the bed next to him looked somewhat feeble, and thus relatively trustworthy, so Nasruddin confided to him, "I'm afraid to fall asleep here. What if I wake up and can't remember which one of these people is me?"

"Simple, my friend," said his neighbor. "Here's an inflated bladder with a string. Just tie it to your leg before you fall asleep. In the morning, you'll obviously remember to look for the person with the balloon, and that'll be you."

"Brilliant!" said Nasruddin, before falling into a snoring slumber. When he awoke, completely disoriented, he got up and remembered to look around for the bladder. He found it tied to the leg of the friendly old geezer lying asleep in the cot next to him and thought, *That must be me.*

A moment later Nasruddin was pummeling the old man with both fists, yelling, "Wake up! Your idea was no good! Something has gone terribly wrong, as I feared it would!"

The old joker sleeping soundly, who didn't expect such a violent response, and who at first didn't remember playing the trick on Nasruddin, jumped up and asked the Mullah what in the world was the matter with him.

"I-I-I can tell by the bladder that you are *me* over there," stuttered Nasruddin, "but for the dear sake of God, please tell me: who am *I* over here?"

AT THE MILL, WHICH all the local villagers shared, Hamza the miller caught Nasruddin taking handfuls of wheat from his neighbors' sacks and putting them into his. Hamza was furious and started shouting, "What do you think you are doing?"

"I am an idiot," replied Nasruddin nonchalantly, "I do whatever comes into my head at the time."

"You don't say?" snarled Hamza. "Then why don't you take some grain from your own sack and put it into others'?"

"Sir, I am just an average, ordinary fool," Nasruddin replied calmly. "I would have to be a complete moron to do something *that* stupid."

TIME AND AGAIN NASRUDDIN passed from Persia to Greece on donkey-back. Each time he carried two bales of hay, and trudged back without them. On every border crossing, Daoud, the customs guard, checked Nasruddin from turban to toes, and even poked the bales of hay with a pitchfork, but found nothing amiss.

"What business do you have outside of the country, Nasruddin?"

"Among the many things I do for work these days, I am a smuggler."

But try as he might, Daoud could never find any contraband on the Mullah.

Years later, much more prosperous in appearance, Nasruddin was traveling in Egypt, where he happened to run into his old friend Daoud, the customs officer, who had also retired and was on holiday. They agreed to take a cup of tea together and catch up on old times.

"Now that we are out of the jurisdiction of Persia and Greece," whispered Daoud, "living here in the lap of luxury, please, Nasruddin *effendi*, tell me at long last — what were you smuggling that we could never catch you?"

Nasruddin answered, "What was it, Daoud *effendi*, you ask, that I was smuggling all those many years that you never discovered?" He smiled, sipped his tea, and said, "Donkeys."

ONCE FATIMA BECAME DEATHLY ill, but Nasruddin seemed rather unconcerned with the matter. The neighbors noticed that he was neglecting his sick wife. Finally his friend Faik asked the Mullah why he didn't take his wife to see the doctor, Berrak, who could prescribe some medicine to alleviate her suffering.

Nasruddin replied, "Don't be ridiculous. We are poor, simple folk who don't need a doctor. In fact, for many generations our people have managed to suffer and die without the least help of doctors or their medicines, thank you very much."

ONCE WHILE NASRUDDIN WAS chopping firewood in the forest near Akşehir, he climbed up a mulberry tree. By the time he reached the high branch, he was panting and sweating, but he edged out carefully onto the branch he wanted to cut down. He caught his breath finally and pulled the axe from his belt, turned toward the tree trunk, and began chopping at the base of the branch he was sitting on.

The village physician, Berrak, happened to be walking by when he noticed the Mullah's folly and cried out, "I say, Nasruddin, you are cutting the wrong side of the branch! Be careful — you are going to fall if you keep chopping it that way!"

Nasruddin paused, scoffing at the man, "Perhaps you know medicine, my dear Berrak, but not trees. I have been cutting wood since long before you were practicing medicine. Do you take me for a fool that I should believe you, or are you some sort of seer who can predict the future?"

"Nasruddin *effendi*, you are really going to fall if you cut the limb that way! Just look where you are sitting and where you are chopping."

"And you, Berrak *effendi*, should look where you are walking," replied Nasruddin. "Those who walk with their eyes in the treetops are likely to stub their toes on the roots."

Berrak shrugged and left Nasruddin to resume cutting the branch. Not even two minutes later, the limb cracked, gave way, and crashed with Nasruddin to the ground.

"*Ai vai!*" groaned Nasruddin. "Big head, big headache," he said, rubbing the lump swelling under his turban.

More astonished at Berrak's prediction coming true than hurt from his own bruises and scratches, Nasruddin limped to catch up with the sage who had accurately predicted his imminent disaster. "Tell me, O great seer Berrak!" he called. "How could you have foretold of my fall from the tree? Your prediction has been fulfilled! You are a prophet and the son of a prophet!" Nasruddin caught up to Berrak and grabbed his cloak. When Berrak turned to face him, Nasruddin dropped to his knees, clasped his hands, and said, "Tell me now, O great seer and sage, Berrak, I implore you to reveal the truth of my future — when will I die?"

However much he tried, Berrak could not convince Nasruddin that he was no prophet and would not foretell his death. After several minutes of haranguing by Nasruddin, however, Berrak became so irritated that he blurted out, "I predict that you shall die when . . . when your pathetic donkey is carrying you and brays four times!" And with that, the doctor turned on his heel and strode off.

Bruised and shaken and unable to work any longer, Nasruddin dusted himself off, adjusted his turban, grabbed his axe, and swung his leg over his little grey donkey's back to head home.

After a while, Karakacan, the donkey, began thinking of the sweet hay and of her baby waiting for in the manger back home. She stretched out her neck and brayed. Suddenly Nasruddin remembered Berrak's prophecy and a chill of horror ran up his spine. "*Aman, aman!* I am one-fourth dead," he thought.

A bit farther down the road, they encountered another donkey and rider, and Karakacan brayed a short but enthusiastic greeting.

The noise nearly paralyzed Nasruddin, thinking this braying thing had gone far enough. "*Vai, vai!*" shuddered the Mullah. "I am now half-dead!"

As they treaded toward home, Karakacan began thinking of the cool clear water that she would drink when they returned home. She was thirsty from the day's work, and brayed in anticipation. Nasruddin tried muffling the third bray, but the bray of a donkey is not easily suppressed.

"*Aman, aman!*" wailed Nasruddin, his cries like a dirge, "Now I am three-quarters expired!"

The doomed Mullah began chatting to his little grey donkey Karakacan to distract it from anything that might make it bray again. He tried to think how he could possibly muzzle the donkey for the rest of her (and his) days to keep it from braying again one final, fatal time.

Ahead on the road, just outside the village, the Mullah could make out the gruff voices of men shouting orders to their donkeys and the clop-clop of small hooves. Karakacan's little grey ears pricked up and turned forward, and she sniffed the air. She must let her friends know she was coming. The agonizing sound piercing Nasruddin's heart, the fourth bray of the donkey sounded as if the donkey were laughing, long and loud.

Nasruddin dropped his axe, clutched his chest, and declared loudly, "That's it! That's all! I have run out of brays. I am completely dead! I am perished! I am deceased! I am no more! I am really dead. Really, really dead and gone. Allah be praised." He dropped to the earth once again — this time, taking care to lay himself out comfortably flat on the ground.

Nasruddin's friends, Mali, Jafar, and Faik, who were the men traveling along with their donkeys, heard Nasruddin's wails and rushed to the scene. They tried to revive him, but Nasruddin was unresponsive and limp as an empty saddlebag. "He was shouting that he was dead," observed Faik, "and if anyone should know if he was dead or not, it's Nasruddin."

They loaded the inanimate Nasruddin on his donkey's back, carried him to his house, washed him, put him in a simple shroud in a casket, and carried him toward the graveyard. Halfway along the funeral route, the road forked and the procession halted, unsure of the road to the cemetery.

Mali said the better road was to the left, and Jafar countered that the right fork was a shorter route to the graveyard. In minutes an argument broke out among the mourners as to the better route to bury their poor friend Nasruddin.

Just as it seemed the funeral-goers were about to come to blows, Nasruddin sat up in the coffin and cleared his throat. "Listen, friends, when I was alive, I always used to take the road to the left to get to the cemetery." The villagers, long accustomed to letting the Mullah have the final word, took the left fork and made their way to the gravesite.

The funeral procession removed Nasruddin's remains from the casket and lowered them into the freshly dug grave. The service, conducted with proper respect for the Mullah's exalted position in the community, included many lengthy and stirring eulogies and much weeping and beating of chests, in the poignant memory of their beloved Nasruddin. The interment at last concluded and the mourners left the Mullah to mull over his untimely and tragic death, in the eerie quietude of the cemetery.

Just as the silence started to press in upon Nasruddin uncomfortably, there was a heavenly tinkling sound. Although it was actually the sound of camel bells and of ceramics clacking together, in a caravan of pottery salesmen on their way to market, Nasruddin thought, *Surely that must be the sound of the angels of death as they approach me in my Final Judgment! If they look in the grave and see me laid out like a corpse, doubtless they will deem me doomed and spirit me away!*

As the caravan drew near, the bells around the camels' legs chimed louder. Dumbstruck with fear, Nasruddin shivered in his newly dug grave. He thought, *I must stand up and shout to them when they arrive, to make sure they know I am not truly dead!* His knees knocked so hard that he could barely stand.

Nasruddin — unable to hear over the fearful chattering of his teeth the low patter of the potters' voices, and of ceramics clacking as the camels, laden with large pots, vases, dishes, and other artful handcrafted pottery of every sort, made their way through the cemetery — scrambled to his feet in his grave.

From ground level, Nasruddin peered out and realized it was not the angels of death who were approaching. It was a rowdy band of unkempt ceramics salesmen — cracking all manner of crude jokes — and their filthy camels. In a flash his fear turned to rage.

Imagine the indecency of using the graveyard as a shortcut for camels, Nasruddin fumed, *in the sacred burial ground of myself and my family — and on my funeral day!* This was the gravest of insults and a dirty shame.

Nasruddin's indignation flared, and just as the caravan reached within a few feet, he stood up in his grave, ready to confront the potters. Still dressed in his white gauze burial clothes, Nasruddin began waving his arms and shouting at the scoundrels who had defiled his funeral.

His abrupt outburst, unfortunately, startled the head potter of the caravan, a bear of a man who was nonetheless very superstitious. When the man saw the shrouded apparition jump up from the grave, screeching and waving his arms like a wraithlike *djinn*, he jumped back into the other men, knocking them over and spooking the camels, who in their fearful confusion reared and fled for their lives, shattering and scattering pottery every which way.

The potters, unable to control the runaway camels, saw their wares in shards all around the graveyard. Turning to the Mullah, the potters unleashed their furor on him, the unwitting cause of the loss of their caravan's lode. Sparing none of God's vengeance and offering none of His mercy, they thrashed him until he was black and blue from head to toe, then dumped his body unceremoniously in his own grave, leaving him for dead.

Sore, swollen, and stiff, Nasruddin lay in his shallow grave for what seemed like eternity, and then he decided to try to arise from the dead. As he shakily got to his feet, he spotted a large, dirty mongrel sniffing around the headstone of his new grave, recently decorated with a lovely wreath and other flowers. Devout Muslims consider dogs to be particularly unclean. Adding insult to injury, to Nasruddin's dismay, he watched the dog lift his leg and water the flowers. *White dogs, black dogs,* Nasruddin reflected, *all are born of bitches.*

Nasruddin, waving his arms, yelled at the dog, "Scram! Have some respect for the deceased, you horrid mutt! Stop that at once!"

The nasty dog faced Nasruddin, bared its sharp teeth, growled and snarled and snapped, poised to attack.

Nasruddin jumped backward in fear, then kept backing up. In a soothing voice, he said, "Down, boy! Nice doggy, nice doggy! Terribly sorry to bother you. I'll just leave you to go about your business as you please, and you can stay right there and let me do the same." The dog finished his business and scampered off to defile other gravesites.

By now Nasruddin had experienced quite enough of death, thanks very much. Sore in every pore of his body and humiliated beyond comprehension, he wrapped the dirty, bloody shroud around his abused body, crawled out of his grave, and hobbled home.

Fatima, shocked by her husband's appearance but of course happy to see him alive, hugged him warmly and tended to his bruises and cuts. As he sat soaking in a hot bath, she gently enquired, "So, I hesitate to ask, but tell me: where were you?"

Nasruddin replied wearily, "I died, and was laid to rest."

Fatima clucked her tongue, "*Ai vai!* So tell me: how was the afterlife?"

"Well," The Mullah replied, "things are not so bad, except that you must take great care not to frighten the potters' camels."

5

ONCE NASRUDDIN WAS SITTING with Fatima, contemplating the meaning of life. He thought aloud, "Some people are dead although they appear to be living. Yet others, again, are alive though they appear to have died." He wondered aloud, "Oh Lord! How can one truly distinguish if someone is living or dead?"

Fatima said, "Foolish man! If the hands and feet are stone cold, you can be certain that a man is dead."

That winter, on a bitterly cold day when Nasruddin was in the forest chopping wood, he left his little grey donkey, Karakacan, tied to a tree while he went uphill to fell trees and collect timber. After several hours, he felt his hands and feet, and realized they were nearly frozen. "*Aman, aman!*" he cried, and collapsed next to the tree he had felled, believing himself dead.

Soon a pack of wolves, emboldened by the harsh winter, came upon the solitary, defenseless Karakacan, and thinking the man nearby was mortified, surrounded the donkey. As Nasruddin heard the sounds of the poor animal while the wolves attacked it, he could not believe his bad fortune. "Wolves eat the donkey whose master is dead," he cried aloud as he remained laying on the ground, dead and thus helpless to save his beloved donkey.

Luqman, the town watchman, who happened nearby and heard the ruckus, came upon the grisly scene and scared the wolves away from the donkey's carcass. When Luqman saw Nasruddin lying down in the snow, watching everything, he grabbed him, saying, "Fool, what are you doing? The wolves have eaten your donkey, and now they are running uphill!"

Nasruddin sat up and said, "Well, it turns out I may not be dead, but it's surely too late for my donkey. Why bother the wolves while their bellies are full and they're running up the hill?"

⁊

THE NEXT WINTER, NASRUDDIN asked his brother, Selim, "How does one know if someone has died?"

"A telltale sign, I have heard," answered Selim slyly, "is that his hands and feet turn icy cold."

"Really?" said Nasruddin. "Never heard that before. Now I know."

On a very cold morning after the next winter's big snow, Nasruddin went out to chop wood in the forest, which was one of the things that Nasruddin did for work. Before long his hands and feet became icy cold, and he remembered what his friend had said. He thought, *I must be dead,* and fell flat on the ground.

After an hour or so, after about an inch of snow had fallen, he realized that it was unlikely that anyone would find his body out in the forest, so he got up and walked home. He told Fatima, "Sadly my dear, apparently I have died out in the woods, so you should ask the neighbors to come get my body." Fatima burst into tears as her dead husband walked back outside to return to where he had been chopping wood, then laid back down on the snow.

The grieving Fatima ran next door to their neighbors, Faik and Turan, tearing out her hair and wailing hysterically, "*Ai!* Nasruddin has died while he was all alone, chopping wood by himself up on the mountain! How unfortunate am I! Please have mercy and retrieve his body so that I may prepare it for a proper funeral."

Faik asked, "But if Nasruddin passed away just today in the forest, who came down and told you that he died?"

"May his soul rest in peace," said Fatima, "Nasruddin was so very alone when he passed — can you imagine? My unfortunate husband had to come home himself to deliver the horrible news."

ONCE NASRUDDIN CAME INTO the teahouse wearing a long face and black robes and a turban.

Ali asked him, "Nasruddin, why are you wearing all black?"

He said, "These are my mourning clothes."

"Has someone died?" asked Musa.

"Almost certainly," said the Mullah.

"When was this?"

"Can't say for sure. It could have happened without anyone informing me of the unfortunate event."

Musa said, "But Nasruddin, tell us — who was it that died?"

"Oh, it's not anybody I know, thank God. I'm wearing these mourning clothes just in case."

"So condolences are not needed?"

"Actually, you may offer your sympathy in advance as well. You must always remember that Death may strike at any moment, any one of us — especially myself! As I always say, it is best to be prepared for the inevitable."

ABDUL ASKED NASRUDDIN, "WHEN is the end of the world?"

"Which end of the world do you mean?" asked the Mullah.

"What do you mean, 'which'?" asked Abdul. "How many ends of the world are there?"

"Exactly two," answered Nasruddin, "the Lesser and the Greater. First, when my wife dies, that will be the Lesser End of the World. Then the Greater End of the World occurs when I die."

❦

NASRUDDIN WAS RETURNING HOME from the forest, dusty and dirty, when he passed through the cemetery.

"My clothes are so filthy," thought Nasruddin. "I'd best take them off and give them a good shake to get the dust off them."

As soon as he disrobed, however, Nasruddin saw some soldiers approaching rapidly on horseback. Panicking, thinking they would either imprison him of conscript him to the military, Nasruddin jumped in an empty grave.

When the soldiers reached the spot and saw Nasruddin naked and quivering in the grave, they were startled, to say the least.

"What are you doing here?" the captain demanded.

"You see," said Nasruddin, "I am dead but returned for a visit. I have come from the other world, and this is my grave."

This explanation amused the captain. "If you are dead and have just returned to this world, why did you hide from us?"

"It's indeed a long story, but suffice it to say that I am here because you are here, and you are here because I am here."

❦

As THEY STROLLED ALONG one day, Hussein asked Nasruddin, "While walking in a funeral procession, is it better to walk before the coffin, or following it?"

Faik then asked, "If you are a pallbearer, is it better to carry the casket on the right or the left side?"

Nasruddin replied, "Whether you go before or after, either on the left or the right side, it doesn't particularly matter — just make dead certain you are outside, not inside, the coffin."

❦

FINALLY, AFTER SO MANY years of the Nasruddin's pranks and antics and exploits, and although nobody nowadays can remember the exact reason, the town held a referendum to decide if the Mullah should leave. Unanimously they voted to banish Nasruddin from his home of Akşehir, and the magistrate summoned Nasruddin to court to read the decree.

"Nasruddin, the citizens have spoken as one that you must go. By the will of the people, I must declare that you are hereby exiled from Akşehir. I'm sorry but you must depart immediately."

"For what reason I am to be expelled from my beloved adopted home?" asked the Mullah.

"The people do not like you, and they want to you leave."

"Well, I do not like them particularly either, and I refuse to go away."

"But they are many, and you are one," said the magistrate.

"Exactly my point. There are plenty of the villagers, and only one of me. If they don't like it here, they can all move together any place they like and build another village wherever they decide to settle. But how can you expect me, all alone and at my age, to move someplace else, build a single house all by myself, and cultivate a field out in the country?"

6

O NCE HUSSEIN ASKED NASRUDDIN, "How long is the world?"

The Mullah pointed to a funeral procession and replied, "Better to ask the person in that coffin, for he has already measured it, and knows its true length."

Hussein asked, "So then, what is Fate?"

Nasruddin replied, "An infinite series of interconnected events, each influencing the other."

"Well then, how do you account for cause and effect?" the scholar asked.

Nasruddin pointed to the coffin. "They are taking a hanged man, convicted of killing another man, from the gallows to the grave. Is this the result of his stealing a knife from the butcher, or of using the knife to murder his enemy, or of being caught by the police, or of being prosecuted by the magistrate, or of his being found guilty by the judge, or of being hanged on the gallows? Which event can you point to and say, 'This is the moment in time that caused him to meet his Fate'?"

THE TOWN WATCHMAN, LUQMAN, was a lifelong nonbeliever when he contracted a fatal disease. As his health rapidly deteriorated, he reconsidered his faithlessness. Luqman knew and respected Nasruddin as a mystic who had impressive contacts in the afterlife, so he called the Mullah to his bedside.

"O wise and noble sage," the dying man desperately implored Nasruddin, "you are known far and wide for your amazing psychic ability to communicate with the other side. Please Mullah, give me a simple prayer that will ease my suffering as I transition into the afterlife."

"Delighted," said Nasruddin. "You may repeat this mantra: *God help me! — Devil help me!*"

Scandalized, Luqman sat bolt upright in bed and said, "Mullah, don't be ridiculous. That is utter nonsense!"

Nasruddin replied evenly, "Not at all, my dear fellow. Actually, it makes perfect sense. You see, someone in your position shouldn't take any chances. Seeing two alternatives, a wise person would try to provide for either of these two very likely options working out."

⸎

"How long is transmigration?" Abdul the baker once asked Nasruddin in the teahouse.

"We are born and we die, over and again, ceaselessly until the end of the universe," answered the Mullah.

"How big, then, are heaven and hell?" asked Abdullah. "How many people can the hereafter contain?"

"Transmigration is endless — at least, until heaven and hell are full," said Nasruddin.

⸎

"Where do we come from, and where do we go?" Hussein asked.

"We come from the very same place to which we departed."

"What is the hereafter like?"

Nasruddin observed, "The afterlife must be terribly frightening."

"Why do you say that?" said Ali.

"It is my observation that most babies arrive crying, and that most people die weeping as well."

⸎

Nasruddin was holding forth in the teahouse, extolling the virtues of abstaining from idle gossip and rumor.

"It is important to remember to consider the source of any new information," remarked Nasruddin to his friends. "Don't believe everything you hear, and don't repeat anything you don't believe. Just as there are some things you may hear which you know intuitively are true and right, there are also things you must recognize instinctively as false."

"How can we really understand what is true or false? What is recognizable truth?" asked Mali.

"Excellent question," replied the Mullah. "Well, for example, just the other day, I was walking in the bazaar and overheard someone repeating a rumor — that I was dead."

EARLY ONE SPRING WHILE traveling, Nasruddin was abducted by thieves who forced him at knifepoint to be their lookout while they emptied the contents of the house of a wealthy merchant.

After the robbery, the thieves escaped on swift horses, laughing at Nasruddin as they sped away. Mullah, alone with only his little grey donkey (who could certainly go no faster on four legs than the Mullah could run on two), was apprehended. Nasruddin was taken promptly to jail and booked for the burglary.

At Nasruddin's criminal trial, despite his protestations of innocence, he was found guilty of the robbery as charged. The *qadi*, wanting to appear tough, sentenced Nasruddin to death and told the doomed Mullah that before he was executed, he would be granted three requests.

"Fine," said Nasruddin evenly. "For my first wish, "I wish to have a very large dish of fresh snow sprinkled with sugar."

"Quite odd," said the judge, "but I am obliged to grant your request. Of course, there won't be snow on the ground yet until winter."

"Of course, sir, you are quite right," agreed Nasruddin. "But if it pleases the court to honor my request, I don't mind waiting."

So nine months passed until the first flurries came, at which point Nasruddin was served a humongous dish of cold, pure snow with a delicate topping of fine cane sugar, which he ate with pleasure, only once eating too fast that he got a headache.

When his meal of snow was done, he was brought before the judge, who asked for his second request. "Next," Nasruddin told the judge, "I would like to eat six fresh ripe apples."

"Not such an unusual request," said the judge, "but of course, apples are not yet in season until late summer," said the judge.

"Of course, you are once again correct in that judgment. But not to worry," said Nasruddin, "I'll wait."

So nine months passed until summer, and Nasruddin was given six ripe, delicious, juicy apples, which he ate with relish.

When he finished eating, the Mullah was again brought before the judge. "At long last, Nasruddin," said the judge, "what is your third and final request?"

"My last request," said Nasruddin, "is to be buried next to the Shah."

"But the Shah is not yet dead — he is quite alive, and has just turned forty!" exclaimed the judge.

"No problem," said Nasruddin. "I can wait."

In Nasruddin's final will and testament, he wrote,

> *The law proscribes that my dependants must receive certain fixed proportions of my possessions and monetary assets.*
>
> *Since I have nothing, let it be divided equally among my family according to the law.*
>
> *That which remains shall be distributed to the poor.*

7

When Nasruddin was aged, he became quite sick and infirm. Berrak the doctor came to examine the Mullah, and following the physical exam, recommended an extensive treatment regimen of medicines, all of which were quite expensive.

The Mullah decided to visit the funeral *imam* and inquire as to the cost of memorial services. He found out that the fee for interment was just a fraction of the cost of the prescriptions.

Nasruddin returned home and crawled into bed. He said to Fatima, "Rather than waste money on medicines I can't afford, better that you should just pull the blanket over my head and let me expire. Clearly it's cheaper to die than to live."

The Mullah supervised the construction of his own tomb. It took a long time to complete, as Mali the carpenter and the workmen were inexperienced with this sort of peculiar architectural design and made many mistakes. Finally, after everything was fixed properly and all the finishing touches had been made, Mali came for his payment.

"It is yet incomplete, I believe," Nasruddin told them.

"Don't be ridiculous, Mullah," said Mali. "Everything has been built to your precise specifications, whatever additions you asked for have been accomplished, and all flaws have been righted. What could possibly be left to finish with your tomb?"

"It is still missing one crucial component."

"Well, what is it?" asked the exasperated Mali.

"We still need to supply the body," replied Nasruddin.

As THE AGED, AILING Nasruddin was frail and bedridden, he called his wife Fatima to come to his side.

"You look like you are ready to move on to the afterworld. How are you feeling, Nasruddin?" she asked through her weeping.

"I hope it's because I'm only ill," wheezed Nasruddin. "Anyone who feels as horrible as I do really ought to be dead."

On HIS DEATHBED, NASRUDDIN called Fatima to his side.

"What can I do for you, my dear old sick husband?" she asked.

"My love," Nasruddin said weakly, "go now and wash your hands and face. Put on your new dress, and your finest jewelry. Put on a dab of perfume, and use some make-up. Make yourself as pretty as you can, then rejoin me and sit right at the foot of my bed."

Fatima was shocked and appalled. "Nasruddin, I don't feel like dressing up and looking pretty when you're so ill. Do you want everyone to think that I have no scruples?"

"Oh no, dear, you misunderstand me," the Mullah gasped. "I am hoping that when Azrael, the angel of death, comes to call, maybe he'll notice how beautiful you look and take you instead."

WHEN NASRUDDIN WAS ON his deathbed, Fatima asked him, "How would you like to be buried, Nasruddin?"

"You may inter the body head downward," said the Mullah.

"Don't be ridiculous. What possible reason could you have to impel us to bury you upside down?"

"At the end of the world, it is well-known, everything will be turned topsy-turvy. Then, I'll be the only one who is right-side up!"

"I REQUEST," GASPED NASRUDDIN ON his deathbed, "that my body be placed in an old coffin and buried in a grave with an unmarked tombstone."

"Nasruddin, why in the world do you want to be buried in an old coffin?"

"When Munkir and Nankir, the recording angels of good and bad actions, appear at the gravesite to find me, I'll tell them I died many years ago. They will see the old casket and the dateless tomb and think that they have already judged me, and go back from wherever they came."

MUCH LATER AFTER HIS death, the date inscribed on the Mullah's tombstone was 386. Substituting Arabic letters for the numbers, as per the mystic Sufi tradition, yields the word SWHF, which means "seeing," especially in the sense of "bestowing or restoring one's vision."

Perhaps this explains why it is said, to this day, that dust from the Mullah's tomb can cure blindness, in the same way that invoking Nasruddin's name cures sadness.

As per the Mullah's design, his final resting place in Akşehir was fronted by an immense wooden door, securely barred and padlocked.

This formidable barricade would not keep out anyone who wished to visit the site, however, as the tomb was erected without any walls behind its immense and imposing front door.

In death as in life, the immortal Mullah Nasruddin always got the last laugh.

GLOSSARY

ai vai   alas, alack
Akşehir   village in south-central Turkey; literally, "white plain"
Aleppo   city in Syria
Allah   primary Arabic name for the Deity
aman   woe is me

baklava   flaky pastry made with honey, cinnamon, and nuts
baksheesh   alms for poor, charity
bekche   town watchman; constable

caliph   supreme ruler

dargah   burial shrine of great being
dervish   Sufi adherents, known for whirling trance-dance
dinar   Persian currency
djinn   jinni, ghost

effendi   mister, sir: scholastic or official title; term of respect
     among equals
emir   governor of an Islamic territory, or emirate

hajj   pilgrimage to Mecca, which every able-bodied Muslim is
     required to complete
halvah   sweetmeat made of sesame
hammam   Turkish bath
hammamji   bathhouse attendant
hoca   Muslim preacher, teacher, elder

hoş geldiniz   welcome; "your coming gives joy"

imam   prayer leader in mosque; Muslim leader

Insh'allah   God willing; I hope so

Isfahan   provincial capital in Iran

Islam   monotheistic religion articulated by the Qur'an

Kaaba   cube-shaped building in Mecca; most sacred site in Islam

Konya   city in Anatolia, central Turkey

Mecca   city in Saudi Arabia, pilgrimage site for all Muslims

minaret   mosque spire, usually with onion-shaped or conical crown

mosque   Islamic house of worship

muezzin   Islamic cantor who calls the faithful to prayer five times a day

Muhammad   founder of Islam; the prophetic author of the Qur'an

muhtar   elected mayor of village or neighborhood

mullah   learned Islamic cleric acting as judge, priest, and teacher

Muslim   adherent to Islam

namaz   Islamic divine worship, recitals of praise with prostrations

Nasruddin   name meaning "victory of religion"

qadi   Muslim judge; minor magistrate

Qur'an   Mohammedan holy book; literally, "the recitation"

Ramadan   Islamic month of fasting from dawn until sunset

rebab   stringed musical instrument

sadir   couch in hammam

salaam   hello; peace; greeting with folded hands

shah   king of Persia

sheikh   tribal or village elder; Muslim officiant

Sivrihişar   Nasruddin birthplace in Turkey

Subhan'Allah   praise Allah; "Glorified is Allah"

Sufi   adherent to Sufism, mystical branch of Islam

takkia   small mosque

yufka   flatbread

BIBLIOGRAPHY

Al-Amily, Hussain Mohammed, compiler & editor. 2004. *The Book of Arabic Wisdom: Proverbs & anecdotes*. Northampton, Mass.: Interlink Books. 28 stories.

Ashliman, D. L. 2001. *Nasreddin Hodja: Tales of the Turkish trickster*. University of Pittsburgh <www.pitt.edu/~dash/hodja.html> 23 stories, accessed 8/1/01.

Barnham, Henry D., translator. 1923. *Tales of Nasr-ed-din Khoja*. London: Nisbet & Co. Foreword, Sir Valentine Chirol. 181 stories.

Birant, Mehmet Ali, compiler. [n.d.: late 1980s?] *Nasreddin Hodja*. Ece Birant Sevil, translator. Ömer Dinçer Kiliç, illustrator. Ankara: Egitim Gereçcleri.

Boratav, Pertev Nailî. 1995, 2006. *Nasreddin Hoca*. Istanbul: Kırmızı Yayınları. 594 stories, in Turkish.

Burrill, Kathleen Ruth Frances. 1957. *The Nasreddin Hoja stories*. New York: Columbia University Library, Special Collections, Masters thesis. 76 stories, in Arabic, Turkish, and English.

Bushnaq, Inea, translator & editor. 1986. *Arab Folktales*. New York: Pantheon Fairy Tale & Folklore Library. "Famous Fools and Rascals: Stories of Djuha and his kind," pp. 254–280. 23 stories.

Chukru, Kemaleddin. [n.d.: 1931?] *Vie de Nasreddine Hodja*. Istanbul: Librarie Kaanat. Illustrated, Ömer Nuri, &c. 38 stories, in French.

Crane, Thomas Frederick. 1885, reprint 2010. *Italian Popular Tales*. Cambridge, Mass.: Riverside Press. 9 Giufà stories, pp. 288–303.

Husain, Shahrukh. 2006. *The Wisdom of Mulla Nasruddin*. New Delhi: Scholastic. Illustrated, Shilpa Ranade.

Husseini, Khaled. 2003. *The Kite Runner*. New York: Riverhead Books. A novel, 3 stories.

Jayyusi, Salma Khadra, editor. 2007. *Tales of Juha: Classic Arab folk humor*. Northampton, Mass.: Interlink Books. Translated, Matthew Sorenson, Faisal Khadra & Christopher Tingley.

Kabacali, Alpay. 1992. *Nasreddin Hodja*. Istanbul: Net Turiskik Yayınları. Illustrated, Fatîh M. Durmus. 116 stories.

Kelsey, Alice Geer. 1943. *Once the Hodja*. New York: David McKay Co. Illustrated, Frank Dobias. 23 stories.

———. 1958. *Once the Mullah: Persian Folk Tales*. New York, Toronto, & London: Longmans, Green & Co. Illustrated, Kurt Werth. 27 stories.

Kúnos, Ignácz. 1896, reprint 2010. *Turkish Fairy Tales and Folktales*. LaVergne, Tenn.: Kessinger Legacy Series. Translated, R. Nisbet Bain & Celia Levetus. Illustrated, Celia Levetus.

Leach, Maria. 1961. *Noodles, Nitwits, and Numskulls*. Cleveland: World Publishing. Illustrated, Kurt Werth. 4 stories.

Legman, Gershon. 1968. *Rationale of the Dirty Joke: An Analysis of Sexual Humor*. First Series. New York: Grove Press.

———. 1975. *No Laughing Matter. Rationale of the Dirty Joke: An Analysis of Sexual Humor*. Second Series. New York: Bell Press.

Levett, Yoram, collector & editor. 1982. *Hakmut Nasaruddin*. Jerusalem: Beit Hotzaah Elishair. Illustrated, A. Nikolaiv. 38 stories, in Hebrew.

MacDonald, Margaret Read. 1982. *The Storyteller's Sourcebook: a subject, title, and motif index to folklore collections for children*. 1st edition. Detroit, Mich.: Gale Group.

MacDonald, Margaret Read, & Brian W. Sturm. 2001. *The Storyteller's Sourcebook: a subject, title, and motif index to folklore collections for children, 1983-1999.* Detroit, Mich.: Gale Group.

Mahfuzdur, Her Hakki (?). [n.d.] *202 Jokes of Nasreddin Hodja.* Tepebaşı, Istanbul: Galeri Minyatür. Minyatür Yayınları No. 1b. Illustrated, uncredited. 202 stories.

Marzolph, Ulrich, collector & editor. 2006. *Nasreddin Hodsca: 666 wahre Geschichten.* München: C.H. Beck. 666 stories, in German.

Meade, Erica Helm. 2001. *The Moon in the Well: Wisdom tales to transform your life, family and community.* Chicago: Open Court. 3 stories.

Muktananda, Swami. 1981, 1994. *Where Are You Going? A guide to the spiritual journey.* South Fallsburg, N.Y.: SYDA Foundation. 7 stories in context of a meditation Master's spiritual lessons.

Nesin, Aziz. 1994, revised edition. *The Tales of Nasrettin Hoca.* Istanbul: Dost Yayınları. Translated, Talât Sait Halman. Illustrated, Zeki Fındıkoğlu. 91 stories.

Parabola: Myth, tradition, and the search for meaning. Fall 2001 (26: 3). Issue theme: *The Fool.* Denville, N.J.: The Society for the Study of Myth and Tradition.

Pearmain, Elisa Davy. 1998. *Doorways to the Soul.* Cleveland, Ohio: Pilgrim Press. 4 stories.

Sachs, Susan. "The Funny, but Fictional, Mullah." The New York *Times,* August 20, 2000.

Sawhney, Clifford. 2009. *The Funniest Tales of Mullah Nasruddin: The wittiest stories of the world's best-loved jester.* New Delhi: Unicorn Press. Illustrated, uncredited. 141 stories.

Schiff, Jeremy. 2001. *Hodja Stories.* Ramat Gan, Israel <http://u.cs.biu.ac.il/~schiff/Hodja/> 28 stories, accessed 8/1/01.

Serwer-Bernstein, Blanche L. 1994. *In the Tradition of Moses and Mohammed: Jewish and Arab folktales.* Northvale, N.J.: Jason Aronson. 6 Djuha stories.

Shah, Idries. 1966. *The Exploits of the Incomparable Mulla Nasrudin.* New York: Arkana/Penguin. Illustrated, Richard Williams. 100 stories.

——. 1968, 1993. *The Pleasantries of the Incredible Mulla Nasrudin.* New York: Arkana / Penguin. Illustrated, Richard Williams & Errol Le Cain. 165 stories.

——. 1973. *The Subtleties of the Inimitable Mulla Nasrudin.* New York: Arkana/ Penguin. 99 stories.

——. 1983. *Exploits* & *Subtleties*: two volumes in one, printed back-to-back. London: Octagon Press.

——. 1990. *Las Hazañas del Incomparable Mulá Nasrudín.* Barcelona / Bueños Aires: Paidos Orientalia. *Exploits*, in Spanish.

——. 2003. *The World of Nasruddin.* London: Octagon Press. 438 stories.

Solovyov, Leonid. 2009. *Disturber of the Peace: The tale of Hodja Nasreddin.* Thornhill, Ontario, Canada: Translit Publishing. Translated, Michael Karpelson. A novel featuring Nasruddin as protagonist, incorporating at least 7 popular stories.

——. *Hodja Nasar a-Din.* 1968. Translated, Spiryat ben Chaskin [?]. Tel-Aviv: Am Oved Publishers. 8 extended stories, in Hebrew.

Stevens, E. S., translator & editor. 1913, 2006. *Folktales of Iraq.* Mineola, N.Y.: Dover Publications.

Wesselski, Albert. 1911, reprint 2011. *Der Hodscha Nasreddin.* Charleston, S.C.: Bibliolife. 338 stories, in German.

Walker, Barbara. 1991. *Watermelons, Walnuts, and the Wisdom of Allah: And other tales of the Hoca.* Lubbock: Texas Tech University Press. Illustrated, Harold Berson. 19 stories.

Yörenç, Kemal. 1997. *The Best Anecdotes of Nasreddin Hoca.* Istanbul: Aksit Kültür Turizm Sanat Ajans Ticaret. Illustrated, Kemal Yörenç. 121 stories.

CPSIA information can be obtained at www.ICGtesting.com
Printed in the USA
BVOW08s1837030116

431633BV00002B/140/P